Hello Mother, Hello Father:

Celebrating Summer Camp

Daniella K. Garran

Schiffer Publishing Ltd

4880 Lower Valley Road • Atglen, PA 19310

Library of Congress Control Number: 2014931484

Photo courtesy of Kari Ahern.

Designed by RoS
Type set in Brisa/Korinna

ISBN: 978-0-7643-4645-3
Printed in China

Published by Schiffer Publishing, Ltd.
4880 Lower Valley Road
Atglen, PA 19310
Phone: (610) 593-1777; Fax: (610) 593-2002
E-mail: Info@schifferbooks.com

For our complete selection of fine books on this and related subjects, please visit our website at www.schifferbooks.com. You may also write for a free catalog.

This book may be purchased from the publisher. Please try your bookstore first.

We are always looking for people to write books on new and related subjects. If you have an idea for a book, please contact us at proposals@schifferbooks.com

Schiffer Publishing's titles are available at special discounts for bulk purchases for sales promotions or premiums. Special editions, including personalized covers, corporate imprints, and excerpts can be created in large quantities for special needs. For more information, contact the publisher.

"Summer is like childhood. It passes too fast. But if you're lucky, it gives you warm memories from which you take strength in the cold days ahead."[1]

—Edward Hallowell

"The proliferation of summer camps bespeaks our understanding of the most unique use of summer: education caught rather than taught."[2]

—Chaim Potok

24677

Contents

Foreword

My mom always said that she knew I would be a happy camper. I happily attended a few different day camps until I was old enough to pack my bags and ship off to New England for the summer. I spent two summers at Camp Chinqueka, an all-girls' camp in Connecticut, but, since I attended an all-girls' school, I decided after the summer of 1983 that enough was enough and that I was ready for a coed camp. My best friend, Kathie, suggested that I look at her camp—Cape Cod Sea Camps—and after a slideshow at my house from one of the staff members who lived in the area, I began packing my bags, in spite of the fact that it was winter and that camp was several months away.

In the meantime, with tremendous excitement and not one bit of trepidation, I poured over brochures sent by the camp. Finally, that Sunday in June 1984 arrived, when Kathie and I left our parents at the airport and boarded a plane bound for Boston and then a school bus headed to CCSC. For seven glorious weeks, I was completely independent and blissfully happy. I tried archery, sailing, and windsurfing, among other activities, and made friends from all over the world. I relished the seemingly endless supply of bug juice and s'mores. I celebrated my twelfth birthday with a pizza party held on the floor of my cabin and could not have been happier than when the obligatory camp ice cream cake, frozen solid, appeared, and my bunkmates sang to me. (Please note that even though there is a photo of this event, it does not appear in this book, since a number of people would be ridiculed for their appearance, and because my hair takes up far too much of the picture). I won Best First Year Camper in my unit and, somehow, Excellence in Woodworking, which I remember attending exactly once.

When the last day of camp arrived in what seemed to be the blink of an eye, I cried inconsolably all the way to the airport and for the duration of the flight. The thought of having to relinquish my independence and my new friends was too much to bear. I convinced Kathie that we should be the last ones off the plane. By the time we finally emerged from the jetway, my mother was positively hysterical with worry (remember, this is long before the advent of cell phones) and was, herself, crying. I refused to speak on the drive home and, once there, proceeded to lock myself in my room—after demanding that my ten rolls of film be taken to one hour processing and not to forget the double prints. Eventually, I emerged, puffy-eyed from so much crying, when I was hungry. I repeated this pattern annually and by the third or fourth year, my mother caught on and realized that I needed some time to mourn the end of the summer and readjust to life at home.

To this day, I get teary-eyed when I drive out of camp for the last time each August after the campers have left. Perhaps this would be more understandable if I didn't live twenty minutes away and see many of my friends and colleagues on a regular basis. What I've come to realize, however, is that these tears are mourning for summers past and a way of life that lasts only seven weeks a year. There is no place on earth where fun is more innocent and laughter more genuine than at summer camp. It is truly a gift to have had so many wonderful experiences and to have befriended such incredible people. Summer camp is something like a snowglobe, which is probably why we refer to it as "the bubble." It is a small-scale version of an idyllic world in which all that is right with the world pervades the community.

I finished my twenty-sixth summer at CCSC in 2012 with some serious sleep deprivation, a few wonderful new friends, a strong sense of pride in what I am able to do at camp, and a pile of small scraps of paper that had amassed as the summer progressed. Entire paragraphs of this book would burst forth at the most inopportune times (like while supervising a trip to a Red Sox game with sixty campers in tow) and I had to scramble to write them down before they faded away into the recesses of my mind. Some of these musings are enmeshed in the book, but there were a few key points I want to elucidate.

On the eve of my fortieth birthday, which was two weeks before the end of camp, I said to my husband, "I can't believe camp is almost over. I don't want it to end." My husband said to me, "I know you don't; no one ever does. But everyone has to move on and you have a hard time because you can't." I was completely taken aback by this comment until I realized that he was absolutely right. I cannot and will not let go of camp and everything that it represents to me. What I need, I told my husband, is a pause button. Not just for me but for everyone else. It's difficult for me when friends move on to different stages of life; I feel somehow betrayed and left behind. My husband said, "*Everyone* wants a pause button." Alas, I have chosen to remain at camp in spite of a multitude of other opportunities and in spite of the fact that many of the people I love spending time with have moved on. Camp *is* my pause button.

While many of my closest friends have retained their camp friendships despite no longer working there, I am unable to give up the memories and the place in which they were made. I know that there are a million other things I could be doing with my summers, but the truth is that I don't actually want to do anything other than exactly what it is that I do: work at camp. What better way to stay young, make new friends, and know that you are having a profound impact on others (even more so, I would argue, than in my real world job as a teacher)?

About ten days later, on the night that the campers left, I was chatting with several counselors, two of whom were new to camp. One of them earnestly said to me that he was surprised to find that camp is a place where people can really heal and get over things. He went on to explain how when camp had started that year he had just broken up with his girlfriend and that he hadn't been sure he would make it through the summer, because he wasn't sure he could buy into what we were all about. Once the pace picked up, however, and he got to know the campers, he couldn't even remember feeling sad at the start of the summer. Another counselor explained that he had experienced some significant disappointment professionally that year and was still coming to terms with it. He was so grateful that being at camp had allowed him the opportunity to recover and regroup while considering what to do with his future. Another counselor chimed in that he had had a difficult spring semester in college and had struggled with depression and anxiety. Coming to camp had made him feel like himself again and he was actually looking forward to returning to school that fall. And then I remembered another friend who had told me how instrumental camp had been in his life when he learned that his parents were divorcing just before the camp season started.

As I lay in bed that night, I started to think of all the ways in which camp has helped my friends and so many others heal. My husband returned to camp just a month after his father passed away and, whether he realized it at the time or not, was able to start the healing process in the loving embrace of his camp friends and family. At nineteen, a close friend learned of her father's unexpected death while she was at camp; ultimately she chose to return to camp after the funeral because, she explained, she knew her father would want her to be there. I thought about camps like Paul Newman's Hole-in-the-Wall Gang Camp, which allows children suffering from serious medical conditions to simply be kids and embrace everything that camp has to offer, while still receiving their necessary medical care. I recalled the camps that formed in the wake of 9/11 to provide a similar and healing experience for children who had lost loved ones on that tragic day. I would absolutely have to agree with these sagacious young men who, having no idea I was poaching this conversation for my book, stated something we all have known deep inside, but perhaps have failed to articulate: simply put, camp cures everything.

Showing my mom around Cape Cod Sea Camps on Visiting Weekend, 1984.

Celebrating the final night of the 2012 season (and my 26th summer) at Cape Cod Sea Camps with my friends Ben Bertolino, Abby Berman, Kelly Flanagan, Tyler Turgeon, and Tom Walsh.

I could never have known that my life would change so dramatically when I pulled into the driveway of Cape Cod Sea Camps in June 1984. Not only have I spent virtually every summer there since then, but I also met my husband there, got married there, and made my very best friends there. I have had the good fortune of celebrating countless milestones at camp beginning with the aforementioned twelfth birthday and going on to include my sweet sixteen, my twenty-fifth, thirtieth, thirty-fifth, and my fortieth birthdays. I celebrated my wedding at camp on a day that was so rainy, had it been camp season no one would have dared venture out of the cabins all day. I've attended bridal showers, baby showers, weddings (including my own), and even funeral services at camp. My friends' children are now campers and my former campers are now counselors. Camp is truly the focus of my life and everything good in it.

I have always felt that I have been my best self at camp. I have been most introspective, while being keenly aware of others. I have tried new things that I never would have otherwise, and met amazing people from all over the world because of camp. When I would call home as a camper, my mother always said that she knew I was at camp just by the sound of my voice. I suspect it must have been sense of peace and pure joy I felt as soon as I got to camp each June.

As I wrote this book, I was surrounded by photo collages of many friends, all of whom, I now realize, are from camp. My camp memories are so visceral that when I close my eyes, I can recreate the unique smell of my cabin: a mix of low tide, mildew and teenage girls' hair products. I can feel the wet sand between my toes as I walk out to the boats at low tide. I can hear the scratch of the old record player used in my early camp days over the P.A. system as "Taps" is played. Having the opportunity to write this book, essentially a Valentine to summer camp, has allowed me to reaffirm that fact that life is all about choices and that I have made mine; I choose to remain a part of camp.

Writing this book in the age of Facebook has been a remarkable experience. While I am "Facebook friends" with many past and present campers and counselors, once I began posting questions and asking for photos, I was able to reconnect with many people I haven't seen since we were 14. Threads on my wall were incredibly long as people began to post their favorite memories and anecdotes. I started to realize both the universality and the individuality of the summer camp experience that exist simultaneously. As I reached out to campers and counselors nationwide, I realized that we all share a common bond: a deep, enduring love for camp. Even though it's difficult to understand how things are done at other camps or why someone would choose to attend a camp other than your own, it is clear that no matter where one attended camp, the memories and friendships last a lifetime as do many of the skills acquired. The most significant commonality, however, is that camp changed the lives of everyone who attended it; whether it was a small camp in the mountains or a large camp on the water, summer camp makes its mark.

In her book *Children's Nature: The Rise of the American Summer Camp*, Leslie Paris explains that "camp's importance in American popular culture has become such that even for those who never attended them, the term conjures up nostalgic images of children singing around a campfire and watching marshmallows turn golden over the flames (or, alternatively, of campers sneaking out of their bunks after lights out)."[3] Regardless of your connection to a particular camp or your experience as a camper, counselor or parent, I hope this book will evoke memories of all this and more and that you will be able to relate to the stories and photos in this book and that they will bring you the same happiness that was experienced by those who shared them.

For those of you who are reading this to relive your glorious camp days, I hope that this book will help bring back wonderful memories and motivate you to seek out and reconnect with old camp friends. For those of you who are reading this in an effort to understand the summer camp experience held so dear by your friends and family, I hope that you are better able to relate to them after reading this book (although to truly understand it, you must be part of "the cult").

This is a love letter to summer camps and the possibilities they provide for both children and adults. My greatest hope is that I am able to do the topic justice.

My cabinmates and I return from getting pizza at a local restaurant on my sixteenth birthday.
I recall that I could not have been happier.

Campers enjoy a sunset on Cape Cod Bay, where I learned to sail.
Photo courtesy of Kari Ahern

Acknowledgments

And so, with all of that said, there are many people to thank for their influence, guidance, and friendship, not only while writing this book but also because they have been instrumental in shaping my camp experience and my life overall.

• My mom who sent me to camp in the first place and sacrificed much else to do so. Camp and my education are the two greatest gifts I could ever have received and she made both possible. There are literally no words to express my love and gratitude for her.

• My husband, Jeff, who has always supported me in all of my endeavors and, most importantly, through the writing of two books. He is, no doubt, wondering what intense project is next. I appreciate his willingness (albeit reluctant) to give me up to the camp bubble each summer. Without camp, we never would have met.

• My daughter, Eliza Rhodes Garran, who will, I hope, one day discover the magic of camp as she learns new things and makes new friends to last a lifetime.

• Kathie Guben Wachs, my very best friend, who first introduced me to CCSC when we were eleven. I am thankful each day for the many ways she changed my life. It gives me no greater pleasure than to watch her children, Sophie and Sam, enjoy camp as much as we did.

• Nancy Garran serves as the executive director of Cape Cod Sea Camps and is the third generation of the Delahanty family to run CCSC. She has carried out the vision of her grandparents, Robert and Emma Delahanty, mother Frances Garran, and aunt Berry Richardson each day as she provides a life-altering experience for hundreds of children each summer. There are thousands of CCSC alumni and campers-to-be who thank her for keeping this tradition alive.

• David Peterson, Sherry Mernick, and Stephen Wallace, the directors of CCSC, have taught me everything I know about working with children. I am forever indebted to them.

• My colleagues and close friends, Christie Peterson and Jim Flanagan, make it a pleasure to come to work every day each summer. I wish we shared an office all year long so we could laugh together and teach Jim new vocabulary words and computer skills while filling my swear jar and snacking on treats.

• The ladies of the Roost—Joanna Flanagan, Julie Lindstrom, Kari Ahern, Debby Greenwood—have provided endless support, friendship and laughter. My world is a better place because you are in it, especially when the party lights are on.

• And again to Debby Greenwood whose art graces the cover of my first book, *A History of Collegiate Rowing in America*, and so beautifully illustrates this book as well. She is a collaborator, a colleague and most importantly a friend. Her gifts and talents are unparalleled.

• Hollis von Summer is one of my most cherished friends. Not only does she speak in direct quotes, but she also is one of the most generous people I know. Everyone needs a singing telegram shark on their birthday, a house with good writing mojo to visit, and a friend who is not only brutally honest but also staunchly loyal and supportive. Hollis is largely responsible for inspiring me to take risks that I never would have had the courage to take otherwise.

• My closest camp friends have contributed immeasurably and indescribably to my life. The kind of friendship offered by the following people is something I hope that everyone has a chance to experience at least once in their lifetime. My deepest gratitude is extended to Rob Percarpio, Mike Kennedy, Katie Carpenter, Garran, and Christie Peterson, the entire Flanagan clan (Jim, Joanna, Kelly, Shawn, Erin, Max, and the menagerie of pets), Caitlin Doggart-Bernal, Dianna Lamb Walsh, Jim and Emily Fay, Andy and Christin Sims, Ed Barber, Alice Guariglio, Philipp Luerzer (my favorite Austrian), Julia Luerzer (my other favorite Austrian), and far too many others to list. It is with great excitement that I await the next generation of campers to attend camp in the near or distant future so that they may make friendships like the ones we have developed.

• I have been fortunate to work with hundreds of campers and counselors over my many years at CCSC. It has been awe-inspiring to watch so many of you grow and mature and still love camp in the age of technology in the same way that I did in the 1980s and 1990s. I love the people I've known for decades and those I just met last summer equally as you are all part of the idyllic, utopian compartment in my mind labeled "camp." I am honored to have had a part in your camp experience and hope that I was able to make it as special and meaningful as mine was.

Friend and artist Deborah Greenwood captures the essence of my summer camp experience.

Staff members celebrate a wonderful summer on the last night of camp. *Photo courtesy of Kari Ahern.*

To An Old Camper

Mary S. Edgar

You may think, my dear, when you grow quite old
You have left camp days behind,
But I know the scent of wood smoke
Will always call to mind
Little fires at twilight
And trails you used to find.

You may think someday you have quite grown up,
And feel so worldly wise
But suddenly from out of the past
A vision will arise
Of merry folk with brown bare knees
And laughter in their eyes.

You may live in a house built to your taste
In the nicest part of town
But someday for your old camp togs
You'd change your latest gown
And trade it for a balsam bed
Where stars all night look down.

You may find yourself grow wealthy
Have all that gold can buy.
But you'd toss aside a fortune
For days 'neath an open sky
With sunlight and blue water
And white clouds sailing by.

For once you have been a camper
Then something has come to stay
Deep in your heart forever
Which nothing can take away,
And heaven can only be heaven
With a camp in which to play.[4]

Introduction

Why Summer Camp?

Learning to make s'mores is an important skill for campers (and counselors) of all ages to master.

Camp experts Jon Malinowski and Chris Thurber write, "if you think about it, overnight camping is a somewhat strange concept. As civilization evolved, people built shelters, walls, and eventually towns and cities to shield themselves from the savage wilderness and the uncertainty of nature. Why, then, would people pay money to leave the safety of civilization and go back into the wilderness?"[5] Nevertheless, each summer, millions of American children pack their duffle bags, trunks, and backpacks and head to camps across the nation. Some campers have great trepidation about leaving home, while others can hardly wait to get there. Many parents have a harder time leaving their campers than their campers have leaving them. In spite of it all, this rite of passage has endured and continues to thrive and expand today.

"Summer camps helped to consolidate the notion of childhood as a time apart, at once protected and playful, which required age-appropriate, adult monitored leisure in the company of select peers."[6]

Urbandictionary.com, the go-to Web site for all things relevant in pop culture, defines summer camp as "a place where parents send their children summer after summer. Usually the place where a child experiences their first kiss, first boyfriend/girlfriend, lots of firsts. A place where everyone is your best friend, all the counselors are your family, and you trust everyone. A place where there are no secrets, everyone knows everything."[7] While this is all true, the site ups the ante for sleepaway camp which is defined as:

> ...the most amazing place in the world. A place where kids of varying ages (usually 7-15) make best friends for life and their bunkmates grow to be like sisters or brothers. A place where kids learn or share lots of information about life, particularly stuff that they don't want to ask their parents. This is where many learn about who they are and who they want to become. Campers cry when they go home, and count the days until they come back. They leave each summer with a new outlook on many ideas, themselves or life in general, and great memories that will last them a lifetime.[8]

That's a lot to live up to if you're a camp director. But clearly camps are doing something right, since the summer camp industry continues to flourish. So why has summer camp remained such a vital part of the American experience?

Camp historian Eleanor Eells expertly sums up the importance of the summer camp experience and although her perspective is nearly three decades old, it holds true today.

> Somehow, the out-of-doors serves as a catalyst for group interaction which results in a well-being seldom found elsewhere. The trust generated between adults and youth and the feeling of accomplishment within the camper group is difficult to understand and, thus far, difficult to verify through research. Whatever the ingredients, something seems to happen at a camp that makes the campers feel good about themselves, about others, and about the environment in which they live.[9]

No statement could be truer than this one, and it elucidates why campers and counselors have such difficulty explaining their love of camp and their experience to "outsiders" and friends from home; summer camp simply defies description.

In his article entitled, "Why the World Needs Summer Camp: An Essay to Parents," Jeff Merhige explains, "The world needs the next generation to be more tolerant of each other's views, ideology, and beliefs. Summer camp is an opportunity for children to be exposed to the best of human character."[10] Camps attract fun-loving types who enjoy being around other people and trying new things. Campers and counselors alike have a desire to meet new people who may share the same interests but are quite different than their peers at home or at school. The most significant commonality they share is the desire to be part of a community that is defined by values such as respect, responsibility, and kindness. Merhige continues:

> There is something magical about a summer camp experience. Each and every camp in the world is different. Not merely because of geography or location, but because of the traditions and people who have touched the camp. Every camp has hidden treasures of history and traditions that give it character and identity...Every staff member, alumni camper, and volunteer has memories associated with their time at their camp—memories that stay with them for their lifetime. Most people remember with fondness the counselors, cabins, camp food, camp outs, and special happenings of their time.[11]

So it seems that camps do for children what schools, sports teams, after-school activities and clubs cannot: free kids from time constraints, overwhelming pressure to succeed, and cut-throat competition. In place of these all-too familiar feelings, camps substitute non-stop fun, independence, a choice of unique activities, and sense of security that allows campers to expand their skills and interests. In short, as the American Camp Association asserts, "Camp gives kids a world of good."[12]

Berry Delahanty (second from left) relaxes on the porch of the Big House with friends at her parents' camp, Camp Wono. The site would eventually witness the merger of Wono with Camp Monomoy into Cape Cod Sea Camps.

A camper feels the exhilaration of zip lining. *Photo courtesy of Camp Echo.*

> To most people, "camping" means living out-of-doors or a form of housekeeping in a natural environment. It may suggest living in a tent, a cabin, sleeping on the ground under the stars, or even living in a motorized camper...to camp implies participation in activities related to the natural resources such as hiking, fishing, cooking over a fire, building shelters...Camping generally implies a way of life more simple than that to which the camper will return...*Organized camping* on the other hand is defined as a "sustained experience which provides a creative, recreational, and educational opportunity in group living in the out-of-doors. It utilized trained leadership and the resources of natural surroundings to contribute to each camper's mental, physical, social, and spiritual growth."[15]

Interestingly, the goals of summer camps today are not much different than those outlined by Eells so long ago. But creating an environment conducive to such experiences was a novel and challenging concept in the early years of the summer camp industry. In *A Manufactured Wilderness*, Abigail Van Slyck writes:

> First introduced to the North American landscape in the 1880s, camps were part of a back-to-nature trend that had been developing on both sides of the Atlantic since the middle of the nineteenth century. In this respect, they are like urban parks, residential suburbs, resort hotels and national parks, all institutions aimed at providing respite from what were regarded as the moral and physical degradations of urban life, evils to which women and children were understood to be particularly prone.[16]

Early iterations of summer camps were varied and changed significantly over the first half of the twentieth century. As alluded to above, initially, camp was a means by which to expose urban children to the fresh air and rural lifestyle that so many were missing out on by living in highly urbanized areas. Lance Ozier writes in his article, "Camp as Educator: Lessons Learned from History," "the evolving American school calendar is probably the most distinctive reason for why the summer camp successfully originated and thrived as it did. In pioneer America, children were educated as they lived on farms and learned to help adults with necessary farm work. Schools were introduced for only three months in the winter to supplement the daily education of farm and village life with 'book learning.' The school, with its emphasis on fundamental academic skills, at first merely a supplement to education, gradually came to assume that it was the whole of education."[17] Thus, eventually the concept of summer vacation evolved. "Summers not only became vast resources of unstructured space and time, the season also gave camp educators an opening to offer learning opportunities not available in schools. Camps became intentional learning venues for young people and the adults who directed and counseled them."[18] It is, perhaps, this approach and the acceptance of camps as educational institutions that has allowed them to remain in business more than a century after the first camps were created.

Once the development of many general interest camps was underway throughout the United States in the first few decades of the industry, special interest camps arose as well, serving various religious or political groups. A large number of camps were run by organizations such as the YMCA and the Girl Scouts, which had built-in populations from which to draw, making the camp community relatively homogenous. Without question, however, Frederick William Gunn, headmaster of the Gunnery School, is considered the "father of the organized camp."[19] A graduate of Yale University, a staunch abolitionist and an educator, Gunn sought to prepare his students for participation in the Union Army and believed the best way to do so was by having them experience nature and go on long hikes. At the request of his students, Gunn created an experience that was intended to simulate that of the life of a Civil War soldier. Gunn took his students on a two-week camping trip that became a valued tradition at the school.

> In the summer of 1861, Mr. and Mrs. Gunn took the whole school on a hike, or gypsy trip, as it was called, about four miles to Milford, on the Sound, near New Haven. The trip took two days. The tents, baggage, supplies, etc., were carried in a large market wagon. There were also a few comfortable carriages and two donkeys, but many walked much, and some of the boys all the way. Camp was established on the beach at Welch's Point and named Camp Comfort. Here two happy weeks were spent boating, sailing, fishing, and tramping. This proved such a helpful and delightful experience that Mr. Gunn repeated it in the years of 1863 and 1865.[20]

Gunn's idea was wildly popular and "the success of the Civil War era camps gave way to summer camps in the 1870s at Lake Waramaug, about seven miles north of The Gunnery. A letter, whose author and date are unknown, spoke of the preparations for the summer camp. The writer described camp tasks and activities, such as ball games, swimming, hiking, fishing, and boating. He also wrote about the morning bugle call for the "Family Meeting" where Mr. Gunn would give advice and "cautions" for the coming day: "no swimming alone, the big boys to care for the younger ones, etc." In the evening, they would sing "camp songs" with organ accompaniment played by Mr. Gunn.[21] Clearly, Gunn's wilderness adventures set the tone for future camp programs, which are not so very different from those which he organized so

Campers receive instruction in how to build model airplanes. *Photo courtesy of Camp Dudley.*

Frederick William Gunn, headmaster of the Gunnery School and the "father of organized camping." *Photo courtesy of the American Camp Association.*

Dr. Joseph Rothrock, a botanist and doctor by training, opened a camp for consumptives in Pennsylvania. *Photo courtesy of the Harris & Ewing Collection, Library of Congress.*

many years ago. Gunn's legacy lives on at the Gunnery School where even today students participate in the so-called "Sophomore Saunter," a day-and-a-half hiking trip that is free of electronics and focused on enjoying nature and forming interpersonal relationships.

Inspired by Gunn's approach to education and these legendary trips (though he never took part in them himself), A.S. Gregg Clarke began Camp Keewaydin in 1894. In the wake of the Gunnery Camp's closing in 1879, many Gunnery School students attended Keewaydin in search of the same experiences as those cultivated by Gunn.

In 1876, Dr. Joseph Rothrock took a group of boys whom he considered to be feeble for a "School of Physical Culture," during which they lived in tents near the North Mountain House in Wilkes-Barre, Pennsylvania. Rothrock explained his rationale for the program: "In 1876, I had the happy idea of taking weakly boys in summer out into camp life in the woods and under competent instruction, mingling exercises and study, so that pursuit of health could be combined with acquisition of practical knowledge outside the usual academic lines."[22] Rothrock's campers delighted in typical summer camp activities despite their "feeble" nature. "The forenoon was usually taken up with drawing, gymnastic exercises, surveying, and barometric observations, while the afternoons were devoted to recreation, such as swimming, rowing, target practice, and other sports. The regular routine was often broken by trips and overnight hikes into the woods and by two-or-three-day fishing trips. These early campers discovered the annoyance of gnats and mosquitoes."[23] Rothrock's grand experiment (which cost $200 for four months) lasted only briefly as he moved on to other projects; however, his work clearly contributed to the development of the camping movement.

A group sets up camp in the early days of the Gunnery Camp. *Photo courtesy of the American Camp Association.*

Early campers, like those at the Gunnery Camp, played sports, told stories, and learned about living in the outdoors. There were some big differences though, between early overnight camps and the ones we have today. For example, instead of driving or flying to camp, some kids had to travel by train for several days to get to camp. Fancy sports facilities were rare and some activities, such as water-skiing, didn't even exist. Some basic equipment, such a toilet, was also rare. Often, campers had to dig their own latrines. Another significant difference was that camps were generally more religious than they are now. In part, this was because the YMCA, a traditionally Christian organization, sponsored many early camps.

Overnight camping turned out to be a fantastic way to spend the summer. Kids had a lot of fun, and parents saw the positive influence that camps had on their children. For these reasons, the popularity of camps grew quickly. Only a few dozen camps were operating by the 1880s, but by 1900, that number had grown to several hundred. Most of the early camps, many of which are still operating, were located in the Northeast and upper Midwest.[24]

—Jon Malinowski and Chris Thurber

Ernest Balch proved to be another important forerunner of the summer camp industry; Eells explains that "while William Gunn is seen as the 'father of organized camping,' Balch is often identified as the 'father of the organized camping movement.'"[25] Worried that young boys were susceptible to the negative influences that they would encounter while on vacation with their parents, Balch founded Camp Chocorua in New Hampshire; he sought to provide an opportunity for American boys (especially those coming from wealthy families) to have rustic experiences. As a sophomore at Dartmouth College, he and his brother built a cabin on Burnt Island in Squam Lake in the summer of 1881. The first camper, Charlie Benjamin, arrived and was followed by his cousin and several other boys, all of whom were from densely populated urban areas. Balch was adamant that the campers experience a sense of equality. Every boy would cook, clean, and earn an allowance in a truly democratic environment. No one was above performing manual labor, and all campers were expected to do their part when it came to building huts, cleaning up after meals or helping to maintain the grounds; the experience was truly a group effort. Most of the campers came from an Episcopal background, so Balch, a religious individual, established an acolyte program and choir at the camp. Additionally, Balch felt compelled to teach his campers the importance of being a responsible and engaged member of society while also teaching them to manage their money in "the real world;" hence, each boy was given a weekly allowance and a bank and law court were established.[26] Sadly, Balch faced a hefty debt and was forced to close Chocorua in 1888 after nine years.[27]

However, in spite of the closure of Chocorua, Balch influenced the foundation of other camps. William Ford Nichols, a student at the Harvard Theological Seminary, opened Camp Harvard in 1882 (though two years later, the camp was taken over and moved by Dr. Winthrop T. Talbot who renamed it Camp Asquam. Apparently, Balch was critical of Asquam and Talbot's approach, because he had hired a chef to feed the hungry boys; this ran counter to Balch's idea that part of the experience was to share the responsibilities of providing for the community in ways such as preparing meals.[28] Talbot was also known for helping to advance the First Camp Conference and Leadership Institute which took place in Boston in April of 1903. At this meeting, Talbot put forth the idea that there was a "need for an organization, through which the camps could cooperate in a democratic manner, correlate existing situations, gather and distribute information, establish standards as well as safeguard the principles in camping."[29]

Balch's influence extended in other ways as more and more boys' camps formed. Leslie Paris explains, "Through these personal and regional networks, many elements of Chocorua culture were incorporated into other boys' camps: special uniforms, the "contract" system, a rotating list of chores, Water Sports Day, and the idea of an extended camping trip away from camp."[30] Clearly, many of these practices are still in use today, demonstrating Balch's far-reaching impact on the world of organized camping.

Other less-widely known founding fathers of the camping industry include C. Hanford Henderson who found camps to be an important part of helping children not to regress intellectually over the summer. Henderson named Camp Marienfeld after his mother when he opened it in 1896. While his program was initially more academic in nature, it gradually evolved into an outdoor program in which boys learned about their environment. Marienfeld was divided into three groups: Midget (boys eight to twelve), Junior (boys twelve to fifteen), and Senior (boys sixteen and up). Boys learned their way around a wood shop and a car engine, mastered basic skills needed on a farm, and learned to sail, swim, and ride. Additionally, they gained "economic training." "Under guidance and instruction of a master specially trained for such an organization definite items will be selected to be made for sale. A business company will be set up. The boys will be workers. Producers, owners; they will take turns at labor, management, finance. Although in the past many boys have at camp first come to grips with an art of which they have later made their life work as music and sculpture this plan has no definite intention to teach a vocation, but is a practical attempt to teach business."[31]

Abigail Van Slyck explains that the notion of summer camp, insofar as it was intended to meet childrens' needs and help define American childhood, was largely imagined by the middle class.[32] "Indeed, summer camps provided an important means for this group to address anxieties about gender roles, race relations, class tensions and particularly about modernity and its impact on the lives of children."[33] The latter is certainly worth re-examining in the 21st century, when we find ourselves saturated in technology. Another salient point Van Slyck makes is that camps developed in an era when the needs and rights of children were finally being examined. Child labor laws and required public education were relatively new mandates in society. Children and teens, when not in school or at work, had little free time and few options for fun. Summer camps, then were a logical response to the changing world of the nineteenth century child.[34] These early camps, according to Van Slyck, "were overtly antimodernist, self-consciously celebrating the past in a search for authenticity."[35]

Campers enjoy a swim at North Country Camps' Camp Lincoln in Keeseville, New York, in the 1940s. *Photo courtesy of Camp Lincoln.*

Boys at Camp Nathan Hale, sponsored by the Methodist Camp Service, raise the flag. *Photo courtesy of the Library of Congress.*

Native Americans were an important influence in the early days of Cheley Colorado Camps. *Photo courtesy of Cheley Colorado Camps.*

Ernest Thompson Seton founded the Woodcraft Indians in 1902. *Photo courtesy of the American Camp Association.*

Seton talks with a group of Native Americans. *Photo courtesy of the Library of Congress.*

Native American Roots

Much of the nineteenth century was spent expanding the nation's borders and, in essence, conquering the frontier in an effort to make it habitable and productive. Summer camps, however, were anathema to this, quickly claiming parcels of undeveloped and pristine land that would allow children to commune with nature. Many of the earliest camps assumed Native American names and traditions, which somehow seemed to lend credence to their wilderness setting.

Perhaps not coincidentally, the late nineteenth and early twentieth centuries witnessed the emergence of psychology. G. Stanley Hall asserted that human development was essentially a process parallel to human history (i.e., the theory of recapitulation) in which children "moved through a series of developmental stages from savagery to civilization."[36] Hence, the tendency for white children (who were the ones attending camps at the time) to "play Indian" was not only age-appropriate but also encouraged. Thus, many of the earliest summer camps emphasized Native American themes and practices.

One particularly influential individual with regard to this trend was Ernest Thompson Seton. A native of South Shields, England, Seton and his family moved to Toronto where "he developed an attitude toward life and the society of his time that was quite revolutionary, for it placed significant emphasis on a return to more traditional Native American-based relationship of humans with their surroundings."[37] Seton eventually settled in New York and found much inspiration in President Teddy Roosevelt's environmentalism and keen sense of the outdoors. Whereas Roosevelt promoted the ideas of the Rough Riders, Seton formed the Woodcraft Indians.

Although the group had existed in Seton's imagination only for some time, he saw its formation through to fruition when a group of local boys vandalized his property and killed a number of animals. Instead of responding in punitive fashion, Seton invited the young lads to his home and initiated them into his newly formed "tribe," the Woodcraft Indians. The boys elected representatives: a Chief, a Second Chief, a Keeper of the Tally and a Keeper of the Wampum.[38]

For the boys, the vacation seemed rich in ceremony and tradition, for Seton had carefully thought out all aspects of Woodcraft before they arrived. Central to their experience was a main 'council ring' where the 43 spent most of their time, where the boys listened to stories of the Plains and Indians life, as Seton, as he would later describe it, "gaug[ed] my stories in a steady crescendo till I had renewed the Fenimore Cooper glamour of romance, and heightened it to a blaze of glory." It is clear that it was quite an inspiring affair for the boys which transcended their previous relationship with their natural surroundings, teaching them a new reverence for natural beauty and nature's creatures. Each boy, as part of the process of "think[ing] Indian," was given an Indian name, and was instructed in identification of various plants and animals, as well as in the arts of stalking and trail making, and a variety of other Indian games and rituals. When the holiday was over, some of the boys were reluctant to leave, for the man whom they had once hated because he had fenced in one of their favorite places to hunt had shown them a previously unknown side of the natural world to which they now felt very strong ties. Many came to idolize Seton as "Black Wolf," his chosen Indian name, and some even viewed him as a father figure.[39]

Tentmates at Camp Nathan Hale in Southfields, New York, circa 1943. *Photo courtesy of the Library of Congress.*

In 1903, Seton published *The Birchbark Roll of the Woodcraft Indians* which was a primer outlining his ideals. More importantly, "Seton's development of the idea of Woodcraft in a larger sense also coincided with an emerging trend in the American conscience as a whole at the beginning of the twentieth century, namely, to view Native American life as the model for American society."[40] One of the most significant themes was the notion that Americans' relationship with the land on which they lived could not continue to exist solely as one based on consumerism. Seton sought to promote the idea that Americans needed to develop a symbiotic relationship with their environment, based on respect and appreciation. "Woodcraft teaches young people how to survive in the woods, respect nature, and live harmoniously with all of God's creations."[41]

According to the E.T. Seton Institute, there were a number of ideals emphasized by Seton. Outdoor recreation was the essence of Woodcraft wherein small self-governing groups were essential to the program's success. "Woodcraft gives recognition to all accomplishments by non-competitive standards... Standards are approved by national experts, taking into account the variety of human ability, and the capability of different age groups. The goal is to overcome barriers within ourselves, not to conquer others."[42] Additionally, individuals were encouraged to express themselves so as to boost self-esteem and expression and, to that end, achievements were to be recognized. In short, "The Woodcraft World is an atmosphere in which individuals can find, test, and explore their strengths, where supported by intimate friends they can grow in many directions."[43]

Clearly, Seton was able to capitalize on the new trend of environmentalism modeled by Teddy Roosevelt, who, during his presidency, set aside 200 million acres for national parks, forests, and preserves.[44] "He emphasized the Indian virtues of honesty and forthrightness, outdoor living, council fires, and Indian dances. His program of personal challenges and skills was presumably based on Indian precedents. The Indian heritage persists in many camp programs to this day."[45] Today, however, fewer than a dozen camps in the country still perform the weekly Woodcraft ceremony as designed by Seton and his Native American friends. "Despite drifting away from authentic Native American traditions, many camps still have a natural setting and an educational philosophy that promotes healthy environmental values."[46] Perhaps Seton's most significant legacy is the influence he had on his friends, Luther and Charlotte Gulick, who created the Camp Fire Girls, and on the development of the Boy Scouts organization.

Girl scouts perfecting the art of making a fire, c. 1912. *Photo courtesy of the Library of Congress.*

The influence of Native American traditions and culture is an important part of the summer camp experience to this day. "The Native American philosophies of life—respect for the land and love of every form of life, human and nonhuman" are the very foundation of many camps' programs and core values. Native Americans "believed in harmony between humans and nature rather than conquest and destruction of nature. These are vital characteristics of the Native American way of life. All people can and must learn to live in harmony with the natural world and with one another."[48] It is important that these values are preserved and emphasized, especially for those camps that associate themselves with Native American roots and customs.

Although many camps continue to use Native American names, motifs, and costumes in their programs, this cultural assimilation ranges from the respectful to the absurd. In *Summer Camp Memory Book,* Richard and Kellie Gutman explain the adoption of Native American names for many early summer camps.

> Indian names abound. Some are chosen for their meaning: Unalayee, Cherokee for "place of friends;" Tapawingo, an Indian word for "place of joy;" Chautauqua, Seneca for "one who has taken out fish here." Sometimes the name has a nice ring to it, but the meaning is a bit off: Chippewa, "to roast until puckered up," is a good recipe for marshmallows but not an apt description, one hopes, for a camp. In some instances the true meaning of the Indian word must not have been looked into when the name was chosen. Winona, a Sioux word for "female first born," seems like an odd choice for a boys' camp.[49]

Some camps utilized Native American "guides" who were intended to introduce campers to the native culture, ceremonies, and wisdom. Some may also have participated in various ceremonies including the campers. Campers at Surprise Lake Camp were accustomed to interacting with Vernon Clute, a member of the Seneca tribe. Clute often played the part of different Native Americans in any number of performances including a pageant chronicling Columbus' discovery of America. Charles Eastman, a Sioux Indian, even ran a girls' summer camp in New Hampshire called the School of the Woods.

Children at other camps dressed up as Native Americans, some even performing a sort of war dance. Some campers slept in tipis, which many camp directors found a charming way to incorporate Native American culture into daily camp life. Still other camps put on "Wild West shows" in which the Native American was grossly misrepresented. The study of nature was often associated with Native American spirituality. The unfortunate result of some of these practices was the perpetuation of stereotypes. "As many camp leaders saw the matter, Indian play was particularly suited to children's nature because Native Americans represented a less advanced stage of civilization."[47]

A ritualistic "Indian Ceremony" at Camp Highlands for Boys. *Photo courtesy of Mike Bachmann and Camp Highlands for Boys.*

Although the notion of "playing Indian" dissipated after the Second World War, remnants of Native American culture are still evident in today's camps. The camp fire, for example, was an important Native American tradition that was adopted by camps and used to denote special occasions. Council rings, to this day, play a significant role in one's daily camp experiences. Generally a circle in which a group of campers sits on benches, this is where news for the day is heard, or campfires are held. George Eastman wrote in *Indian Scout Talks,* "The circle is symbolic of life, also symbolic of the day's journey."[50] In the same text, he also explained that "as fire is the symbol of enthusiasm, energy, and devotion, and is with the Indians a strictly masculine emblem, it is fit that the young men gather about it before going upon a journey or 'war path.'"[51]

Campers hike through the Rocky Mountains in the early days of Bear Lake Trail School, now Cheley Colorado Camps. *Photo courtesy of Cheley Colorado Camps.*

Camp Dudley campers pay homage to the Native American values emphasized in the camp experience. *Photo courtesy of Camp Dudley.*

Girls' Camps

Initially, camps were only available to wealthy boys and existed primarily in New England. Over time, however, girls' camps were created and programs began to spring up throughout the nation. Girls' camps in the first half of the twentieth century played a significant part in breaking with the past. Van Slyck explains, "summer camps prepared girls to be better pals to both their husbands and their sons by giving them a camping experience akin...Like boys' camps, then, girls' camps ultimately sought to address the sissy problem by forging a new generation of middle-class white women who knew the value of discipline, while enjoying the hardy outdoors activities that their sons would need to grow into manly men."[52]

Reporter Caille Millner wrote for *The Daily* that "girls' summer camps have gone through just as many incarnations [as boys' camps]. Camps offering outdoorsy life were meant to inoculate degenerate city boys with masculinity and toughness—where did that leave girls, who were supposed to grow into ladies? Well, there was the "rest" model pioneered by that early camp in New Jersey. And there was the solution of Dr. Luther Gulick, who founded the Camp Fire Girls organization in 1910: His curriculum was designed to make housekeeping duties seem like an 'adventure.'"[53]

In a 1914 article for *Outlook*, Anna Worthington Coale wrote, "The girl camper may be twelve or twenty. She usually comes from a home of luxury and hugely enjoys the novelty of sleeping in tents, the unhampered opportunities for learning to swim, to row, to paddle—in short, to live close to friendly Mother Nature—through eight or nine happy weeks of the camp season. And, best of all, she learns the value of girl friendships."[54] She went on to explain, "The girls' camp has proved that there can be just as great esprit de corps among girls as among boys. Not only that, but among girls of varying ages and circumstances."[55] "Girls come to camp 'tired of books and lessons and the dead routine of school,' but they love to work at basketry, pottery, stenciling, jewelry, leather work, bookbinding, and carpentry."[56]

Girls pose on the steps of their platform tent at Wyonegonic Camp. *Photo courtesy of Wyonegonic Camp for Girls.*

Three girl scouts enjoy boating while at camp in 1912. *Photo courtesy of the Library of Congress.*

Merry Meeting Camp Juniors on a hike. *Photo courtesy of Sharon Elizabeth Bramlett.*

Coale explained that attending camp allowed a girl to find her place in the microcosm of the camp community, thereby preparing her more thoroughly for finding her place in the larger world.

> In the democracy of camp life a girl finds herself in an environment of simplicity and freedom which stimulates her to activity. In place of languidly accepting a ready-made programme of play she must provide play activities for herself and others. There is no distinction in dress, for the camp costume is alike for all. A girl is rated by her achievement, not by externals. Moreover, she has a distinct advantage in being rated well at the start, for, as one older brother put it, 'your camp takes it for granted that a girl is a good fellow till she proves that she isn't.[57]

Coale also asserted that "the result of camp training should be, and usually is, a sound mind in a sound body."[58] She goes on to explain that schools and colleges, in her opinion, were not preparing girls for their future; she claims that "the study of dead languages and higher mathematics may be good mental exercise, but may be wholly unrelated to the life of the girl who is preparing to make a home."[59] Coale noted that some of the important qualities that girls who attended camp acquired were a sense of humor, time management skills, adaptability, and sportsmanship.

Campers at Pine Tree Camp in the Poconos play a game of volleyball, c. 1910-1920. *Photo courtesy of the Library of Congress.*

Laura Mattoon, founder and director of Camp Kehonka. *Photo courtesy of the American Camp Association.*

Dr. Luther Gulick, founder of the Camp Fire Girls. *Photo courtesy of George Grantham Bain Collection (Library of Congress).*

The first such program can be attributed to Laura Mattoon, the founder and director of Camp Kehonka (1902). Mattoon's contributions to the camping industry were absolutely critical, as "she understood well the place women were to occupy in the twentieth century and the many ways in which the camp experience could provide preparation."[60] Not only did Mattoon start a reputable girls' camp, she also went on to be influential in the development of many camp administration models. Mattoon was a science teacher in a New York City school and believed firmly that girls needed to commune with nature just as much as boys did. At Kehonka, girls camped out in tents, hiked, swam, and even built their own furniture. "Mattoon also provided her students with bifurcated skirts, similar to today's 'skort,' so that the girls could move more freely in communion with nature."[61] In addition, "Miss Mattoon believed that camping is an important means of building character. She taught her campers the pleasures, values, and skills of outdoor life. She shared in the publication of the *Camper's Guidance Manual* which emphasized character development and skills in outdoor activities, canoeing, swimming, hiking, arts and crafts, music, drama, and nature studies."[62]

Another significant early girls' camp was Wohelo, founded by Luther and Charlotte Gulick in 1907. The name, Wohelo, was short for "work, health and love," three important values that remain at the core of the camp's mission today. The Gulicks later founded Camp Fire Girls, which would become a significant player in the world of summer camps. The Gulicks firmly believed that boys and girls needed to be treated differently and, as a result, they devised a program guided by a set of principles that would help girls prepare for their futures as homemakers. Girls were expected to become self-reliant through their camp experience that was based largely on Native American traditions, environmental awareness, and a sense of community.

The "law" of the Camp Fire Girls, as outlined in the official handbook of 1912, was to "seek beauty, give service, pursue knowledge, be trustworthy, hold on to health, glorify work, be happy."[63] Local chapters were instructed to have their own unique name though urged to include "Camp Fire" somewhere in the title. Members started as Wood Gatherers and then advanced to Fire Makers and finally Torch Bearers.[64] After at least three months, Wood Gatherers had the opportunity to advance to Fire Maker by learning and reciting the Fire Maker's Desire which is as follows:

As fuel is brought to the fire
So I purpose to bring
My strength
My ambition
My heart's desire
My joy
And my sorrow
To the fire
Of humankind
For I will tend
As my fathers have tended
And my fathers' fathers
Since time began
The fire that is called
The love of man for man
The love of man for God.[65]

Girls relax on a pier at Luther Gulick Camps. *Photo courtesy of the American Camp Association.*

Camp Fire Girls hiking. *Photo courtesy of the Bain Collection, Library of Congress.*

Camp Fire Girls at Lake Sebago. *Photo courtesy of the Bain Collection, Library of Congress.*

> "She must also prepare two meals for the Camp Fire meetings, mend knit items, account for all money, tie a square knot repeatedly, sleep outside or with open windows for a month, abstain from soda and candy for a month, spend thirty minutes outside every day, name the main causes of infant mortality in summer and know how to care for various emergencies."[66]

After reaching this milestone and serving as a Fire Maker for at least three months, an individual was eligible to become a Torch Bearer, which meant that she was an assistant to the Guardian. First, candidates had to recite the Torch Bearer's Desire: "That light which has been given to me, I desire to pass undimmed to others."[67] Other requirements included leading girls in camp and achieving additional honors in several different areas including health, home craft, nature lore, camp craft, hand craft, business, and patriotism.

Group leaders were called Guardians of the Fire and, as such, were responsible for organizing and running meetings. The most important and symbolic part of each meeting was the lighting of three candles that symbolized work, health and love, the guiding force behind the Camp Fire Girls and, ultimately, Camp Wohelo. Three important phrases were spoken as the candles were lit.

> "Wohelo means work. We glorify work because through work we are free. We work to win, to conquer, to be masters. We work for the joy of the working and because we are free. Wohelo means work." Next, another girl would say, "Wohelo means health. We hold on to health, because through health we serve and are happy. In caring for the health and beauty of our persons we are caring for the very shrine of the Great Spirit. Wohelo means health." Finally, as the last candle was lit, a third girl said, "Wohelo means love. We love Love, for love is life, and light and joy and sweetness. And love is comradeship and motherhood and fatherhood and all dear kinship. Love is the joy of service so deep that self is forgotten. Wohelo means love."[68]

Anna Worthington Coale wrote at length about the benefits of summer camp for girls in a July 1914 issue of *Outlook*. She asserted that not only was camp beneficial for girls in terms of providing them an opportunity to experience the outdoors while forming friendships but also that it was critical in preparing them for college and life thereafter.

> The camp girl is taught how to divide her time. Play has a large place in her programme, and it furnishes valuable educational training.

> Through play she learns some of the first principles of the fine art of living—adaptability, reliability, initiative, and good fellowship. She also realizes the great value of rest—sometimes solitude—and its relation to work and play...And then the camp girl works. She goes in for things, and works for the sake of working. It may be organizing sports, or some unfinished craft work, or a part of the domestic work of the camp assigned to her. Sometimes she puts in an hour or two on lessons which have to be made up for school in the fall. With superb health, exuberance of spirits, and pleasant companionship, she gets joy out of working. And a definite part of each camp day is sacredly devoted to work. Because she has learned the importance of accomplishing what she sets out to do and the advantage of team-work, the camp girl is depended on in college for the executive work in non-academic activities...Camp life gives a girl also a good store of knowledge as a preparation for her academic work. She knows not only how to bandage a cut and right an overturned canoe, but also how to recognize the stars and appreciate the poetry of scenery. Contact with the real world of nature develops an interest in scientific explanations and theories.[69]

Kehonka campers in 1931 sport their uniforms and strike a serious pose on Lake Winnipesaukee in Wolfeboro, New Hampshire. *Photo courtesy of Roy Ballentine.*

More specifically, Coale discussed the differences between "sports and occupations" at camp. She explained that girls engaged in sports simply for fun, dismissing the competitiveness of their male counterparts. However, when it came to "crafts," campers were advised not to take on challenging projects that exceeded their skill level; in fact, she recommended that they begin with "the simpler arts, such as basket making" before moving onto more complex skills like jewelry making."[70] She discusses at length the notion of "camp crafts," which seem to fall under the heading of nature. So called "camp crafts" included hiking, bird watching, astronomy, and sleeping under the stars. Coale recommended that some sort of expert be brought in for this special aspect of camping so that the girls might learn something in addition to simply having fun while enjoying nature.

Coale wrote a great deal about "camp spirit," which she explained as putting aside one's individual needs and interests in favor of the common good. But she also understood intimately the different types of girls who attend camp. "A great many stories might be told of the experiences of different types of girls in fitting into the camp environment. Of the shy, sensitive girl who only needs to be brought out, and who responds at once to the friendliness of camp; of the over-confident girl who has a great many jolts before she finally finds herself, and wins the friendship of others; of the self-centered girl and the spoiled darling; and the girl who is just naturally lovable and is sure to find a warm place in the hearts of everybody."[71]

Girls participate in warm-up exercises at Camp Kehonka, circa 1910. *Photo courtesy of Roy Ballentine.*

Girls engage in vigorous exercise at Camp Kehonka circa 1910. *Photo courtesy of Roy Ballentine.*

The outbreak of World War I was felt by summer camps in a variety of ways. Anna Worthington Coale wrote in *Summer in the Girls' Camp* about how camps were impacted by the war. "We had heard rumors here and there that the camps would be closed, or offered to the Government for military purposes, but that would have been a great mistake…the summer camp is the very best place in the world to develop patriotism among boys and girls, for the spirit of the camps has always been the spirit of service."[72] Girls received Red Cross training in a number of skills including first aid which could, if need be, help with the war effort.

Some boys' camps emphasized a military-like, regimented discipline in their daily schedule while girls' camps, which had begun to appear on the camp landscape, taught campers first aid and other skills that could be useful on the homefront during or after the war.[73] Critics, however, were skeptical that the summer camp experience would detract from a girl's proscribed future as wife, mother, and homemaker.

The 1960s and 1970s were a tumultuous time for this country, which precipitated a great deal of change, but Camp Kehonka remained true to its values and ideals. The camp's literature cited the following among its goals for campers: "Realization of potential for spiritual growth in everyday living relationships, development of essential character attributes like self-reliance, unwavering integrity and emotional stability, experiences in group living that confirm home training, and facilitate social adjustment, appreciation of democratic freedoms and privileges as interpreted through discussions, a voice in determining program, and acceptance of individual and group responsibilities."[74] Throughout Kehonka's existence, Mattoon's wish that girls'

Campers stretch in preparation for swimming and canoeing at Camp Kehonka. *Photo courtesy of Roy Ballentine.*

Girls at Camp Kehonka perform *You're a Good Man, Charlie Brown. Photo courtesy of Roy Ballentine.*

camp experience would complement that which they learned at home, school, and church was realized through a rigorous and diverse program.

Today, girls' camps remain a vital option for many campers. A 1993 *New York Times* article ("A Last Goodbye to Camp, and to Just Being a Girl") featured interviews with several girls who had attended Camp Fernwood for Girls for a number of years. The girls all emphatically believed that they were better able to be themselves and were more inclined to try new activities without boys around. They could go skinny dipping, raise bras up the flagpole, and form genuine female friendships all without the pressure of having to impress boys. It is thanks to pioneers of the industry like Mattoon and the Gulicks that girls were afforded the same camp experiences that were extended to boys in the late nineteenth and early twentieth centuries.

Girls at Camp Kehonka enjoy their friends on an idyllic summer day. *Photo courtesy of Roy Ballentine.*

Religiously Affiliated Camps

Camps with religious affiliations have also had a rich history. Reverend George Hinckley is typically cited as the founder of the first church camp. A newly minted pastor, Hinckley organized a camping trip in order to get to know some of the boys in his new congregation in 1880. The boys camped on Gardner's Island near Wakefield, Rhode Island, and their days consisted of campfires, swimming, physical activity, and religious studies. The experience was a positive one, and Hinckley sponsored a similar trip the following summer, before moving on to start Good Will Farm, an institution dedicated to providing assistance for struggling boys and girls. Good Will Farm was founded on ideas similar to those of camps; following religious education in the mornings, the children would have an opportunity to swim, play games, and enjoy nature. Religiously affiliated camps like the one started by Hinckley continued to become more and more popular over the years and often grew out of existing organizations such as the YMCA and the JCC. Today, the American Camp Association reports that one-fifth of all ACA accredited camps are religiously affiliated.[75]

Memorial Service

Conference Boys' Departments, Y. M. C. A.

Albany, May 29th, 1897

In Loving Memory of

Sumner F. Dudley

Died March 14, 1897

The program for Sumner Dudley's memorial service. Dudley was the founder of the earliest YMCA camp. *Photo courtesy of the American Camp Association.*

YMCA

Sumner Dudley was an important figure in the development of both the summer camp and YMCA traditions. In the summer of 1885, Dudley took a group of boys camping for eight days at Orange Lake where they fished, hiked, swam, and engaged in Bible study. Dudley, financially backed by George Peck and Rudolph Leypoldt, referred to this as the "Boys' Camping Society" and thus YMCA camps were established.[76] The experience was a positive one and, once word got out, twice as many boys enrolled the following summer. Dudley led the 1886 trip and the five successive trips to Wawayanda (near Newburgh, New York). After Dudley's unexpected death in 1897, "Camper #1" George Peck assumed the role of director. In 1907, enough money was raised to procure a permanent site for Camp Dudley and, in 1908, it set down roots in Westport, New York, where it remains today. Some significant changes took place under the leadership of Herman "Becky" Beckman (to whom the campers affectionately called "Chief") who took over Camp Dudley in 1908.

The entrance to Camp Dudley. *Photo courtesy of Camp Dudley.*

Beckman altered the camp's daily schedule to reflect more structure and greater supervision. He added a number of sports to the camp's program offerings and insisted on daily inspection of the campers' living quarters. He also instated an awards system that allowed campers to earn Camp Dudley emblems after completing certain tasks or activities. Although the camp continued to

Campers and staff perform at Camp Dudley. *Photo courtesy of Camp Dudley.*

grow in terms of both physical plant and enrollment, its fundamental values and approach to caring for boys remained the same. Today, Camp Dudley remains one of the oldest and most successful YMCA camps in the country. Matt Storey has been the camp's director since 2011 and strives to uphold the camp's early motto of "the other fellow first."[77] The four pillars of the Camp Dudley program are athletics, the arts, the outdoors, and spirituality.[78]

Camp Becket, another early YMCA camp, was opened in 1903. H.W. Gibson, Becket's founder, penned *Camping for Boys* in 1913. Nearly three decades later, Henry and Ina Gibson opened Becket's sister camp, Chimney Corners Camp for Girls. One of Camp Becket's most enduring traditions is the annual Dads' Weekend. "Since 1922, dads and sons have shared a weekend at camp, with boys taking their dads—or other relatives, friends, or mentors—through two full days of their camp experience. Dads' Weekend offers the chance to enter your boy's world, free of the distractions of day-to-day life."[79] The weekend is sponsored by the Dads' Association, which is comprised of the fathers of current Becket campers. Camp Becket continues to adhere to the same values and traditions as those upon which the camp was founded.

Most YMCA camps had a number of things in common. First, they set aside Sunday as a day of rest, when most campers would attend chapel services, read, and write letters home. "Whites" or more formal clothing was generally worn, particularly for chapel. Second, camp chapels were often outside, providing campers for an opportunity to appreciate God in a natural setting; this emphasized the importance of the transcendent aspects of nature. Third, most YMCA camps were somewhat formulaic; in 1946, the organization published *Layout, Building Designs, and Equipment for Y.M.C.A. Camps.*

What is most significant about the YMCA camp movement, however, is that it made camping accessible to a larger segment of the population. Abigail van Slyck writes, "Explicitly intended to foster Christian conversation, these early YMCA camps also implicitly aimed at intervening in Victorian gender roles. In addition to extracting boys from their mother-centered homes, these camps sought to introduce young campers to muscular Christianity, a new mode of manhood that melded masculinity (a new term in the late nineteenth century) and religious sentiment (reclaimed from the feminine sphere)."[80] While much has changed about the Y's approach to summer camp programming over the years, the founding goal of Camp Dudley remains relevant: "to provide children with a positive developmental experience through making new friends, building confidence and growing in self-reliance."[81]

Today, there are 335 Ys that conduct overnight camps and 245 resident camps (sites or properties) that collectively serve over 196,000 youth each summer.

YWCA

According to the American Camp Association, the first YWCA camp, Sea Rest, was organized by the Philadelphia chapter and was located in Asbury Park, New Jersey. The camp, which predated any YMCA camp, was intended as a place where, "'tired young women wearing out their lives in an almost endless drudgery for wages that admit no thought of rest or recreation'" would have a chance to relax.[82] *The New York Times* reported the following on August 4, 1874:

> A Philadelphia paper of yesterday says: "About three months ago a lot of ground in Ausbury Park [sic], N. J., was donated by Mr. Bradley, of New-York, to the Women's Christian Association of this city for the purpose of erecting a boarding-house for the use of the numerous overworked female employees of our city stores and manufactories, whose slender means will not admit of a sojourn by the sea at the high rates usually charged. The lot comprises 125 feet of ocean front, extending in depth 75 feet. Upon this has been erected a handsome house, capable of accommodating from twenty-five to thirty inmates. A fine verandah extends around two sides, affording both a lake and ocean view. The rooms are furnished with the good taste to be expected from the ladies in whose hands the matter was placed. White Swiss curtains, with blue trimmings, drape the windows of the cozy little bed-rooms, iron bedsteads, hair mattresses, covered with white counterpanes, toilet tables, mirrors, chairs, and matting, complete the cool Summer furniture. Situated on the edge of a grove, it has the uncommon advantages of well shaded grounds with the cool sea breezes, while the lake within two minutes' walk affords fine opportunities for rowing or sailing. The rate of board has been fixed at $3 per week, thus affording an opportunity to many a weary seamstress or saleswoman of spending her two weeks' vacation where renewed health and many happy hours may be attained period."[83]

Many notable individuals were a part of this early effort to provide some sort of camp experience for girls; among them was Abbie Graham, author of *The Girls' Camp: Program Making for Summer Leisure*. Graham wrote, "probably the greatest social contribution which the camp vacation can make to any group of campers is an experience of successful cooperative life in a group diverse in interests, skills, abilities, but all enjoying common activities...To realize that everyone has something to give and that the best life is possible for all when every person has opportunity to make his contribution."[84] These values are still emphasized in much of the YWCA's work and outreach.

Another early camp to be affiliated with the YWCA was Camp Hochelaga. Founded in 1919 by the Vermont chapter of the YWCA, Hocehlaga was initially located in Burlington, but moved to its current location, South Hero, Vermont, in 1926. Today, Camp Hochelaga, located in South Hero, Vermont, is the only remaining all-girls' YWCA camp in the United States.

Girls perform exercises at a Maryland YWCA camp.
Photo courtesy of the Library of Congress.

Jewish Camps

Jewish camps, like most other camps, were started to alleviate the "symptoms" associated with city living and to avoid the scourge of rampant diseases like polio. However, with the tremendous influx of immigrants, more camps were established to help children acculturate to their new environment. "The quest for a Jewish identity in an overwhelmingly non-Jewish nation, the growing affluence of Jewish families, and the willingness of city-dwelling Jews to send their children to 'the country' for the summer contributed to the camps' enormous popularity."[85] A number of Jewish social service agencies helped establish camps for Jewish children, which "combined Jewish identity building with athletics, arts & crafts, nature experiences and general fun."[86] Ultimately, the goal is to help Jewish youth develop into passionate, practicing adult Jews.

The late nineteenth and early twentieth centuries witnessed an influx of European immigrants, many of who were Jewish. This growing population was looking for a way to assimilate their children into American culture. Hence, a number of Jewish camps developed, especially along the East Coast. Writer Jeri Zeder explains the origin of summer camps created for Jewish children.

> The early Jewish camps were motivated by two concepts: Bring inner-city kids out to the country, and "Americanize" the children of Eastern European immigrants. What made these camps Jewish was their demographics, not their programming. Their campers were Jewish, and the camps were run under Jewish auspices. But beginning in the 1920s and through the '30s, '40s and '50s, a trend emerged that ran counter to the emphasis on acculturation at many Jewish camps: the growth of camps with consciously Jewish cultural and educational missions...In addition to Yiddish camps, camps with Zionist, Hebrew, and socialist identities came into existence. While sporting different cultural and ideological missions, they all offered in common Jewish experiences inextricably linked to the pleasures of friendships forged in outdoor summer fun.[87]

Researchers Amy L. Sales and Leonard Saxe explain in their book, *How Godly Are Thy Tents: Summer Camps as Jewish Socializing Experiences,* that "camp exposes campers and staff to Jewish leaders and role models who exhibit Jewish identity, *ruach* (spirit), and *menschlichkeit* (being a good person)."[88] These early Jewish camps were generally run by Jewish agencies and organizations and, soon after, Jewish community centers and federations began to organize camps as well.[89] The result of this movement was the development of community camps, Zionist camps, denominational movement camps and private camps.[90] Sales and Saxe assert that so-called "community

Older campers perform a traditional Israeli dance at Camp Ramah. *Photo courtesy of Camp Ramah.*

Girls at Camp Ramah enjoy a traditional camp experience while also celebrating their Jewish heritage. *Photo courtesy of Camp Ramah.*

camps" account for one-third of the Jewish camps today. "Zionist camping arrived on the scene in the 1930s and spread during the 1940s and 1950s."[91] Not surprisingly, there was a distinct increase in the creation of denominational movement camps following World War II. This, Sales and Saxe claim, was "the time when the field shifted from camps with social welfare or ideological aims to those with educational or religious missions."[92]

The experience of American Jews vis-à-vis the events unfolding overseas that ultimately led to the rise of Nazi Germany provided an interesting backdrop against which the Jewish summer camp movement strengthened. "That a uniquely Jewish summer camp movement developed during this period must be understood both as an expression of national trends and as reaction to a growing nationalism. Referred to by historians as nativism, this nationalism expressed fear and hatred towards people deemed not-American, including Jews. This prejudice resulted in social policies and immigration legislation that hampered Jewish-Americans' access to elite educational institutions and social clubs, effectively barred Jews from entering the country, and undoubtedly shaped the lives of some Jewish children in America."[93] Jewish children were given the opportunity to develop a strong sense of cultural identity while engaging in traditional camp activities. The development of private camps geared towards wealthier Jewish families began slowly in the 1920s and 1930s and significantly increased after World War II as well. Among the earliest of this type of camp were Androscoggin, a boys' camp established in Maine in 1907, and Blue Star Camps, begun by the Popkin family in 1948.[94]

That the majority of Jewish camps are located in the Northeast Triangle (New York, New Jersey and Pennsylvania) and New England (Connecticut, Massachusetts, Maine, New Hampshire and Rhode Island boast the most in that region) is the direct result of twentieth-century immigration patterns.[95]

> Among the first were the Cejwin Camps in Port Jervis, N.Y., which were founded by the Central Jewish Institute, an independent Jewish community center on Manhattan's Upper East Side, and Camp Boiberik, a Yiddish camp near Rhinebeck, N.Y...Brandeis University professor Jonathan Sarna explains that before 1940, about two-thirds of all new Jewish camps were either philanthropic or community based. From 1940 to 1960, that number dropped to less than a quarter, while 40% had explicit educational and religious missions. Ninety new Jewish camps opened during the 1960s, but then growth stopped abruptly. "There was stagnation of new camps from the late 1960s to the early 1970s until the mid-1990s," Silverman said. There are no clear explanations for these trends. Some speculate that the stagnation was related to the push to build congregations and day schools, and that the subsequent new growth is related to the redirection of resources to Jewish summer camping after studies suggested that camps are good investments for the Jewish future because they are effective at making Jewishness "stick" to kids.[96]

Camp Boiberik, affiliated with the Sholem Aleichem Folk Institute, was run by Leibush Lehrer from 1923 until 1964. Lehrer, a well-known Jewish educator, worried about too much assimilation and the potential loss of Jewish culture and tradition among the next generation. "Boiberik was established to imbue Jewish children with 'the educational values of wholesome fun, recreation and cooperative living' and to give campers a 'consciousness of Jewish belonging and have the feelings arising there from translated into meaningful activities,' according to its founding director Leibush Lehrer ... The camp was named Boiberik after a mythical summer place referred to in one of Sholem Aleichem's stories."[97] Marla Sokolsky recalls, "Going to Boiberik was not an 'American camp experience.' Although there was lots of swimming and sports, there was an East European, socialist, Yiddish cultural overlay that permeated everything we did."[98]

Longtime camper and former White House Liaison to the Jewish Community Noam Neusner explains that there are three experiences Jewish youth must have in order to maintain a vibrant Jewish community in America: Jewish sleepaway camp, Jewish day school, and an extended trip to Israel. "The elite Jewish community leaders like rabbis and community directors invariably have gone to summer camp and have been involved as adults. It is a defining characteristic of being a Jew in America: sending your kid to camp. In order to strengthen the community you've got to send people out of it."[99]

Today, about 120 non-profit Jewish camps exist throughout the United States, which are staffed by approximately 18,000 Jewish young adults and attended by over 70,000 children. While Jewish camps today have a wide variety of approaches to the incorporation of Jewish traditions, they all share one goal: the desire to promote and keep vital Jewish culture and practices with each new generation. "It is Jewish tradition to give children candy when they study the Torah so that they will associate the sweetness of the candy with the sweetness of Torah. The educational theory of summer camping is similar: if children come to associate Jewish life with sweetness—the smell of pine trees, the closeness of friends, laughter in the bunk—what they practice and learn at camp will remain with them for a lifetime."[100]

Like the rest of the camp industry, Jewish camps are facing challenges as they navigate the twenty-first century. First, capital funds are needed to establish more camps and offer scholarships. Many philanthropists have spent time and resources over the past decade to improve the facilities at Jewish camps to help them compete for clientele with the larger, more extravagant camps.[101] One area to which they have dedicated resources is the creation of some specialty camps that focus on specific activities like drama and sports; this is an important marketing strategy because many Jewish camps lose would-be campers to these types of camps. Second, attracting qualified Jewish staff poses a difficulty. Third, these camps need to improve and maintain a high level of quality so as to not lose campers to regular camps that might have better facilities or superior programming.[102]

Neusner reflects on the relevance of Jewish camps in today's world. "As long as camps provide kids and families as a way to grow they will still be relevant. Kids have more opportunities now [but] they lack independence and the ability to control their own lives and show leadership. We put up more and more guardrails in schools [and in society] and camp is an escape from that. The institution is able to adapt to what families need."[103]

What stands out from the national census of Jewish residential camps is the complexity of the system of camps that have been built over the past century by and for the American Jewish community. Both structurally and programmatically, the variety of Jewish camps is vast. There are nondenominational private camps and camps organized by the religious movements. There are East Coast camps and West Coast camps, old camps and camps newly built, camps that create small communities during the summer with fifty campers and those that create small cities with five hundred campers…there are camps with minimal Jewish programming and those in which Jewish life and education pervade the entire day.[104]

Campers and counselors enjoy spending the summer together exploring their Jewish identity. *Photo courtesy of Camp Ramah.*

It is especially important to promote a strong sense of Jewish identity among teens so that as adults they remain committed to their faith. The Ramah camping movement has had great success in terms of promoting Jewish ideals within a summer camp setting. This is likely the reason that Ramah camps boast so many marriages among former campers and counselors. *Photo courtesy of Camp Ramah.*

Fresh Air Camps

"Fresh Air" camps, though not labeled as such initially, were started in 1872 by the Children's Aid Society of New York on Staten Island. This program was designed to give children from the city an opportunity to escape city life and commune with nature. In addition, it was also intended to serve children suffering from tuberculosis since fresh air was believed to aid in recovering from this affliction.

Reverend Willard Parsons delivered a sermon in 1877 in which he asked his Sherman, Pennsylvania, congregation to open their homes to a small group of impoverished children from Brooklyn. The parishioners did just that and a group of children enjoyed the Poconos that summer. By 1881, the Fresh Air Fund, as it came to be known, was so popular that Parsons sought funding from *The New York Tribune* to help with his efforts.[105] Parsons remained the director of the program until his death in 1906.

Today, the Fresh Air Fund organizes a volunteer host family program and also operates five camps, Camp Mariah (coed camp for 12–14 year olds), Camp Hidden Valley (coed camp for 8–12 year olds with and without special needs), Camp Anita Bliss Coler (for girls ages 9–15), Camp Hayden-Marks Memorial (for boys ages 9–5) and Camp Tommy (for boys ages 12–15). A 2006 *New York Times* article showcased the purpose of the Fund: "the city children who venture into the countryside as part of the Fresh Air Fund say it best. One rhapsodized about 'how it feels to live without violence and gangs on the city streets.' Another talked about how, beyond the city limits: 'It's really quiet and you see the stars at night here. At home, you only see street lights.'"[106] In many cases, Fresh Air host families are the only people that these inner-city children meet who have attended college and are not prey to substance abuse, gangs, and violence. One fortunate camper explained to *The New York Times in 2012,* "'getting away from the city was not just a breath of fresh air for me...It was a geography, history, economics, agriculture and sociology lesson all rolled into one.'"[107]

Today, the Fresh Air Fund works hard to reach out to all groups in New York City whose children might benefit from the program. Literature is distributed in Spanish, Mandarin, Korean, Albanian, Polish, and French, in an effort to reach out to new immigrant groups and ever-changing city demographics.[108] There are a host of generous corporate sponsors including Payless Shoes which sold the "Friendship Shoe." This white canvas sneaker comes complete with a set of markers that can be used to design the shoe while at camp "to celebrate friendships, as children can have their friends and counselors sign and illustrate the shoes, creating a perfect one-of-a-kind memento of their time with The Fresh Air Fund."[109] All profits from the shoes' sales go directly to the Fresh Air Fund. To date, the Fresh Air Fund has provided free summer vacations for over 1.7 million inner city, low-income children since 1877.[110]

Trail Blazer Camps

Trail Blazer Camps were founded by John Ames Mitchell, editor of *Life* magazine, with the same idea that children should have a respite from city living. In the summer of 1887, Mitchell raised enough money to send twenty children to a ten-acre farm in Connecticut for a vacation. The concept was so popular that even the railroads contributed to the effort by lowering the fares for the young travelers. Within three decades, almost 40,000 children had enjoyed a summer in the fresh air thanks to Mitchell. The program expanded when, in 1923, James Cox Brady opened his estate in New Jersey to children for a Life's Farm parallel program.

Lloyd B. Sharp took over as the executive director of Life's Farm in 1925, changing the organization's name to Life's Camps and dividing the program by gender; girls enjoyed the Branchville, Connecticut, location (Life Girls Camp) while boys journeyed to the farm in New Jersey (Camp Raritan). However, as the economy of the United States began to decline and the nation was engaged in two World Wars, funding for the Trail Blazers' programs became more difficult to procure. In the post-war era, *Life* magazine's parent company, Time, Inc., decided that the camps were "no longer an appropriate corporate mission," and consequently withdrew its funding. Time, Inc., did, however, bestow $100,000 as an endowment before severing ties.[111] The name Trail Blazer Camps was applied to the camps after the magazine withdrew its financial support.

In 1951, an individual donor by the name of Doris Duke financed the summer so that the programming could continue. She was able to do the same in 1952, but then announced that the camps were closing. Sharp, however, was unwilling to give up his vision and continued to seek support elsewhere. Lois Goodrich, equally committed to the future of Life camps, was able to effectively raise funds with the oversight of a new board put in place by the St. John's Guild. Over the next decade, Doris Duke remained a benefactor as well. It was during this era that boys' and girls' camping was separated and they remain so today.

Today, Trail Blazers calls 1,100 acres of land on the Mashipacong Bogs Preserve in New Jersey home. The goals of the program are to "experience the wonders of nature firsthand, build confidence and independence in a supportive, communal environment, explore and develop new skills and interests, form close bonds with staff and fellow program mates [and] develop a love of learning and deep connection with the outdoors."[112]

The Camp Industry Responds to Changes in Society

Once they became an established industry in the United States, summer camps found themselves having to change in response to global and national trends and events in the first half of the twentieth century. The entire movement of camping can be divided into several eras.

The Recreational Stage: 1860s–1920s

On the heels of Romanticism and Transcendentalism, trends that had defined the nation for a number of years, the Recreational Stage lasted from the inception of summer camps in the 1860s until the 1920s. During this seminal period, a number of important movements occurred including the Fresh Air, Conservation, Settlement, Playground, Scouting, and Child Study movements. Camps founded during this era were run mainly by educators and parents with the intent of providing wealthy children a respite from city life and the rigors of formalized education.[113] It is important to note, however, that "whereas private independent camps developed around the strength and personality of individuals, agency camps developed as part of the overall programs of larger church denominations and social service agencies."[114] This was also the era during which a number of agencies such as 4-H, Camp Fire, YMCA, YWCA, and the Scouts also began their own camps (see above).

A group of campers relaxes on the porch of Camp Kehonka's loom house in the 1930s. *Photo courtesy of Roy Ballentine.*

The Cove at Camp Kehonka, circa 1920. *Photo courtesy of Roy Ballentine.*

The Educational Stage: 1920–1950

The Recreational Stage was followed by the Educational Stage (1920–1950). Over these three decades, the summer camp industry expanded westward, as the idea of organized camping spread from New England; this was aided by the simultaneous improvements being made in transportation. Although some believed that public schools should be responsible for operating camps so as to ensure their educational merits, camps remained separate institutions, though there was a concerted effort to connect camps with schools. Camps solidified their independence with the creation of a number of different organizations during this era such as the Camp Directors Association of America and the Camp Directors Association.[115]

Lance Ozier describes the decades of the 1920s through the 1950s as being the "educational stage of camping" (first described as such by Penny James of North Carolina State University) which was heavily influenced by the influx of professional educators into the summer camp industry.[116] This era saw the rise of the Child Guidance Movement, Progressive Education Movement, and the School Camping movement. Conferences were held to discuss which approach to education was best for camps and whether or not certain standards should be adhered to. In the early 1920s, the Chicago Council of Social Agencies met to address character education at summer camps. It was widely agreed upon that, while it was important for camps to adhere to universal standards in terms of health and safety, leadership, program and administration, it was equally important for camps to maintain their individual identities; "doesn't the essential genius of the summer camp lie in its independence, its freedom, its flexibility, and its individuality?"[117]

Campers enjoy a friendly game of tug-of-war at Camp Chipinaw in 1957. *Photo courtesy of Camp Chipinaw.*

By the late 1920s, summer camps were seen as a legitimate and viable social endeavor. *The New York Times* reported in 1928, "Forty-seven years ago the first summer camp was a rather laughed at experiment. Today, characterized as 'the most important step in education America has given the world' by the late Charles W. Eliot, President Emeritus of Harvard, the summer camp has become a vital part of American life."[118] Two years later, the *Times* ran another article in which Eunice Fuller Barnard stated, "Camping for children in America has long ceased to be a desultory, sporadic or mainly commercial affair. For poor and rich, from coast to coast, in the last ten years it has evolved from a mere escape from city life and a relief for harassed parents, to a recognized institution consciously aiming at a status beside school."[119] Prolific writing and discussion of the merits of summer camp ensued and in 1930, a summit was held at Teachers' College at Columbia University where the importance of education gained at camp was addressed. "Ben Solomon's speech 'Camping as a National Movement' was later printed in the March issue of *Camp Life*, establishing five comprehensive values of camping: recreational, physical up-building, character-building, educative, and spiritual."[120] This initiated a long discussion about potential partnerships between camps and schools, the relationship between the two, and whether it should be formalized. As Dr. Beulah Clark Van Wagenen stated several years later, "because camps have the child twenty-four hours of the day and partly because they are not bound by tradition as are the schools, they have even a better chance than the schools to do a really educative job."[121]

The Second World War posed a particularly challenging time for camps for many reasons. First off, staffing camps was difficult since many potential staff members were off fighting in the war. Second, many families experienced economic hardship and were unable to afford to send their children to camp. Third, rations affected many camps, making it difficult to feed the camp population. Helen Herz Cohen served as the director of Camp Walden in Denmark, Maine, from 1939 until 1995. In an article entitled, "A Camp Director Remembers World War II," Cohen reflects on the challenges of operating a girls' camp during wartime. She explains that the kitchen and food service experienced the most significant impact. As food for all Americans was rationed and stamps were issued for items like meat and sugar, Camp Walden "required each camper and staff member to send us the allotted stamps for the eight weeks of camp…We turned these stamps into the federal agency in charge and were given checkbooks with a total number of credits for all the stamps we had submitted. When we purchased any of these items, we wrote a check for the amount to be delivered."[122] Cohen also explained that since it was wartime, the campers felt strongly about contributing to the war effort and helping those abroad. The girls helped local farmers by picking beans, sent their earnings to refugee camps abroad, and made dresses and overalls for children in Europe. Knowing that rations were far more severe overseas, campers included a bar of soap and a toothbrush in the pocket of each article of clothing. Finding qualified staff and, in the case of a girls' camp, maintenance men, proved difficult during the war since young men were off fighting overseas. The result for Camp Walden and many other camps of that day was to hire younger staff who were likely less qualified and would probably not have been hired had there not been a war on.[123]

Health-related issues also played a role in the mid-century summer camp industry. The polio epidemic ran rampant through America in the 1940s. Parents, worried about their children contracting the debilitating disease (especially in congested urban centers), had mixed reactions to how they ought to handle the situation. Some sent their children far from the cities, where their risk of getting sick was much greater, into the woods and mountains, while others kept their children at home for the summer, fearful of possible exposure to germs at camps. Camps were completely sealed off from outside visitors, and, in many cases, visiting weekends were canceled so as to minimize campers' potential contact with germs.

> So compelling was the threat that, on Visitors' Day, no outside children were permitted to enter the camp, not even the young siblings, relatives, or friends of the campers, lest they be carriers of the disease. And one grim summer, when a particularly virulent polio epidemic raged in the distant city, visiting parents were forbidden to approach too close to their children and restrained behind a roped-off area. Campers and parents shouted greetings and conversations across a wide sunlit meadow bordered by tall embowering trees. And so, as I grew up, chief among the uses of summer camp was the saving of young lives. [124]

The director of Camp Catawba in Blowing Rock, North Carolina, Tui St. George Tucker, worked hard to assuage the fears of parents at home. In a letter dated, August 1, 1948, she wrote:

> Dear Parents: I know perfectly well that all of you are following with anxiety the newspaper reports on the polio epidemic in this state. Yet keep in mind: your children are in the safest place and the most complete isolation on our hilltop. We receive reports and advice from the State Board of Health twice a week. We take all possible precautions such as: mopping, spraying, dish washing with disinfectants; no visits of the boys in Blowing Rock; no visitors on camp grounds; every adult who has been to the village gargles and washes before coming into contact with the children."

A week later, she wrote again: "The responsibility for the boys is weighing heavily on us these days. I can absolutely reassure you about their safety while they are at camp."[125]

Renowned author Chaim Potok reflects on his experience during the epidemic.

> I grew up in New York, where the fear of that illness was so overwhelming that my father, a deeply religious man brought to ruin by the Great Depression, would send me to non-kosher Jewish overnight camps sponsored by local community centers, the only free camps available to us. Breathe the fresh air, he would say. Have a good time. He did not say what I read on his face and in his eyes: I am sending you out of the city so you will be far away from this sickness that is crippling children.
>
> Those polio epidemics, as we called them, would begin with the coming of late spring and hang over us like shrouds all through the summer months, and fade only with the end of the summer camp season and the first cold weather of autumn. A train or bus would carry us away from that invisible killer and the streets it menaced, and only when we were out of the city across the bridge or through the tunnel would I feel myself begin to shed the miasma of dread under which we lived. Each summer a dreamlike world presented itself to my innocent eyes: vast green fields and rolling hills and dense stands of trees and the sky an astonishing blue, open, enormous. My family--left behind. My street and neighborhood and city—vanished. The threat of paralysis or death—gone; for the time being, blessedly gone."[126]

Some camps were even forced to close because of outbreaks of the dreaded disease. Overall, however, the experience did more than just expose children to fresh air; it helped buoy the industry as camps became an appealing option for a wide variety of reasons.

Girls enjoy a sing-along in in their cabin at Camp Kanata in Wake Forest, North Carolina. *Photo courtesy of Camp Kanata archives.*

The post-war era brought about not only a change in the way that camp directors thought about the layout and organization of their camps but also in how they approached their clientele. "With the number of competitors growing steadily, camp directors could not always afford to offer a rugged sort of camp experience that might not appeal to campers accustomed to the comforts of home."[127] Additionally, this era saw a shift in the role and mindset of the American teenager. "By the 1930s, however, it was increasingly acknowledged that 'teenagers' (who had only been recently recognized as comprising a distinct phase of human development) considered themselves too old for camp."[128] The result was the development of counselor-in-training programs that were age-appropriate and developmentally beneficial to this unique age group.

The Social Orientation & Responsibility Stage: 1950–1970

The Social Orientation and Responsibility Stage followed the Educational Stage and lasted until 1970. This somewhat explosive era saw the Civil Rights, Women's Liberation, and Disability Rights movements play out on the national stage. The most notable change during this era was a move towards standards development and implementation. "There was a systematic and collective effort to formulate and apply standards to the operations of camps, thus recognizing that camps could no longer be run out of the scrutiny of the general public."[129]

New Directions Stage: 1970–Present

Camping has been experiencing the New Directions stage since 1970. Some of the hot button issues that have been addressed during this era include "fiscal responsibility, increased competition for campers, diversity in camp programs, environmental responsibility, and an increased emphasis on standards and certifications for staff."[130] The changes in the camping industry continue and parallel those in society. It is hard to imagine where camps will be in another few decades and what will be emphasized then (see 21st Century Challenges).

Changing Notions of American Leisure

The concept of summer camp is wholly American and seems to have had no influence from other cultures. "Outdoor living by young people in small groups within larger camp communities, isolated from city distractions, dedicated to free and joyous experiences with educational values, with leaders especially selected for their understanding and guidance skills: this is the American concept of camping."[131] Summer camps, ultimately, are intimately enmeshed in the social fabric of American life. While many early camps were intended to provide an escape from overcrowded, germ-infested urban centers, sending children to camp may have been somehow connected to a once-popular theory asserted by psychologist G. Stanley Hall that children had to go from savage to civilized via barbarism.[132] Camps were also a response to the Victorian-era worry that boys were not manly enough (see page 69, *Single-sex vs. Coed: what's the difference (besides the obvious)?*).

In his formative 1925 text, *The Camping Ideal: The New Human Race*, Henry Wack pontificated,

> Leisure becomes one of the foremost problems of our time. Indeed it is already such. Crime of every description and degree is multiplying in the proportion that leisure, unemployed, idle and mischievous leisure, is increased and placed at the disposal of individuals who have never learned what to do with time except to "kill" it. In this direction camp-trained boys and girls, men and women can see what is coming to add to the explosive character of our social complexities. They can see a day already dawning when human beings will run amuck destructively with more leisure than they can assimilate. Men and women intelligently employed in legitimate occupations and recreations do not commit the crimes which infest the world.[133]

Wack intimated that in order to save the nation from a future of crime and disaster, camping was a necessary force for teaching Americans how to use their leisure time effectively. Moreover, Wack asserted that camping was critical to maintaining the health of Americans who were faced with the threat of disease. It is as though Wack believed that camping was essential to the survival of the human race. He continues:

Campers move around the grounds from one activity to another at Camp Wa Wa Segowea. *Photo courtesy of Camp Wa Wa Segowea.*

Campers arrive and depart from Camp Kehonka in 1924. *Photo courtesy of Roy Ballentine.*

> "We stop playing not because we grow old, but we grow old because we stop playing." All recreation is, however, not playing. There are many forms of recreative activity which, while pleasurable, are far from sheer play. Angling, mountain climbing, wilderness walks, botanizing, geological investigations, canoe and auto cruises, camping, land and aquatic sports, forestry, gardening, fruit culture, raising furbearers, animal breeding, traveling here and abroad, outdoor sketching, floriculture, nature studies, photography and hundreds of other avocational pursuits bring new joy into the leisure day and make the tasks of the work-day sweet and spirited.[134]

Campers and staff pose while taking a break from a busy day. *Photo courtesy of Cheley Colorado Camps.*

Wack advocated for "camp-trained boys and girls" to take the lead in petitioning the government to fund more national parks, playgrounds, and camp sites so as to prevent Americans from certain destruction. He believed that "the proper relation of leisure to labor, of work to play, is there rationally worked out and maintained. In the camp the problem of leisure vanishes in the coordinated activities of work and play each day. Camps have learned to recognize that leisure is either a constructive or a destructive opportunity; either a period of wholesome and progressive generation or one of malignant degeneration."[135]

Wack points to the work of Dr. Luther H. Gulick, the founder of Sebago-Wohelo Camps in Maine, who opined:

> There seems to be something almost magical in the common things of life to draw people together. Doing those things which all the people of all the world have done together; experiencing the common feel of the earth under one's foot, the look of green trees, the touch of fresh water; cooking in the open; sleeping on the ground about a campfire; carrying the pack; standing the strain of the long trail—somehow human nature seems to come right to the top and look around under such conditions as these. You somehow don't need to become friends—you just are friends. It seems as if sham, insincerity, false courtesy and other pretenses are swept away by the sweat that pours from the body, and you and he stand before each other for what you really are. Under such conditions souls fuse.[136]

Wack had a clear view of the role that camps were to play in American society.

> From this time forward, American camp directors who are camping for service to the youth of the nation more than for a financial self-service have a new, a civic cause to labor for in solving the problems of leisure. They can solve them by making their camps the laboratory of resourceful and efficient boyhood and girlhood. If they produce self-reliant, handy-fingered, thoughtful, physically fit boys and girls to go forth and lead the mob to employ its leisure sanely and profitably, they will have rendered a public service to the whole nation.[137]

Van Slyck remarks that even during the Depression, "summer camps were considered so essential to the production of good citizens that the federal government used New Deal programs to sponsor the construction of state-of-the-art campgrounds earmarked for the use of charitable agencies serving poor children."[138] The Cold War era saw the development everything from Communist camps to Jewish camps (the latter of which remain vibrant in today's camp culture). After a brief decline in the 1960s, summer camps enjoyed a resurgence. In fact, today there are summer camps specializing in just about everything from watersports to landsports to circus performing to serious theater and visual arts and, of course, there are plenty of general camps that offer a wide variety of activities and experiences.

Not surprisingly, camps were also affected by the development of technology and modern conveniences. For example, as Van Slyck points out, "before World War II, camping would not have been possible were it not for the existence of an extensive system of rail lines...After World War II, most children arrived at summer camp by bus or car along new and improved highways... As early as the 1930s, however, camp brochures no longer mentioned the streetcar and provided only driving directions."[139]

Van Slyck astutely points out that camps began to stray from the militaristic feeling held by earlier camps and began to assess camper's needs based on

Boys at Camp Nathan Hale in Southfields, New York. *Photo courtesy of the Library of Congress Prints and Photographs Online Catalog.*

their age and developmental stage. This had a significant impact not just on the organization and administration of camps, but also on the layout and design of camps in the 1940s. Camps also began to deviate from the previous models that embraced camps as communing with nature and the wilderness in tents in favor of electricity and cabins.[140] The benefit of having a facility with electricity and plumbing was that it could be used year-round. Today, many camps offer a variety of programs throughout the year and rent out their facilities to schools, church groups, and the like to bring in extra income during the off-season.

But with more freedom and leisure time than ever before, how will the camp experience remain vital and relevant for today's children?

Camp Sebago-Wohelo's first Blue Birds enjoyed a nest in the treetops, 1913. *Photo courtesy of Camp Wohelo*

2 The Benefits of Camp

Campers take a break to enjoy the majestic scenery on a hike. *Photo courtesy of Gold Arrow Camp*

What does camp offer children?

In his editor's letter in the June/July issue of *Town & Country*, Jay Fielden wrote about the difference he had noted upon the return of his close friend who had attended camp. "Lloyd came back a little different, having seen and heard things I hadn't. And worse, I seemed to have missed his company a lot more than he'd missed mine."[141] Anyone who has ever attended camp can attest to the fact that Lloyd likely had changed and that his re-entry into the real world had been a difficult one. Further, Lloyd most likely struggled to find the words to adequately describe his camp experience to Fielden and his other friends; one's camp experience simply defies description.

The majority of early boys' camps were founded with the idea that groups of boys should "camp together for moral and physical betterment."[142] Ernest Balch pioneered many of the ideas that came to characterize boys' camps including, "special uniforms, the 'contract' system, a rotating list of chores, Water Sports Day, and the idea of an extended camping trip away from camp."[143] Although Blach's camp focused primarily on the outdoors and a more rugged, rustic experience, other camps emphasized a more academic approach. Some early camps were more like outdoor schools and stressed the study of science in addition to tutoring in a number of other subject areas. This is likely the result of so many early camps having been founded by educators. As scholar Leslie Paris points out, "The first camp directors evidently took enormous satisfaction from the experience of leading boys in the woods and away from idleness and dissipation."[144]

Many early boys' camps were intended to counteract what some viewed as the "overly feminized home" in which many were being raised.[145] Camp leaders believed that if boys became homesick that their mothers were to blame "for overindulging and overprotecting their sons."[146] Clearly, the aim of summer camps today is quite different. Now, more than ever, America's youths are being treated as adults-in-training rather than as children and teenagers. Parents are rightly concerned about preparing their children for college and a career, but often forget to allow their children enjoy childhood. In today's schools, teachers are forced to focus on content mastery and standardized tests rather than on fostering creativity and curiosity among their students. However, being able to solve calculus problems, recite the Preamble to the Constitution, and achieve high standardized test scores does not necessarily mean that one is prepared socially, emotionally, or even intellectually for what lies ahead. Summer camps fill this very important void.

How many times in children's lives today do they truly get to be masters of their own destinies? How often do adults step aside and let them figure out things for themselves?[147]

Camp director and ACA member Audrey Monke explains in her article, "Why Kids Flourish at Camp," that camp helps children to achieve PERMA, an acronym devised by Martin Seligman.

- P: Positive Emotion—"At camp, positive emotions are the norm, not the exception. We're singing; we're dancing; we're doing skits that don't make sense but that cause us to laugh so hard our stomachs hurt."

- E: Engagement—"At camp, kids are constantly exposed to new experiences and challenges — both recreational and social — that get them interested and excited to learn. They're pushed to get outside their comfort zone and really engage."

- R: Relationships—"Everyone comes to camp to see their old friends, make new friends, and just spend quality time connecting with others and building positive relationships. And camp is like no other place for that. You don't have any of the competition or stress that often accompanies kids' relationships at home...The relationships at camp, without all the competition and "baggage" that kids have in some of their relationships at home, grow strong quickly."

- M: Meaning—"Being a member of a cabin group at camp helps kids gain an understanding of how they are valued by others. For some kids, camp is the first place where they understand what it means to be a valued and accepted member of a community. Unlike at school, where some kids can be 'invisible' and go through a day without connecting with others, camp forces integration. Kids learn that they are an important and valued member of their cabin group, and they discover their character strengths through recognition from peers and counselors."

- A: Achievement—"Every day at camp, kids have the opportunity to try new things and master new skills. Some kids arrive at camp with a specific goal: a bull's eye at archery or getting up on a slalom water ski. But others simply practice and work towards improving or challenge themselves to try something that frightens them — like completing the ropes course."[148]

The sound of laughter fills the air at summer camp as old friendships grow stronger and new friendships are made. *Photo courtesy of Roy Ballentine.*

Campers learn the importance of teamwork and supporting one another. *Photo courtesy of Roy Ballentine.*

Camp Wyonegonic Junior Unit Director Barbie Cobb and her daughters. *Photo courtesy of Barbie Cobb.*

There are few other settings in which children and teens can develop life skills better than they can at camp. For many children, coming to summer camp is the first time they experience being on their own. Each day, they are given opportunities to work with other people, take responsibility for themselves and for their actions, display leadership among their peers, behave in an ethical fashion and adapt to a variety of situations, some of which may be challenging for them.

Barbie Cobb, Junior Unit Director at Camp Wyonegonic explains why camp is so important in today's world.

> Camp is important for kids today because it allows them to truly be children without outside influence. We don't allow any electronics or cell phones at camp, and we have a uniform. By taking away things that can cause peer pressure (especially with girls, clothing can become an issue), everyone is much more equal. Campers at Wyo use their creativity and imagination, they exercise their muscles in a non-team sports way (hiking, canoeing, playing capture the flag). They sing songs, they play in the stream, and they support each other in drama. Learning to entertain yourself (without a screen to watch) is a lost art, and our campers have the opportunity to do just that.[149]

Sherri Maxman attended Camp Hochelaga from 1973 to 1980. Camp, she says, is "a way to reinvent yourself. I was no one special at school, but somehow managed to be somewhat of a star at camp. I was allowed to try different things and find out that I was good at some of them, like swimming and acting. Also, the people I met at camp were so different from the people at home and I really appreciated that difference."[150] This phenomenon holds true for many; children who are especially awkward and even unpopular at school often come to find themselves something of a cult figure in a camp setting. Camp is one place where differences truly are celebrated. These ideas are reinforced in an article penned by writer Ombretta Di Dio entitled, "What Happens in Summer Camp Doesn't Necessarily Have to Stay There." Reflecting on her first summer at camp, she wrote, "my first summer at camp amazed me...nobody there knew how much of an outcast I was in the real world. I had created a wild character, made of funny jokes and self-confidence. Summer camp taught me that you can really be whoever you want to be...It doesn't matter how cool or ridiculous I ended up being when summer camp was over, the following year nobody would remember me...The following year, I had a brand new character to build, plenty of new stories to tell and tons of new adventures to live."[151]

Gina Malanga explains that "things in my household were very bad when I was in high school and, for me, camp was a break from that and a chance to live without constant worry or pressure. When I was older and had no 'escape' like camp I often reflected on those days fondly. I wish I was still better friends with people from camp today but those people helped me through a very tough time in my life even if they didn't know they did. Camp will always have a very special place in my heart!"[152]

In their essay entitled, "Some Historical Backgrounds of Camping," L.B. Sharp and E. DeAlton Partridge wrote, "In camp...it is not possible to shirk individual responsibility, sharing, and cooperative planning. It is not possible for a youth to hide behind a curtain of make-believe and keep his real self from emerging. He cannot dodge or fake for long. The necessities of living in the camp environment force his hand. This comes quickly in camp, and when it does, there can be real tolerance, understanding and happiness, the essentials of good citizenship."[153] Although written in 1947, this still holds true.

Jenna Bergmann of Pennsylvania reflects on her experience as a junior counselor at Cape Cod Sea Camps. "For me, camp has never just been a place where I spend seven weeks during the summer. Camp means everything to me; I'm completely obsessed. I always have a hard time explaining it to my friends at school. At the mention of having to complete requirements at a four year leadership program that I pay to go to, I usually just get funny looks. The thing that's hardest to explain, however, is how completely rewarding all the work is."[154]

> *No grades. No permanent records. Just authentic connections to the real world. Play is the work of childhood; it's how children invent and re-invent themselves, find their place in the universe, and learn what they are good at and where they need to practice. Life is the quintessential test tomorrow's leaders need to pass.*[155]
>
> —Marla Coleman

Some families may be reluctant to send their children (especially teenagers) to traditional camps because they believe that an internship or long list of experiences will look better on a college application or resume. But parents must ask themselves what they want their children to gain through such an experience. Are they looking for work experience? Are they hoping to pique the child's interest in a certain field? Or are they simply trying to keep the child occupied for the summer? In fact, summer camps provide a set of experiences and skills that may prove to be even more valuable than an internship at a law firm or volunteering for a political candidate. In fact, research shows summer camps to be proven training grounds for success.

The Partnership for 21st Century Skills (P21) is a national organization of leading world employers that advocates for twenty-first century readiness for every student. By fusing content with learning and thinking skills, ICT (information and Communications Technology) literacy and life skills, P21 strives to educate the whole individual. In fact, there is no better place to develop and master these skills than at summer camp.

P21 advocates the need for *21st Century Content,* which includes global awareness, financial literacy, civic literacy, health and wellness awareness, and environmental literacy. Camp provides the perfect setting in which to learn about these important themes. Campers must take responsibility for maintaining their health while away from home. Keeping their bunk and cabin clean, sorting their laundry, and eating healthily are just a few examples of the opportunities camp provides children that they may not otherwise have at home. Further, many American summer camps attract international campers, providing an amazing opportunity for raising cultural awareness and sensitivity. In fact, many campers make lifelong international friendships that are often rekindled during family vacations and college semesters abroad. Whereas twenty years ago, letters were sent to overseas camp friends via air mail, today the click of a mouse allows an instant transcontinental visit via Skype, e-mail, or Facebook. Finally, many camps are located in spectacular environments where campers must have respect for the lake, pond, forest, beach, or mountain. Raising awareness about the environment and how to protect it can be an especially valuable lesson for campers from urban areas who may not necessarily be as aware of environmental hazards and the need to recycle and preserve the environment.[156]

Another theme advocated by P21 is the development *of Learning and Thinking Skills.* This involves honing critical thinking and problem-solving skills, communication skills, creativity and innovation skills, collaboration skills, information and media literacy skills and contextual learning skills. Campers are given daily opportunities to problem solve and think critically while enhancing their communication skills. For example, they may participate in a variety of team building activities that require them to think logically, troubleshoot, incorporate others' ideas and so on. While some individuals may be reluctant to engage in sports at school because of their competitive nature, camp provides a great opportunity for "low stakes" participation in intramural sports and activities (e.g.: Color Wars, gaga, dodgeball, ultimate Frisbee). This kind of activity is extremely beneficial with regard to fostering communication with peers and developing one's analytical abilities).[157]

Camp also exposes children and teens to new activities and skills that they may not have the opportunity to develop in school. For example, many camps offer sailing programs, tennis instruction, pottery classes, and drama. Campers' schools may not have the resources or facilities to offer watersports (which generally aren't offered in the winter months anyway), or their schedules may not allow them to take an arts elective. In short, camp offers access to new and different activities while also providing instruction at different levels for more traditional interests such as swimming.

P21 also emphasizes the importance of *ICT Literacy* and although most camps do not allow cell phones or access to social media, this time away from technology can prove to be quite valuable to today's wired youth. Campers learn to engage with one another face to face rather than by texting, messaging, or tweeting. Furthermore, counselors are reminded about the importance of posting appropriate content to their Facebook pages, blogs, and the like, particularly if they are "friends" with their campers.

Finally (and perhaps most relevant to camps), P21 focuses on the critical nature of *Life Skills.* This category includes leadership, ethics, accountability, adaptability, personal productivity, personal responsibility, people skills, self-direction, and social responsibility. These are intangibles that cannot be graded or assessed and which have been virtually eliminated from most school curricula. Not coincidentally, these are the areas in which camps excel. Gaining a sense of how to work with others and how to take responsibility for one's actions is an essential part of learning how to be a productive member of society. There is no place better to learn the importance of teamwork than summer camp.[158]

There are few other settings in which children and teens can develop life skills better than they can at camp. For many children, coming to summer camp is their first time on their own. Each day, they are given opportunities to work with other people, take responsibility for themselves and for their actions, display leadership among their peers, behave in an ethical fashion, and adapt to a variety of situations, some of which may be challenging for them.

In a recent *USA Today* article by Peg Smith, CEO of the American Camp Association, she expounded on the ability of summer camps to fill a void in development that seems to have been lost in recent school-aged populations. "Without a doubt, we need citizens who think in optimal ways—producing original concepts, processes, and changes that will enhance a future beyond what we have experienced in the last century....There is a great deal of research that validates the educational, social, and emotional impacts of a positive camp experience—impacts that address the precursors needed as well as the 21st century skills required for success."[159]

Campers and counselors take a few moments to talk during an otherwise busy day of camp. *Photo courtesy of Camp Towanda.*

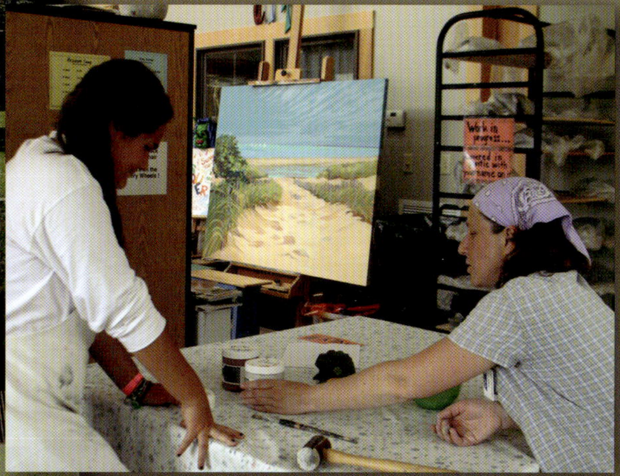

Summer camps are instrumental in developing 21st century skills and giving campers access to activities they might not otherwise have a chance to try such as pottery. *Photo courtesy of Kari Ahern.*

Soccer is among the most popular landsports at most camps. The sport is a great way for campers to learn the value of teamwork. *Photo courtesy of Kari Ahern.*

Campers learn teamwork and trust from activities like the crate stack at Camp Kupugani. *Photo Kupugani.*

A camper masters the art of hiking out to keep her boat flat so as to maximize speed while sailing upwind. *Photo courtesy of Roy Ballentine.*

Why are parents willing to send their children away for as many as eight weeks each year?

> *A month apart from parents... is that really allowed? I'm not sure I would have embraced traditional summer camp as a kid (I did not see myself as the outdoorsy type) but I would have welcomed the idea of so much time away from my parents with enthusiasm. I should want my son to feel the same way—but that feels like a lot to ask. On the flip side of that now, I will miss my son in the week he is gone, and yet when he is gone, that will be one less child to tend to in various ways (the laundry, I'm told, will return with him). I know parents whose entire packs of children will be gone for weeks or even months this summer. That's a prospect that makes me want to weep, partly from sorrow and partly from envy.*[160]
>
> —KJ Dell'Antonia

Deciding to send one's child away for as many as eight weeks can be nerve wracking for many parents. Parents worry about whether their children will make friends, if they will eat enough, if they will have fun, if they will listen to the counselors, if they will learn new skills, and, above all else, if they will be safe. As camp staff will attest, there seems to be a new breed of parents who are too afraid to send their children to camp for anything more than a few days because of a host of fears (some of which are realistic, while others are not). Judith Warner wrote in the summer of 2006 that "parents today, apparently, don't want their kids out in the wilds, where they might walk in the paths of potentially tick-bearing Bambis. They don't want the kids out of reach, where they can't take a mood reading at each and every at-risk moment of the day."[161] Camp directors spend much of their off season reassuring parents over the phone that their children will be just fine, that the staff is

Campers take in the spectacular scenery offered by Cheley Colorado Camps' location in the Rocky Mountains. *Photo courtesy of Cheley Colorado Camps.*

Chris and Rachel Horn met, married, and continue to work at Cape Cod Sea Camps. They are shown here with their daughters, Frances and Elizabeth, both of whom now attend CCSC.

Alison Guben Waldman drops off her boys, Ethan and Eli, while Kathie Guben Wachs drops off Sophie at Cape Cod Sea Camps. Both Alison and Kathie attended CCSC. *Photo courtesy of Kari Ahern.*

Jessica Flaxman, Stacey Ingraham Loscalzo, and Lindsey Mead Russell, who became friends at Cape Cod Sea Camps in the 1980s, sent their daughters to camp together in the summer of 2011. *Photo courtesy of Kari Ahern.*

well-trained to handle homesickness should it arise, and that every possible safety precaution is in place. However, when opening day arrives, all bets are off. Some parents have great difficulty leaving their children at camp even when the children seem perfectly ready and well-adjusted. Author Leslie Paris explains, “to temporarily relinquish control over their children’s day-to-day lives, parents had to identify with...the sponsoring organization or a camp leader’s vision of community life. Parents expected their own values to be fortified or, in the case of charitable camps’ clients, at least not usurped by the camp socialization process.”[162] While leaving one’s child at camp takes a huge leap of faith, it is an important rite of passage for both child and parent.

According to the American Camp Association, there are three main reasons why parents send their children to summer camp. They believe that “camp helps build self-confidence and self-esteem, camp is a safe environment [and that] camp is a place to build social skills and make friends.”[163] And although there is a great deal of learning that takes place at camp, summer camp is almost the antithesis of school. For the most part, kids *want* to be at camp. For one, the atmosphere is relaxed; there are no high stakes tests or assignments. Second, there are no parental pressures. Lastly, although camp days are highly structured, they don’t feel like it at all. Camp experts Chris Thurber and Jon Malinowski explain that there are five main goals of overnight camps: To have fun; to improve athletic, artistic, and intellectual skills; to gain independence; to make friends; and develop social skills and finally to experience a new environment.[164]

Lindsey Mead Russell, a longtime camper and counselor herself, recalls the agony of dropping off her daughter, Grace, at camp for the first time. The most difficult part owas “saying goodbye and leaving her in tears, even though I knew she’d be fine in a matter of minutes.”[165] In her blog entitled *A Design So Vast,* Russell revealed how difficult it had been to leave Grace at camp. “Last Thursday we dropped Grace off at camp. My heart was still soggy from the night before, but I put on my sunglasses and got in the car and off we headed. As we drove the familiar roads on Cape Cod, turned into the driveway with the archery range and sun-bleached grassy front fields, I was flooded with memories. The smiling, white-clad Junior Counselors looked *so young*, and I choked up inside. I was trying to reconcile the fact that I was *just* them with the knowledge that that was more than half my lifetime ago.”[166]

Ten days later as she was about to head back to Cape Cod to pick up Grace, Russell blogged, “Absolutely my primary motivation in signing her up to go this summer was my firm belief in the importance of independence and my certainty that she would have a terrific, and valuable, experience. But it was also that I wanted her to share a place that had been so incredibly meaningful to me. When I am there the memories rise up, as evanescent but as tangible as puffs of sand blowing off of the dunes.”[167]

Kathie Guben Wachs and her husband, Jon, both had strong ties to their respective summer camps. When it came time to choose a camp for their daughter, Sophie, they had to think long and hard about what was right for her. ”As difficult as it is for a parent to send a child away for part of the summer, it was and is very important to us that our children experience life on their own, even at this young age. We wanted Sophie to have an experience all her own, something that she could be proud of and cherish, something that is only hers, not ours. Both of us had that experience as kids at our respective summer camps, and as hard as it is to have the house so quiet in the summer, we would never want to deprive her of the camp experience. We also wanted her to be with people who did not know her, who did not have any preconceived notions of who she is, and we wanted her to see that she can make it on her own, and be a little more independent.”[168]

But how did Kathie and Jon know that the time was right for Sophie to go to camp? “She announced to us that she would be attending camp the following summer. Quite bold! But we were happy to oblige. I think hearing all the wonderful things about it from me and after visiting so many times, I think she sensed the magic and specialness of it, and I think she wanted to experience that herself.”[169]

Kathie explains that the most difficult thing about sending Sophie to camp is that her younger brother, Sam, misses her terribly (though Sam joined Sophie at camp in 2013 and had so much fun that both children extended their stays) and that the family misses the sound of Sophie’s laughter filling the house. However, the temporary hardship of missing Sophie is far outweighed by the benefits that a positive summer camp experience offers. “She is more willing to try new things now and I can see that she is pushing herself a little harder when doing so. It also helped her transition to a new school. If she can go away to camp, a new school is easy!”[170]

Laura Monfried Egerman explains that when looking for a first-time camp for her daughter, Caroline, she and her husband, Josh, looked for “a place that had seemed to have a structured response plan for first time campers with homesickness.”[171] One of the selling points for the Egermans was Rookie Day which provides prospective campers and their parents a chance to experience a day in the life of the camp. “When we arrived, the kids were broken into groups based on age and went off with a counselor or two to do a day’s worth of activities... swimming, crafts, sports, etc. The parents got a separate tour of the camp and then were free to leave; we came back at the end of the day to pick them up.”[172] Not only did this experience prove to ease Caroline’s fears about going away for the first time but also those of her parents. “As an only child, she has no idea what it is like to live with other kids and share like you would with a sibling. I hope she gains confidence and learns independence and self-reliance.”[173]

Carol Ann and Tom McCurdy explain their top priorities when they looked for a camp for their children.

> Safety and references were at the top of the list. Putting your kids in the hands of others who are unknown is terribly unsettling. Therefore, references from those who we trust were critical. After that we looked for an overnight [program to] provide an environment of independence and diversity, meaning the fewer kids from home the better. We also appreciate the international campers and staff. We wanted to introduce them to different ways of seeing, living and enjoying life. We looked for new activities that are not likely to be readily available during their 'normal' routine at home. Day trip destinations to unique locations influenced us as well. And finally, we looked for a "family feeling" and warmth... the feeling of closeness they experience is most reassuring for parents.[174]

Upon dropping off his youngest daughter, Cami, at camp in 2012, Tom McCurdy mused, "At camp, it doesn't matter if you screw up. Your peers help you up and dust you off. In high school, they step on you. There, it's all about skinny jeans, straight hair, and UGG boots."[175] This sentiment is exactly why so many families nationwide send their children to summer camp: the sense of self-worth, the independence, the acceptance, and an environment in which it is safe to try new things.

Perhaps the best way to understand why parents are willing to send their children to camp is explained by a camper. Tommy Cusano, a native of Morristown, New Jersey, explains why camp is so important to him:

> To me, camp is all about building and learning from different relationships. Living and working with my friends, aside from being fun, shows me the value of cooperation and shared responsibility. At the same time, I learn to be strict but playful and patient while teaching younger campers. Finally, I get to work with and learn from caring and friendly counselors from around the world, an aspect of camp that I truly value. Most of all, though, and I know this answer is rather cliché, camp is a home away from home. It is a place where I can truly be myself and meet up every year with friends that I would have never met if not for camp. It is difficult to describe the camp experience unless you have lived it yourself, but I can say with certainty that camp has definitely changed who I am for the better.[176]

With an endorsement like that, it's hard to imagine that any parent would not choose to send their child to camp.

Sam Wachs joined his sister, Sophie, at camp in the summer of 2013.

Cami McCurdy poses with her sister, Kendall, who also attended and worked at camp. *Photo courtesy of Kari Ahern.*

Every child who goes to camp has the absolute right to be emotionally and physically cared for. No exceptions. Having raised four children and worked at camps for most of my adult life, I know the incredible trust that parents place in counselors and directors to care for their children. Caring for another person's child is a responsibility, a privilege, and a gift. Those are not just words; let me repeat. Responsibility, privilege, and gift. None of the three should be treated lightly.

Childhood shouldn't be—but can be—tough. Each child brings to camp their own life story: the super athlete, the child who just lost a mom, the mischievous ten-year-old, the child who is bullied, the popular boy, the shy, awkward girl, the overweight thirteen-year-old...you get the idea because the list could go on and on. The point is that every one of those children has the exact same indisputable right to be emotionally safe. Every one. And don't be fooled. Sometimes the popular athlete needs your nurturing and support just as much as the shy, awkward child. Camp must create an environment that not only includes, but celebrates, every child regardless of their story. For some kids it is their break from the mold they live in at home. Imagine being twelve years old and going to school with the same kids for the last seven years. Everyone has a "place" and it's hard to break out of that sometimes. At camp, they can be who they want to be, make new friends, or create a new definition of themselves.

When I first started as a director, I know that I frustrated many counselors because of the way I viewed child behavior and because I refused to quit on a child—even the difficult ones. No child comes to camp in the morning thinking, "I can't wait for camp. I hope I get into trouble. I hope I get punished and yelled at." There is always an underlying reason for negative or unacceptable behaviors. I am not saying that you "shush" it away or ignore it. I am saying we must put in the time to find out why and help the camper work through the issue to find success. It happens ALL the time.

Sometimes it is as simple as the crying six-year-old who has to be pried away from mom. Scared, she just wants to go home. Step number one? Build trust. After spending time with her, getting on her level, and asking lots of questions about her siblings and puppy, you come to find out she doesn't know where she is going to get lunch. Cue the golf cart. A quick tour around camp settles her fears, and by 3:00 mom returns to a child bubbling with excitement over an awesome day.

Sometimes it is more difficult. One time, I was called to the pool to help deal with a very stubborn and rude eleven-year-old. James refused to get in the pool and was angry. Really angry. We left the pool area after it was obvious he wouldn't be splashing around anytime soon. A lot of time spent talking amounted to nothing. Calling his mom to see if she had any insight and to make her aware of his behavior, I was taken aback by her description of a very kind and gentle boy. It was obvious that something was wrong here. The next day I found him well before swimming and we talked...again, cue the golf cart. Far away from the pool, I saw that kind and gentle boy. The root of James's behavior was not that he was afraid of the water; he was absolutely petrified beyond measure. It took a lot of work from a swim instructor (also a counselor in his unit) and me, but we slowly got him in the water. It was all about showing him that we understood his fear and that he could trust us. Days later he was splashing in the shallow end, incredibly proud of himself. I am not going to lie; it was exhausting and took a lot of time, but I cannot describe how awesome it felt when he burst out of the water after dunking his head for the first time and with a huge smile said, "Why have I waited so long to do this?" But it gets better. Because his swim teacher and he bonded, he would hang out with her in unit. Soon, that shy, awkward eleven-year-old who could have been teased or excluded by his peers because of his initial rudeness and crying made lots of friends and had a great time at camp.

It is so important to work hard to help every child overcome homesickness or fear and experience a positive, healthy, and incredibly happy time at camp where so many important life skills and lessons are learned. I look at the child who is misbehaving and just hope that if that were my child, somebody would be willing to invest in them, to believe in them. In fact, I truly believe that a part of my own children's personalities and character is a direct result of their positive experiences at camp.

In the end, it comes down to three things. Validate a child's feelings without judging and build the trust needed to help them succeed. That is our responsibility. Show them, with your actions, words, and time, that you care. That is a privilege. Then watch a child thrive and flourish before your very eyes. There is the gift—the most amazing gift you will ever receive.[177]

—Joanna Flanagan

Campers learn many skills that will last for a lifetime. Here, a camper at Wekeela shows off the fish he caught with the help of his counselor. *Photo courtesy of Camp Wekeela.*

Campers prepare for a day hike in California's Sierra Nevada Mountains. *Photo courtesy of Gold Arrow Camp*

Choosing a Summer Camp

When considering camps, perhaps the most salient question is whether a day camp or an overnight program is more appropriate for the camper-to-be. There is one main consideration when determining whether sleep-away or day camp is right for a particular child. First, does the child want to attend overnight camp? If so, how much structure does he or she need? How far away from home is he or she going to be comfortable being? What session length is right?

Deciding which camp is right for a child can be an overwhelming experience. Day camp or overnight? Coed or single sex? Large or small? Near or far? General activity or specific instruction? Fortunately, there are many resources and guidelines to help families make the right choice so that camp is a positive and fulfilling experience. Thurber and Malinowski believe that when selecting a camp, families need to evaluate camps in terms of the following: features, character, quality, service, and cost.[178]

Bette Bussel, the American Camp Association's Executive Director, offers the following sage advice to families packing for camp. "Visit camp web sites. Pay attention to session length and activities and all your family's important search criteria. But, try to dive a little deeper and explore each camp—from their culture to their facilities. Check out the photos—they tell a lot about what the camp looks like, what campers do there, and about what's important in this particular camp. Watch the videos, read the newsletters or the blog written by the director, and even check out their social media."[179]

Most experts warn against sending children away with their friends because any cliques or conflicts that may characterize the school year are likely to follow them to camp. Parents who attended camp may be inclined to send their children to the same camp, but it is important to assess whether the camp is actually the right place for the child; for example, if the father went to sailing camp, is this something that his son would enjoy or would he be happier at an arts camp?

There are many things to think about when choosing a summer camp, but programming should be among the most important considerations. Parents should consider what their child already likes to do (baseball, arts and crafts, sailing) and be sure that it is offered. This can be an especially important consideration for first-time campers as doing something familiar or something that they are already good at will make the adjustment to a new camp easier. While this is significant, parents should also consider what opportunities to try new activities are available. A related question is whether the camp has activities to which the child does not have access at home; archery is a great example of an activity that is not generally offered at home but that is readily accessible at camps.

A camper races to shore trying not to lose too much water from his bucket during a wacky relay race. *Photo courtesy of Camp Wekeela.*

Learning to swim and waterfront safety is a critical aspect of nearly every camp's program.

Campers tally up their score on the archery range as they pursue their next award.

Evening sail on a pond is simply spectacular.
Photo courtesy of Kari Ahern.

Another important consideration is what type of experience and instruction parents want for their child. Families looking for highly competitive tennis and lessons that will help their child significantly improve his or her game may not be satisfied with a camp offering general activities; instead they may want to consider a program which is geared specifically towards tennis. Many parents wish for their children to spend a good portion of the summer sailing. Again, it is important to assess whether the goal is for the child to develop general skills and knowledge or to participate in a highly competitive racing program. Regardless of what is sought, there is camp to suit everyone's needs and interests.

It is also essential to be sure that there is a balance between instructional activities and less structured time, as this is often when friendships are fostered and memories are made. Daily down time (e.g.: rest hour) is just as necessary as structured activities, especially when campers are so busy and active all day long. Additionally, parents should feel empowered to ask camp administrators about programming options for their children. Parents should be confident that there are age-appropriate programs for evening activities, rainy days, and special events rather than a "one size fits all" approach. They should determine whether campers can focus in a particular activity area (e.g.: sailing) and if campers can try out a new activity but change if he/she doesn't like it. Parents should also be clear about whether there are prerequisites for any activities (e.g.: a certain swimming level needed in order to waterski) or limits on the number of times a camper can participate in a certain activity. Most important, however, is determining that the camp staff provide direct instruction to campers, especially when they are trying a new activity. Finally, parents should understand how they will be notified about their camper's progress in specific activities.

Another influential factor in selecting a camp is the length of sessions offered. Some families may be happy with the traditional four- or eight-week programs offered by many camps, but others may be in search of shorter sessions, which are becoming more and more popular in the camp industry for a variety of reasons. Camps have found that shorter sessions are a great way to fill beds and to create a bigger pool of campers who may return for a longer session in the future. Many camps elected to offer shorter stays in response to the weak economy of recent years. Families who wanted to send their children to camp were unable to because a longer session was cost prohibitive. Shorter sessions at a lower cost have proven to be equally appealing to families either because they are seeking an introduction to the overnight experience for their child or because of other summer commitments like family reunions, sports camps, or trips.

Although shorter sessions are an appealing option to many, there are also more benefits to staying for a longer session. The American Camp Association asserts staying at camp for a longer session "allows relationships between campers and their peers to develop at their natural pace, as well as providing many opportunities to connect with other campers and staff, fostering a broader community spirit." In addition, there is "time for skill development in both activity and social areas, cementing learning and instilling confidence among campers, which spills over into other areas of their lives," and it provides campers with "a longer break from the digital world and a sustained period without reliance on home support systems, fostering greater independence and resiliency in participants."[180]

There are a multitude of activities to enjoy at camp each day. Here, girls at Camp Kehonka swim and sail. *Photo courtesy of Roy Ballentine.*

Parents who were not themselves campers may have an even more challenging time saying goodbye to their children as they may not fully understand the benefits of camp and all that it has to offer. In her *New York Times* blog, "Is It Too Late to Send Myself to Camp?" KJ Dell'Antonia wrote, "Do I really want my children to fall in love with a world I can't share, and credit it with giving them things I can't? Both my inner green-eyed monster and my inner helicopter parent are yammering. If I'd gone to camp, would I be a better swimmer or a stronger person, one with deeper friendships and the ability to use a compass? I envy those summers at camp, and in an odd way, I question whether my children can belong in a place I've never been."[181]

Once parents adjust to being childless for a few weeks, however, their perspective may shift. "It is the time when parents of children away at summer camp have finally adjusted to tiny loads of laundry, sinfully small grocery bills, and plenty of peace and quiet, and it precedes the period when they start dashing off to concert halls, R-rated movies, getaway weekends for two and other ''adult'' activities—before the kids come home. By the middle of summer, the family dog has reluctantly left his post at the kitchen door, having given up hope of seeing his favorite people trooping in at 3 o'clock."[182] In 1985, *The New York Times* ran an article about "the Joys of Summer Camp—For Parents." It talked about parents holding "thank God-they're-gone parties" and frequenting museums and restaurants that wouldn't be tolerated or appreciated by their offspring.[183]

While it may be hard for parents to deposit their children into the hands of college students who seem impossibly younger than said parents were when they were that age, cutting the proverbial cord is generally positive for both parent and child.

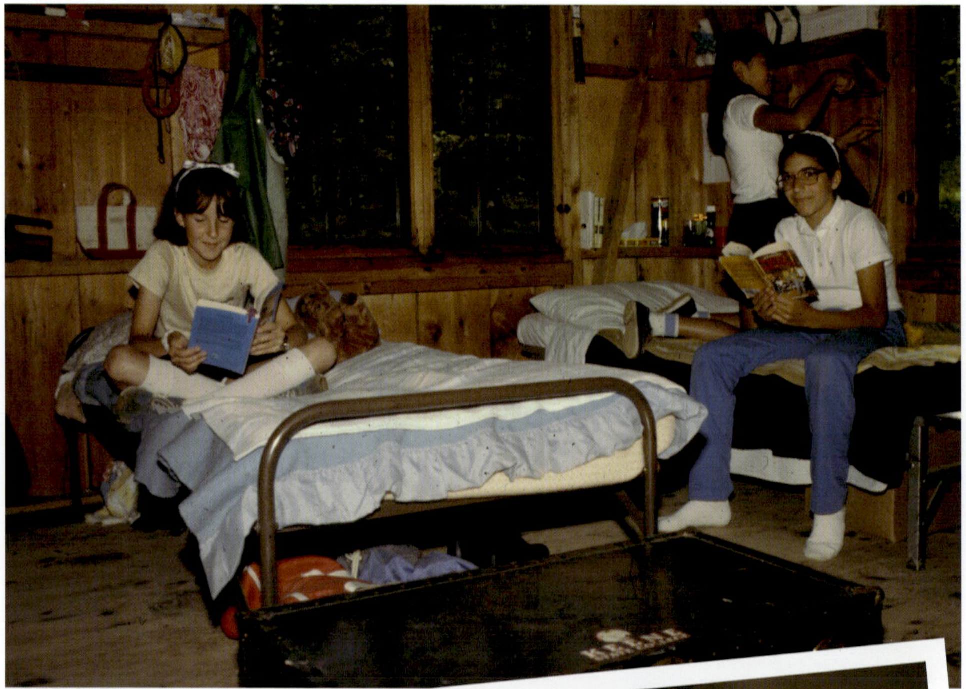

Campers relax in their bunks, enjoying a chance to read and relax with friends. *Photo courtesy of Roy Ballentine.*

Patriotism is often an important part of the summer camp experience. *Photo courtesy of Camp Towanda.*

WHAT WONDERFUL EXPERIENCE COULD I PROVIDE for our two young sons who lived with my husband and I in the heart of suburbia?! That became my dilemma and mission as our sons left the age of toddler playgroups and had that "expansive" summer break from their busy school routines. I grew up in a "little pink house" in a South Jersey development and my summers were filled with going to the local swim club, riding bikes, and hanging out with friends at their houses to play board games, etc.; no computers, no video games, and nothing on television that was remotely interesting to me. I was determined that our sons would not "hang around the house" all summer! I wanted them to meet new people, discover new abilities! I thought about how much I enjoyed my stay at a girls' camp in the Poconos one summer, so I started looking into summer camps for our sons. Summer camp turned out to be a life-altering experience for our entire family!

Our sons are similar in so many ways, yet their personalities, talents, and interests could not be more opposite—the older one is a non-conformist in every way—and is comfortable being different. He is not at all competitive, has a great sense of humor and had yet-to-be-discovered (more about that later!) talents. The younger son was a "jock" from the beginning—soccer, baseball, tennis, lacrosse—competitive. He certainly fulfilled the suburban profile of an athletic kid who was aware of what it took to "fit in" and be liked by his peers.

As it turned out, seven weeks of the same multi-activity summer camp for both of them was far more of an influence on who they have become as young adults. Both sons have since graduated from college. The older one discovered confidence in his talents as a performer at camp and is now a member of Artists Equity and supporting himself as an actor in NYC. I attribute his experience at camp and the influence of his wonderful counselors and department heads as being a major influence. Our son learned how to be a team player and was exposed to campers and college students from different parts of the country and different parts of the world. Being at camp gave him confidence beyond what suburbia could provide—everyone at camp was not the same and that was okay!

Experiencing so many different personalities in such a condensed time and place gave him the tools of his craft as an artist. At camp, he acquired experience with a full range of emotions as both observer and participant—and I feel that these authentic experiences for seven summers have added to his amazing ability to connect with audiences.

The younger one realized that although being a great athlete is an admirable goal, he too had other talents—woodworking, art, windsurfing—and that everyone at camp applauded the "individual" and cheering others on for their unique talents was fun and felt good! He became less of a conformist and more confident as an individual. He learned tolerance, compassion and also gained an understanding of how to interact with campers of all ages. He embraced the opportunity to become a junior counselor and developed outstanding leadership qualities that he continued to apply in his role as a mentor, coach, and after-school teacher throughout his years as a college student. He will be entering the Peace Corps in a few months and we could not be more proud of his commitment to making the world a better place!

I consider my husband and I to be good parents and we have tried to do our very best to provide our sons with experiences that enrich their lives and prepare them for the future. But I think that the opportunity to live with other campers and counselors at summer camp provides a very different and important experience that doesn't happen in many family situations. The counselors were important role models for our sons. Campers lived in cabins with college students from different parts of the world and this experience previewed "times ahead" for our sons—what it would be like for them as they grew older. Their examples of how to inspire enthusiasm, resolve conflict, show empathy, and support others were important life lessons that will be invaluable to our sons in their chosen careers and as parents.

I became the art department head at the camp our sons attended after that first summer and my summer job at camp enabled us to send both boys for many summers. The expense of sending children to camp can be costly, but the investment is well worth it. I started adding up the cost of the activities they would participate in at home and then considered what they would be missing if they did not go to camp and although many of my fellow teachers would use summer to "take a break," I decided that the personal sacrifice was well worth it.

My husband's and my life has changed considerably as a result of summer camp—we have since relocated very near camp and its beautiful surroundings—with big career changes for us both. I was a high school art teacher in New Jersey and I am now teaching art at a local public charter middle school. He left his job as a manufacturer in a big city and is now a counselor in a local residential school for disabled adults. After seventeen summers, I am still looking forward to the end of my school year and the opportunity to share my love for making art with campers and my even greater love of helping to make each summer an amazing experience for campers who will, hopefully, gain as much from their time at summer camp as our sons did![184]

—Deborah Fowler Greenwood

Dan and Phil Greenwood first came to camp with their mother, Debby, in 1997, when she began her career as the art director at the Cape Cod Sea Camps.

3 Types of Camps

Tufts University professor of child development David Elkind, writes,

> The traditional camp experience was, and still is, a particularly powerful example of the integration of play, love, and work. Camp activities are created to meet the needs, interests, and abilities of the children. In addition, children have choices as to the activities in which they will participate. Some may prefer swimming to hiking, while others may prefer spending much of their time participating in crafts. Because children have a choice and can choose the activity they prefer, it gives them the opportunity to express themselves and is a form of play. And because the camp respects their personal tastes and aptitudes, they admire and respect their counselors (for the most part) and as a result learn a great deal about themselves and others.[185]

Today, there are a multitude of different kinds of camps. So-called "traditional" camps include a variety of sports, adventure, and arts activities, while specialized camps may be devoted to the performing or visual arts, sports, or horseback riding for example. There are overnight and day camps, single-sex and coed camps, and brother-sister camps. Regardless of each camp's approach, philosophy, and focus, it is proven that the experience summer camps provide for children is life-altering and positive.

What's a camp without a fully functioning pirate ship? During the day the children can become pirates! The speakers blare *Pirates of the Caribbean* music as the children man the eight water cannons. Other children defend the docks with their trusted water blasters and balloon launchers. In the evenings groups go into Pirate Cove where they roast marshmallows and make s 'mores while telling pirate stories. The children then come aboard and get to sleep on a real pirate ship. *Photo courtesy of Camp Echo.*

A Word About Day Camps

Day camp programs provide excellent options for many. Day camp programs are of equal value and often pack as much activity into six or eight hours as overnight programs pack into a whole day. The first day camp in the U.S. was Pierce Country Day Camp which was opened in 1918 by physical education teacher Forester Pierce, who "envisioned a unique summer recreation program for children that would instill them with a lifelong commitment to health and fitness."[186] Many other day camps were founded by teachers who obviously had their summers free and were seeking to achieve the same goals as Pierce. Initially, day camps were "looked upon first as an alternative to resident camp. Some independent day camp owners affiliated with a resident camp to provide older campers with a sleep away experience. Others bought deteriorating resident camp properties in high density locations to remodel as day camps."[187] The ACA adopted standards for day camps in 1956 at its national convention, holding day camp programs to the same high standards as resident camps.

Girls play a game of volleyball in the water at Camp Kehonka. *Photo courtesy of Roy Ballentine.*

Campers of all ages are bound to make friendships that will transcend both time and distance. *Photo courtesy of Coleman Family Camps.*

Campers and counselors develop important relationships over the course of a summer. *Photo courtesy of Kari Ahern.*

The demand for day camps grew throughout the 1970s and 1980s, when families experienced a new dynamic as many women entered the work force. This created a need for child care during the summer that was neatly filled by the explosion of day camp programs nationwide. Camps also found that they had to diversify their offerings and sessions in order to accommodate families seeking options for their children all summer long; the result was the creation of specialty camps, half- and full-day programs and teen programs.[188] Connie Coutellier explained in a 2011 article entitled, "Years of Adventures and Challenges: The History of Day Camp," that the rise of day programs was in direct response to the stresses experienced by children. "In her 1980 book, *The Day Camp Program Book*, Virginia Musselman stated: 'Today's child grows up under many pressures . . . so that the child is pushed rapidly into maturity. . . The day camp is uniquely qualified to offset and relieve such pressures. It is relaxed, informal, and noncompetitive, yet stimulating and adventurous. Day camping does not have to cling to the coattails of resident camping or to the apron strings of the playground. It has its own unique contributions to make—to home and community, to education and conservation, but most of all, to childhood.'"[189]

Coutellier also points out that "in the last fifteen years there have been major cultural shifts in some communities served by day camps. The attitudes and values of the new population may not be interested in day camp. They may want more of an academic or other emphasis, or require more modern facilities such as heated pools and air-conditioned buildings."[190] Staying current and relevant while also maintaining the integrity of the camp experience is, perhaps, the most difficult of the many challenges facing camp directors today.

Marla Coleman, co-owner of Coleman Camps and a past ACA president, explains, "Day camp can begin as early as age three and is geared to children who get to experience camp and still return home each evening! They have the best of both worlds—the camp community, which is built exclusively for kids, and their own home, which provides the security they need at a tender age."[191] She goes on to explain that day camps are "reminiscent of less complicated days, when people connected with nature, thrived on inter-generational relationships, and made new discoveries...everything is designed and scaled to ensure that children feel included, cared about, and capable. Beginning camp at an early age provides important advantages."[192]

The American Camp Association reinforces the idea that day camps offer just as much value as overnight programs. Not only are day camps close to home, often eliminating transportation issues, and easier on the family budget, they also "offer a wide range of programming and activities, from sports to arts to science and education. Like resident camps, day camps offer team-building activities, leadership training, and wilderness programs."[193] The ACA also points to "research [which] indicates that participation in intentional programs, like camp, helps reduce learning loss during summer months. Camp is the ultimate classroom, using experiences to teach problem-solving and skill-development."[194]

Program specialist Christina Quirk Peterson equates the day camp program with a treadmill; "we never stop, there is no down time [and] we are always on the go."[195] She explains that day camps face the unique challenge of not being with their campers around the clock so that it is difficult for staff to know what their campers are experiencing from the time they leave camp in the afternoon until they return the next morning. If something is happening at home, campers who were fine on Monday may act out on Tuesday, which makes the counselors' job more challenging. Additionally, creating a strong sense of community can be a challenge, especially with a higher camper turnover rate than resident camps experience; some campers may only attend day camp for one week but it's just as important to foster a sense of belonging for them as it is for campers who come for the entire summer.

Psychologist Michael Thompson, a well-known advocate of the camp experience, believes that sleepaway camp is not only still relevant in today's "competitive, resume-building world," but also key to child development; he argues "that children develop in profound ways when they leave their parents' house and join a camp community."[196] However, for those who opt for day camps, the benefits are equally great and the impact equally profound.

Single-sex vs. Coed: What's the Difference (besides the obvious)?

Attending a single-sex or coed camp will largely determine the nature of one's overall camp experience; this holds true not only for the campers but for the counselors as well. Eliminating the pressure of having to impress the opposite sex allows campers to express themselves in ways they might not otherwise. Boys might choose to participate in activities that they'd be reluctant to if there were girls around to see them, while girls will surely spend less time on their hair and more time on their friendships. For those who attend single-sex schools, coed camps are a great way to experience positive interactions with the other sex, while single-sex camps may provide a much-needed break from a school year spent in a coeducational classroom.

The oldest girls in camp have a special role. They are responsible for promoting camp spirit, leading songs, and setting a positive example for younger campers. *Photo courtesy of Kari Ahern.*

Assistant counselors set the tone for the fun to be had at one of the summer's all camp dances at Cape Cod Sea Camps. *Photo courtesy of Kari Ahern.*

In our youth camp setting we are very lucky to provide a day and/or overnight program on the same campus. To explain the difference between managing the two different programs, I would tell the story of one summer's day on Cape Cod Bay during a sandcastle contest.

The tide was at its lowest in the afternoon with sand flats spreading as far as the eye could see, dotted with puddles of salt water teaming with marine critters in the bathtub temperature water. The task given to the campers and staff was to divide into teams of six and create a sand sculpture. The groups of campers scurried across the flats to pick the perfect spot to build their creation shouting out their imaginative designs. Once they agreed upon a plan, their buckets, shovels and hands began constructing with furious speed against the tide and counselor imposed time limit. Working together, mermaids, castles, volcanoes, whales, and pirate ships emerged from the sea bed. Creativity, cooperation, along with a fierce sense of ownership for the best idea shaped out of sand surfaced. At the end of the activity, decisions were made using a camp-like democratic process choosing suitable verbal awards for each sculpture. Everyone congratulated each other and commented on the inspirational sand carvings displayed.

While watching the events happening on the beach, there was no obvious sign of which program—day or resident—was thoroughly entertained by nature and counselor-inspired quests. The lessons learned would be the same for a resident or day camper who was being challenged to work on a team, collaborating with peers, making something out of sand and items found on the beach, problem solving, communicating, sharing in the joy of a completed project, and receiving praise from their counselors and friends. The learning, growth, and pure pleasure gained are relevant to all children. The major difference between a resident or day camp is only in the amount of time a child has a chance to participate in the magic of camp.

Day camp is characterized as a fast-paced non-stop treadmill for eight hours each day. Families drop off enthusiastic, excited campers in the morning and meet sometimes exhausted and always satisfied children in the afternoon, interacting with camp on a daily basis, bringing issues to resolve more frequently and immediately, and sharing joys and concerns with the staff continuously. In addition, staff leave for home every night, to another job or responsibilities, and then return refreshed, or maybe call in sick. Day camp is a whirlwind of experiences in a short amount of time.

On the other hand, a resident overnight setting has the opportunity to be more leisurely paced. It can be a "home away from home" where campers and staff are encouraged to reconcile squabbles, confrontations, and mishaps independent from parents. Campers can develop friendships while watching a campfire at night, deal with sick days, or share the thrill of reaching a goal over a longer, more extended amount of time. There seem to be more opportunities to savor relationships and bond closely with cabin mates and counselors. However, the richness of the camping experience happens in both programs, no matter the length of time. The management of each program is predominantly the same and differs only in the amount of time spent at camp![197]

—Nancy Garran,
Executive Director, Cape Cod Sea Camps

A counselor helps a camper construct a sandcastle.

A camper gives a helping hand to a friend at Camp Nathan Hale. *Photo courtesy of the Library of Congress.*

Campers prepare for a hiking trip.
Photo courtesy of Camp Dudley.

Girls formed strong bonds at Camp Kehonka which was in operation from 1902 to 1985. *Photo courtesy of Roy Ballentine.*

Thurber and Malinowski expound on the benefits of single-sex camps. "There tends to be less showing off, reduced self-consciousness, and fewer broken hearts. At a single-sex camp, children support each other and bond together in ways that reinforce the best parts about being a girl or the best parts about being a boy. Plus, the staff at a single-sex camp is primarily the same sex as the campers. This provides kids with many adult role models of the same gender."[198] However, advocates of coed camps emphasize the authenticity of the friendships developed between boys and girls. The ACA cites that gender stereotypes are often broken at coed camps where "girls interact with women in positions of authority and boys interact with men who act as nurturers."[199]

Psychologist and camp expert Dr. Chris Thurber explains the benefits and potential hazards of both coed and single-sex camps.

> "We live in a coed world," one camp director astutely pointed out to me at a recent camping conference. "Kids should attend coed camps so they can prepare themselves for that world." At a high quality coed camp, boys and girls may learn interpersonal skills that depart in healthy ways from the gender-role stereotypes they may have learned at school or elsewhere. Boys have an opportunity to see girls as leaders and athletes; girls see boys in nurturing, expressive roles. At a poor quality coed camp, flirtation and flaunting overshadow and undermine opportunities for respectful relationships and genuine growth. Therefore, the special responsibility of the staff at any coed camp is to model the kinds of non-romantic, polite, genuine male-female interactions they want campers to adopt.
>
> "We live in a coed world," a different camp director astutely replied at the same camping conference. "Kids should attend a single-sex camp so they experience something different and uniquely supportive." At a high quality single-sex camp, boys and girls see balanced role models and largely avoid romantic distractions. Boys interact with men who are both strong and compassionate, assertive and attentive. Girls interact with women who are both tenacious and tender, confident and caring. At a single-sex camp, boys and girls can not only be themselves, they can be their whole selves and reenter the coed world with renewed confidence and empathy. High quality single-sex camps nurture that which is stereotypically feminine and stereotypically masculine, and they do it in an environment where boys and girls feel an enhanced sense of emotional safety. At a poor quality single-sex camp, staff model only those behaviors stereotypical of one sex, sometimes even in an exaggerated, unhealthy way. Bravado and machismo reign at such boys' camps; gossip and diffidence at such girls' camps.[200]

Regardless of whether a camp is coed or not, campers are sure to engage in plenty of same-gender activities. Girls will always enjoy counselor makeovers and trashion shows (where all fashions must be made out of trash bags) while boys will enjoy water gun wars, flag football, and playing cards on rainy days. Building relationships with one's own gender is important and not always emphasized in a classroom setting. For girls, spending time together is a great opportunity not to worry about appearances and boys while for boys, spending time together allows them to focus on building bonds while not trying to impress girls.

Arts

While many traditional camps include arts programs, there are many camps dedicated to the visual and performing arts across the country. Psychologist, author, and camp consultant Dr. Michael Thompson penned an article for the American Camp Association's magazine *Camping* in 2008 in which he discussed arts camps. "My experience is that arts camps really are different. Different in the way they use time, in the amount of autonomy given to campers, and in the relationship between campers and counselors, and naturally, in the nature of the children they attract. Arts camps are trying to bring out the creativity in children, and that is a delicate matter."[201]

Thompson explains that those who are drawn to arts camps are, in general, nonconformists who enjoy an atmosphere devoid of competition. He wonders, along with many others in his field, "who is creative and under what circumstances that creativity will emerge. Despite more than a century of research it remains ineffable, a mystery. Who is creative? How do you create the conditions for creativity to emerge? Some great artists emerge from art schools; others seem to appear from nowhere. What is clear is that you cannot force art to happen; you have to create an environment and hope that it emerges. That's the challenge for a creative arts camp. How do they meet that challenge, and can they do it for every child?"[202]

Laura and Mickey Morris, directors of Buck's Rock Performing and Creative Arts Camp explain their views on running an arts camp. "Every summer at Buck's Rock Performing and Creative Arts Camp, we witness triumphs and achievements that our campers have experienced which will be monumental to their personal growth, future endeavors, aspirations, and achievements throughout the rest of their lives. Inevitably, there are also struggles, disappointments, and setbacks that become equally valuable life lessons and learning experiences, but most of all they have dared to try and explore any and all that inspires them. As camp directors, that courage and passion is what is most fulfilling to witness."[203]

Arts camps are dedicated to allowing campers freedom of self-expression in a non-competitive community of like-minded individuals seeking to pursue their creativity. An emphasis is placed on honing the individual's creative process be it in the visual or performing arts. Today's arts camps offer more than just painting, theater, and ceramics. Also included at many arts camps are circus skills, film editing, rock band, cartooning, and stage combat.

Though not an arts camp, Kehonka placed a heavy emphasis on the visual and performing arts. *Photo courtesy of Roy Ballentine.*

Campers at Buck's Rock Camp enjoy a guitar jam. *Photo courtesy of Buck's Rock Camp.*

Sports

At the other end of the spectrum are sports camps which are, by their very nature, competitive. Sports camps have become extremely popular in the U.S. While there are many that offer instruction in a variety of sports, there are just as many specialty sports camps offering coaching in tennis, hockey, baseball, lacrosse, basketball, football, volleyball, horseback riding, and any number of other athletics. There is much value to attending a sports camp. Children have the opportunity to develop and hone their skills in a given sport while also having the opportunity to experience a variety of coaching styles. Campers may have a chance to experiment with a new position on the field, switching from offense to defense or vice versa. They may also have a chance to participate in both team and individual sports whereas at home they may have to commit to one or the other. Most sports camps offer a variety of different sports, thereby allowing campers to sample other sports they may not have had the opportunity to try at home or at school. Campers receive quality instruction from college athletes and professional coaches; this may not always be the case in school settings where coaches may often be parents or volunteers who are not necessarily that knowledgeable about the sport they are coaching. Additionally, sports camps promote the values of sportsmanship and teamwork which cannot always be said about today's high-stakes teams and clubs.

Anyone involved in the field of education will attest to the fact that sports foster a sense of higher self-esteem, positive self-image, and a boost in self-confidence. Sports camps are able to deliver this in spades through developmentally appropriate sports and athletic competitions.

Campers hone their soccer skills under the tutelage of their counselors. *Photo courtesy of Kari Ahern.*

4-H

Camps affiliated with 4-H programs, while based on their ideals, are not just for 4-H members. The 4-H organization emphasizes head (managing and thinking), heart (relating and caring), hands (giving and working), and health (being and living). The 4-H motto, "to make the best better" and creed, "learn by doing," provide a solid foundation for camping. Many 4-H camps have an environmental focus and educate campers through experiential learning. A majority of 4-H camps are run through land grant institutions in affiliation with larger entities such as colleges and universities. The camps are typically organized at the state level by the 4-H chapter.[204]

Camp Fire USA

Founded in 1910, Camp Fire Girls offered important programs for girls; at the time, society lacked resources and programming for girls. However, the organization recognized the importance of expanding its membership and in 1975, the organization went coed and became Camp Fire USA Today, Camp Fire USA offers both resident and day camp programs that emphasize an appreciation for nature and the environment. A significant component of Camp Fire USA's summer camps is service. Like many of their peers, Camp Fire USA campers have a history of contributing to this country's war efforts and reaching out to those less privileged.

Camp Fire camps offer many typical summer camp activities like swimming, land sports, boating and archery but many Camp Fire camps also include outdoor living and environmental education in their program. Camp Fire USA boasts 41 resident camps and 70 day camps throughout the United States and continues to adhere to the organization's founding principles of work, health, and love (Wohelo).

YMCA

As referenced above, camping became an integral part of the YMCA's programs in 1885, with the establishment of Camp Dudley. Each Y has its own camp history such as Camp Seymour in Gig Harbor, Washington. This Y camp got its start when W.W. Seymour allowed a small group of local boys to camp on his property in 1903. Two years later, the program was more formalized and by 1908 more than 60 boys attended camp there. Seymour deeded 125 acres to the Tacoma YMCA and Camp Seymour was dedicated in 1926.[205] Providence, Rhode Island's YMCA Camp Fuller got its start in 1887 and after moving from site to site for several years, settled on a waterfront property named for Frederic Fuller, who facilitated the Point Judith Pond purchase. Becoming coed in 1978, Camp Fuller boasts a strong leadership development program for teens and prides itself on the "rusticity" of the Fuller experience.[206]

Today, many YMCA camps offer programs for at-risk youth, special needs populations, and teens; according to the American Camp Association, there are over 400 YMCA camps nationwide.[207] The camp facilities are often used to run off-season programs for families and group camping. Overall, however, YMCA camps remain committed to the ideals on which Sumner Dudley founded the earliest YMCA camp: spirituality and leadership.

Campers listen to a sermon at Sunday chapel. *Photo courtesy of Camp Dudley.*

Leatherworking and ceramics are taught at Camp Dudley. *Photo courtesy of Camp Dudley*

Boy Scouts and Girl Scouts

Boy Scouts and Girl Scouts of America both offer summer camps nationwide. A recent study of Boy Scout campers reveals that their summer camp experience included development in the following areas:

- Strong Personal Values and Character
- Positive Sense of Self-Worth and Usefulness
- Caring and Nurturing Relationships
- Productive and Creative Use of Time
- A Desire to Learn
- Social Adeptness[208]

Currently, the Boy Scouts of America offers 420 camps nationwide while the Girl Scouts boast nearly 200 camps. Their approach to camp is that it's "an experience that's bigger than any video screen."[209]

The first Girl Scout camp took place in Savannah, Georgia, in 1912, under the guidance of Juliette Gordon Low. A decade later, the Girl Scouts began chartering summer camps nationwide. According to Eleanor Eell's *History of Organized Camping,* "the philosophy of the Girl Scout organization has been basically the same: camping is part of the program, not an addition to it; camping extends opportunities for girls to develop as individuals and as members of groups, providing experiences not usually or easily found in troop meetings and activities in town."[210] By the 1960s, Eells notes, there was less direction of the camps from the national office and their operation was largely left to regional and local organizers. Today, some Girl Scout camps are run by volunteers and some allow parents to attend with their daughter in exchange for their willingness to volunteer their time and skills to help run a certain aspect of the camp.

Most Scout camps are focused on helping campers attain a certain rank or master Scout skills in order to achieve badges. However, some Scout camps are attended by campers who aren't yet part of the Scouts and the camp experience is used as something of a marketing tool for the organization.

Born out of the Progressive Era, the Girl Scouts' and the Boy Scouts' camp programs played an important role in breaking down both gender and racial stereotypes in the first half of the twentieth century and the same can be said about their efforts today. Conservation and environmental education as well as civic duty remain important aspects of the Boy Scouts' and Girl Scouts' summer camp programs to this day.

Boy Scouts at Camp Roosevelt, July 9, 1925.
Photo courtesy of the Library of Congress.

4 Who Will You Find at Camp?

Camp Directors

The stereotypical image of the camp director for many is that of Morty, the bumbling director of Camp North Star in the 1978 film *Meatballs*. Today, camp directors are committed professionals, most of whom possess advanced degrees in education or psychology. The American Camp Association offers a host of professional development opportunities for camp directors including a New Director Orientation and a Basic Camp Director Course. Education is provided in fourteen core areas including business and finance, food services, health and wellness, human resources, leadership, marketing, mission and outcomes, participant development and behaviors, program design and activities, risk management, site and facilities, strategic planning, target population and diversity, and transportation.[211]

There are as many leadership styles among camp directors as there are camps. Some directors take a very hands-on approach, walking the grounds and interacting with campers and counselors day in and day out. Others allow the staff to work its magic, choosing instead to remain behind the scenes. Regardless, the role of a camp director in the twenty-first century is drastically different than it was a century ago.

In 1935, the Chicago Council of Social Agencies hosted the sixth annual Institute on Character Education with the intent of defining standards for summer camps. Among the suggested standards for camp directors were that the individual have an interest and degree in the field of education, maturity, a sense of values, administrative skills and an "understanding of the place of the camp in society."[212] Today, camp directors are often preoccupied with risk management, assuaging parents and disciplining campers. Living in the litigious society that we do, running a summer camp is, quite literally, a risky business. Nevertheless, many camps have endured and remain vital, robust organizations in the business of educating children.

Executive director camping services for the YMCA of San Diego County Tom Madeyski explains in *Camping* magazine, "once upon a time, the resident camp directors spent the off-season preparing for a few intensive summer months. When summer ended and campers were back at school, directors returned to the home office to catch their breath and begin planning next summer's season. How the camp field has changed! Many of today's camps operate year-round, have expanded to conference and environmental education centers, and thrive with progressive programs and thousands of students, campers, adults, and families."[213] Camp directors, he explains have a great deal on their plate in order to keep twenty-first century camps not only relevant but also operational.

Captain and Mrs. Robert Delahanty, founders of Camp Monomoy for Boys and Camp Wono for Girls. *Photo courtesy of Cape Cod Sea Camps.*

A. Cooper Ballentine teaching shop at Camp Kehonka. Ballentine was hired by Laura Mattoon, the camp's founder, in 1911. "Bally" went on to serve as the owner and director of Kehonka. *Photo courtesy of Roy Ballentine.*

This expansion of the traditional youth camp has brought with it challenges. No longer will spaghetti and hot dogs suffice as food service; no longer will campers accept antiquated plumbing; no longer do summer huts suffice as housing. Times have changed. Even with these challenges, the future holds exciting prospects for resident camping. As natural space and environmental preservation become more important to society, camps stand ready to serve as ideal experiential teaching centers. While social interactions transform to an impersonalized on-line world, the simplified outdoor lifestyle found at camp will prove more valuable. Camps provide powerful hands-on experiences. The camp director of tomorrow will utilize technology to shape and extend their service, yet will maintain a traditional high-touch experience.[214]

Madeyski points to the most effective camp directors as those who have come up through the ranks, often starting their camp experience as campers or counselors themselves. Gaining perspective as a unit leader, activity head, program director, and the like gives executive directors the perspective needed to oversee all aspects of running a camp.

Today, the American Camp Association holds a New Director Orientation each year which provides training with regard to supervision of the camp, staff, and campers, behavior management, and risk management. Camp directors must oversee recruiting, marketing, human resources, and program management in addition to any number of other aspects of general camp management.

The author with fellow assistant directors Jim Flanagan and Christie Peterson. *Photo courtesy of Kari Ahern.*

Nurses

Camp nurses and health care managers are responsible for the health and well-being of the camp community. Not only do they administer band aids and aspirins, but they also are in charge of dispensing daily medications and a healthy dose of TLC for those campers (and sometimes staff members) who are struggling, often with homesickness. Camp nurses have a challenging job vis-à-vis communicating with parents, triaging difficult situations, and reacting in an potential emergency. They must also train the staff with regard to how to treat emergent situations until they arrive on the scene. In short, the health center of any camp is a bustling place all day long.

Many camp nurses are nursing students, school nurses, or nurses who enjoy flexible schedules and can take time off in the summer. Some camp nurses work in different and more stressful environments during the year and enjoy the chance to work with children, spend some time outdoors, and experience a more relaxed atmosphere than critical care or an ICU might offer.

In her book, *Camp Nurse*, Tilda Shalof reflects, on why she wanted to experience being a camp nurse. "I longed to learn the secrets of successful campers. It was much easier for me to understand why someone might *not* like camp, what with the non-stop, exhausting activities, the noisy silliness, the bothersome bugs—not to mention the lack of books, solitude, and quiet time. I wanted to see for myself why so many loved it."[215] And despite her significant training and work as a nurse in Toronto hospital intensive care unit, she worried about her ability to serve a camp population. "I had never even seen a case of poison ivy. I could start an intravenous drip, measure central venous pressure, and analyze arterial blood gases, but I'd never removed a splinter or taped a sprained ankle."[216] And although she had a wealth of intense experience treating serious health concerns, nothing quite prepared her for the "guidance" and suggestions she would receive from campers' parents. One parent wrote, "Jay is in tune with his body. He will let you know which pills he needs and when" while another wrote, "Madison experiences strange sensations at times. She'll tell you when this happens."[217]

The job of a camp nurse has become exponentially more challenging in this age of allergies and medications. Camp nurses must serve as liaisons with local doctors and hospitals if need be, as well as with parents who are far away from their injured or sick child. What all camp nurses have in common, however, is a love of camping and a love of kids. Shalof explains, "the most challenging aspect of being a camp nurse is soothing, counseling, conflict-resolving, and stress-busting with parents who are at home, anxious and worried (usually needlessly) about their children. "The 'helicopter parents' who hover and the 'snowplow parents' who are used to clearing the path of obstacles for their children—both have difficulty when their kids are at camp. There have been many days when I have spent more time on the phone reassuring parents than I have treating campers in the infirmary."[218]

Kitchen Staff

Twenty-first century children are certainly much more savvy about their nutrition than their parents were when they were at their age. Today, many camps offer extensive salad bars at lunch and dinner, fresh fruit, soy milk, and granola. Some camps have deli bars available at lunch and pasta bars available at dinner. Managing so many options requires a bigger staff than many dining halls had even just a few decades ago and purchasing higher quality food also means a bigger price tag for the camp, which, in turn, gets passed on to families in the form of an increase in tuition. Nevertheless, healthy dining is a vitally important component of the camp experience and one for which parents have high expectations.

Camp cooks are generally accustomed to providing massive quantities of food for a range of palates for campers and staff alike. Increasingly, however, campers' dietary restrictions have become a factor in camps' standard fare. For example, most camps are now nut-free and many offer gluten-free and vegetarian options. Many cooks are certified food safety managers. Gone are the days of giant vats of peanut butter and jelly and one entrée option.

Jan Hoffman explains in her article, "At Camp, It's Not Grub, It's Cuisine," "certainly there are camps that still serve 'hello muddah' steam-table food: chicken nuggets, Sloppy Joes, and French fries, with salad bars freighted with cottage cheese, Jell-O, and iceberg lettuce (emphasis on the "ice")...But in the last few years, camp food has increasingly become camp cuisine, transformed from an afterthought to a prominent place at the table. Camps no longer hire cooks; they hire chefs."[219] This, Hoffman explains, is largely in response to parents' concerns about their children's health and nutrition. "When a child spends weeks away from home, parents worry: how will the camp nourish my child? During the school year, many parents strive to control their children's meals; they don't want that hard work to collapse as campers are loosed upon twice-a-day desserts and thrice-daily snacks. So parents are increasingly insisting that camp food be more healthful. That means 'bug juice,' the sugary color-enhanced punch drink of yesteryear, is out; water is in."[220]

Today, many camps are hiring international staff to work in their kitchens. This is challenging because it is an extra group of people that must be recruited, paid, housed, and fed. Another option that many camps have pursued is hiring a food service company. This ensures that the chef is properly trained in food safety and preparation. It offers additional peace of mind for parents of campers with food allergies, knowing that the chefs are knowledgeable and have access to virtually any kind of ingredients needed.

CITs (counselors in training) / JCs (junior counselors)

Among the happiest campers of all are those who have finally reached the ranks of CIT or JC. These campers have generally been at their respective camps for a number of years and are "experts." Often, these individuals know more about the daily operations at the camp and the camp's traditions than newly hired staff members. Nevertheless, these individuals are the poster children for what it means to be a happy camper. As counselors in training, it is their responsibility to motivate younger campers and show them how much fun camp can be. They are the ones to teach younger campers the requisite camp songs, pass on camp traditions, and lead activities. Younger campers look up to these teens with respect and admiration, looking forward to the day that they are among the ranks of junior counselors. Grace Benjamin, a longtime camper at Cape Cod Sea Camps, reflects on her experience transitioning from a camper to a junior counselor.

> As a younger camper, having a JC know you by name, or even wave to you in passing is better than chocolate chip muffins for breakfast, and that's saying something. These seasoned campers seem infinitely more fun, composed, responsible, and older than you will ever be. When eventually, as a JC, you have the ability to make a younger camper's day or summer by forging a connection, the gratification intensifies given your own past. Striving to be a role model comparable to those who defined your personal experience is remarkable—you never feel as accomplished or influential as they were. Yet, you know you are.[221]

Warren Davis reflects on the moment that she realized the influence she could have on younger campers.

> I remember teaching art one day and looking over and a little kid was doing the same thing as I was. That is when it hit me; I am the one that I always looked up to when I was little and it is now my turn to be the older kid. It also really had not occurred to me how much of an impact you can have on a child and how much fun it is to make this impact. It was so adorable when my little 12-year old campers knew what I liked and didn't, would say little phrases that I would say, and would respect me if I asked them to clean [up the cabin]. It was my turn to be the role model to them that I had always looked up to. It was amazingly fun but scary at points not knowing if I was doing it right."[222]

The beauty of a teen leadership program is that it is intentionally structured and age appropriate. Many camps offer multi-year programs which give teens more responsibilities and freedoms incrementally, which are commensurate with increased age and maturity. For example, some programs offer time off and allow the teens to go into town for a movie or pizza. Other camps offer special trips and travel programs like white water rafting or hiking opportunities. Additionally, it is often also the responsibility of the CITs or JCs to serve as team captains in Color Wars or significant games and intercamp competitions. Many teen leaders can be found teaching activities or working with younger campers who may be homesick or struggling with the camp experience.

Many campers who become junior counselors say that the best part about their role in camp is the opportunity to set an example and share their love of camp with the rest of the community. They have the chance to employ the skills they have developed in certain activity areas and the chance to counsel younger campers, knowing that if they need help they can turn to staff members. The optimal outcome is to help these teens develop the skills and knowledge they need to be effective camp staff in the future.

Being a JC or CIT is the equivalent of being a senior in high school and is often more significant and meaningful to the individual than their elevated school status is. Junior counselors embrace their role at camp and wear it like a badge of honor. They have many stories to tell about past Color Wars, camp legends, and special events. They recall the time there was no electricity for two days and all camp meals were cooked over open fires. They laugh about the camp director's performance in the previous summer's talent show. They plot and scheme to pull off the most epic prank in the camp's history. In short, they are walking, talking compendiums of recent camp history and they are proud of it. Advancing through the camp's ranks is a great honor for those who are truly invested in the camp experience. And that experience is made richer by the fact that this group of campers has been together for a significant portion of their childhood and ascended to their vaulted status as a tight-knit group of friends.

Junior counselors enjoying their time in the art room and the opportunity to work with younger campers. *Photo courtesy of Kari Ahern.*

Here, a junior counselor helps a younger camper master his strokes in the pool. *Photo courtesy Kari Ahern*

Junior counselors can be found helping out all over camp. Here, two JCs assist in the Cape Cod Sea Camps office. *Photo courtesy of Kari Ahern*

A camper glazes her project. *Photo courtesy of Kari Ahern.*

Counselors / Staff

In the 1920s, Henry Wack conducted a cross-country trip with the goal of learning more about the camp movement. Along the way, he asked camp directors to describe their ideal staff member. H.W. Gibson, director of Camp Becket-in-the-Berkshires, responded, "a counselor is one who is desirous of investing his or her life and times in genuine character-building and looks upon camp as a great field for such an endeavor."[223] Lotta Broadbridge, director of Camp Bryn Afon, replied, "one mature enough to use sane judgment, and young enough to share in the joys resultant from camp activities; sympathetic, with an understanding of the demands of youthful enthusiasm, but firm enough not to permit herself to be imposed upon, unafraid to offer constructive criticism, and quick to recognize the futility and danger of gossip."[224] And Louis Lamborn, director of Camp Red Cloud and Camp Red Wing, pontificated, "his impulse to be a councilor must be based upon the sincere desire to help mold the lives of young people."[225]

> *And with my counselors, whom I learned to trust as I did no one else, I would hold long conversations in which I talked openly of my deepest fears and fantasies. And afterwards the counselors too would disappear: What was it about those summers that so opened us to strangers?*[226]
>
> —Chaim Potok

Arguably, counselors have the most important job at camp. It is exhausting, rewarding, entertaining, frustrating, and altogether wonderful. Most counselors are college students who have never really had to think about putting the needs of others ahead of their own. The responsibility can be daunting for some; suddenly being in charge of a cabin full of ten-year-olds can be overwhelming for even the most skilled and patient eighteen-year-old. "At 7:30 a.m., when your supercool counselors come to wake you up, it doesn't matter how tired you are—you cooperate, enthusiastically. It's like getting woken up by a celebrity every day."[227]

It can be shocking, to some, how quickly they lose any sense of privacy as a counselor; the campers want to know every little detail of their counselors' lives including but not limited to what they like to do in their free time, who they have a crush on, and whether they have tried drugs and alcohol. Today's campers are incredibly savvy and setting boundaries (especially around sensitive issues) often proves to be a challenge for some counselors. However, being a camp counselor is one of the best and most meaningful jobs one can ever have. Lindsey Mead Russell says that one of the greatest challenges is "being emotionally present and available for all the girls in the cabin all the time."[228] Jillian Gundersheim explains that her "greatest challenge was giving specific attention to every camper and catering to their individual needs. I do feel like I succeeded, however, at times it was extremely hard especially when there were conflicts with campers that were not as 'outgoing' or 'cool' (according to the others)."[229] The result? "It was also awesome to watch my campers learn how to work together and figure out conflict with independence. I definitely feel like I made an impact on their summer in a positive way."

John Gabordi explains his experience sharing a cabin with campers.

> There is never a dull moment when it comes to living in a cabin full of teenage boys. Sometimes the adjustment from normal living situations to a cabin can be difficult. Fortunately, I had just come from living in a house full of college seniors and the environments are surprisingly similar. It can be loud, smelly, and if the occupants had their way they would probably sleep till noon.
>
> However, close relationships can often form from a group living together. It's a similar dynamic to a sports team who spends a lot of time together in practices, on trips, in the locker room, etc. While some privacies are sacrificed, it is those sacrifices that can make people comfortable with each other and provide the perfect atmosphere for close relationships.
>
> Living with campers can also be beneficial because the kids know you are going through an experience that is almost the same as theirs. It would be different if counselors went home and slept in their comfortable bed every night, or saw their family and friends at the end of the day. Living with campers means that a counselor can relate much better to a homesick child or a kid who is having a tough time adjusting to a new environment.[230]

Acclimating new staff is just as important a challenge as doing so with campers. Gundersheim explains, "especially as a new counselor, I was extremely surprised at how welcoming and friendly the staff and campers were. It was really nice to feel like I belonged and was part of a team that was geared toward making the kids happy and comfortable."[231] It is most challenging for camp administrators to indoctrinate new staff who have never even been campers before. Mike Gomez looks back on his experiences as a counselor new to the entire camp experience.

I had never been a camper growing up since my parents always wanted to take us on vacations during the summer. Little did I know how much I would've loved going to camp. For my first year, I was 21 and just out of college. I felt as if a huge void in my childhood had been filled. I was initiated into a second family, a wonderful community of all ages that shared so many different kinds of experiences together in just a couple of months out of the year. And what's left at the end of one summer is easily picked up at the next as if no time has passed. I discovered a special kind of life experience that everyone should have no matter how old they are. [232]

Not surprisingly, new-to-camp counselors are often the staff members who become camp's greatest advocates and often return the following summer with several friends in tow.

Barbie Cobb, director of the Junior Camp at Camp Wyonegonic, explains the significance of counselors' impact on the lives of children with whom they work.

The greatest reward for a camp counselor is knowing that you are making a difference in a child's life. The counselors that I had as a child taught me about respect, responsibility, the importance of tradition, and the joys of laughter. Granted, these are things that a parent can teach, but a camp counselor does it without even realizing it. Just by being at camp, wanting to spend the summer with children, speaks volumes about the level of commitment and love that the counselors have for the camp, and it influences the campers in wonderful ways. As a counselor you love your kids—the quirky, the quiet, the goofy, and the serious—and you get so much love in return. It's incredible."[233]

As a staff member, you are on call 24/7, sleeping six hours a night and spending the remaining 18 outside, running around with your campers, planning programming, catering to every need of your cabin and getting more mosquito bites than you thought physically possible. The dedication to your work, the happiness of your campers and their personal growth is incalculable. You want an easy, restful summer? Go get an internship. You can sleep all weekend long and get paid a lot more, too.[234]

—Talya Minsberg

Jessica Werlin comments on her experience as a counselor at Gold Arrow Camp. "As a counselor, my experience has been entirely different, and leaving camp is hard for a whole different host of reasons. It's funny; in many ways I feel like the experience I 'should' have had as a camper I have gotten as a counselor instead. Camp for me now provides a great freedom to be myself, in all my goofiness. Heck, if I want to walk around singing Disney songs at full volume, that's not only fine, it's encouraged! At camp, instead of raising an eyebrow, everyone joins in. I find it hard, and disappointing, to leave behind this kind of atmosphere and compress myself back into a socially acceptable box when I go back into the real world.[235]

It is vitally important to have a range of counselor "types" at camp. While spirited extroverts are often a natural fit for the position, it is equally necessary to have more mild-mannered staff around whom quieter campers may be more comfortable. Certainly, it is essential to have a staff with a wide range of interests and skills; this, of course, is often driven by the program (i.e.: does the camp need sailing counselors, musicians, etc.?). However, it is also helpful to have staff members with unusual skills such as the ability to juggle or ride a unicycle. And certainly, all staff members must come to camp with a positive outlook, a sense of humor, and a willingness to be flexible. There are so many qualities that are necessary to do a good job as a counselor. Werlin expands on this:

The counselors who were out to have the most fun were always the greatest. A counselor who was vibrant and lively guaranteed a good time. Friendliness and openness were important too, particularly from the counselors in your cabin. A good counselor would also be excited when you were, excited *for* you. Behind all of these qualities really was, more than anything, a genuine counselor. It was all too easy to see right through the false enthusiasm, to identify the hidden disinterest, in a counselor who didn't really want to be there all that much. It was this counselor who made an already slightly outer-edge kid like me feel all the more discouraged. A good one though would personally invest and really, honestly, want to get to know you and make your experience great. That attitude really was reflected in every interaction with the counselor, and kids pick up on that, without a doubt.[236]

Campers enjoy getting to know their counselors at Camp Wa Wa Segowea. *Photo courtesy of Camp Wa Wa Segowea.*

Counselors are often viewed by their counselors as veritable superheroes. *Photo courtesy of Justine Darmanian.*

Camps work hard during the winter months to hire fun-loving and hard-working counselors to care for their campers. *Photo courtesy of Justine Darmanian.*

Living together in a cabin can be a difficult adjustment for some or it can be like a giant, two-month sleepover. In any case, cabin life requires a great deal of patience and understanding while also fostering a sense of camaraderie and community. *Photo courtesy of Kari Ahern.*

The friendships formed at summer camp are an essential part of the camp experience, providing a second family for many. *Photo courtesy of Kari Ahern.*

The best counselors are compassionate, considerate, energetic, and enthusiastic. *Photo courtesy of Kari Ahern.*

A staff member shows a group of campers how to properly paddle a canoe at Camp Wa Wa Segowea. *Photo courtesy of Camp Wa Wa Segowea.*

Camp...is an environment designed explicitly for trying out new behaviors and exploring questions of personal identity and values. Camp founders intended this environment to serve campers' developmental needs. However, they unintentionally created a near-perfect environment for young adult counselors who, perhaps even more than the campers, are in the process of exploring options and setting the pathway for their future.[237]

Just as there are different groups of campers (veteran campers and new campers), there are groups of counselors. There are returning counselors, new counselors, and campers-turned counselors. Camp directors are thrilled when they are able to retain their best staff members from year to year. These individuals are spread throughout the various units of campers in order to share their expertise, knowledge of camp, and accumulated wisdom.

Like so many other aspects of the camp experience, the demands of society and the economy have affected camps' staffing. Sherry Mernick, one of Cape Cod Sea Camps' resident camp directors, explains:

> Many of our Department Heads and Activity Specialists have been with us for 10-20+ years. Most are teachers during the school year and they have children or grandchildren enrolled in our program through age 17. The trend with counselors, however, is much different. Even just ten years ago, college aged counselors stayed with us on average for three years...and many stayed even longer, almost approaching the "lifer" designation. With today's current emphasis (demand one might say) on internships, we are lucky to have staff return for two or three years. We, as other camps, do partner with colleges to offer internships in the form of hours spent working with children in an educational/ recreational setting for various majors, i.e. social work, education, physical education, sports management, psychology, nursing, drama, etc. Too, the cost of a college education now has many students taking summer classes to hasten their graduation date or insure that work is completed within 4 years.[238]

Staff members who were once campers and have risen through the ranks often present and interesting challenge for camp administrators. While they are experts on all things camp, knowing the routine, the culture, and the policies and procedures, they are also generally very eager to assert themselves and their newly acquired power as a full-fledged counselor. While many do an excellent job transitioning to staff member, others struggle with how to get campers to follow directions, perform their cabin chores, and participate in activities. Renee Tucknott comments on the challenges presented: "The most challenging part about going from camper to counselor is that you now have a new responsibility and a new place at camp. As a camper you are responsible for yourself, but as a counselor you have sometimes 15 kids who are depending on you to make the right decisions. You want to have fun like the other campers, but you still need to be the adult and the person setting the good example."[239] Kelly Flanagan explains, "The hardest thing about going from camper to counselor is the added responsibility. You no longer have your rest hours to yourself; you are now responsible for watching your campers to make sure nothing goes wrong. You have to constantly be counting and watching everyone. You can still have just as much fun, but it definitely puts pressure on you to make sure everyone is where they are supposed to be and that no one is misbehaving."[240]

Corrinne Loder, a camper-turned counselor at Gold Arrow Camp explains how rewarding being a camp counselor is. "There are countless rewards to being a counselor. Seeing how happy the kids are that you're spending your summer with them, encouraging them to push themselves and to do well, you know that they really appreciate you. A kid's excitement when they reach the top of the rock wall is enough to keep you going for days, and you literally get those positive reactions all summer."[241] Flanagan says, "The greatest reward of being a counselor is the friendship you create with your campers and how much your campers look up to you as a role model. My girls ask me about advice and come to me if they are having an issue with anything. Their relationships mean so much to me and I would seriously do anything for any one of my girls."[242]

Many American camps have taken to hiring international staff. The main reasons that American college students are unable to work at camps even if they'd like to are: first, the salary is quite low compared to what they might make elsewhere; and, second, many college students feel pressure to complete internships prior to graduating. Hence, the market for counselors from abroad is an active one. BUNAC was, for many years, one of the best-known work abroad organizations and has placed 250,000 staff at more than 2,000 camps since 1962.[243] The majority of BUNAC's applicants hailed from the United Kingdom, Australia, New Zealand, and Canada, bringing an important international perspective to American summer camps. "Summer sleep-away camp is still a quintessentially, even peculiarly, American institution. Color wars are seldom fought on foreign soil, and in most countries, scions of the middle and upper classes do not associate summer with name tags sewn on underwear and enforced dips in freezing lakes."[244]

Alison McCarlie, a native of Scotland, reflects on her summer camp experience. "Camp was very different from what I expected. I thought it would all be little kids and hadn't anticipated there being a [teen] leadership program. I also had not anticipated the level of independence the children get at camp...

Proper supervision on the water is critical...and perhaps one of the most coveted jobs on a hot summer day. *Photo courtesy of Kari Ahern.*

Sherry Mernick reflects on the value of having a diverse and international staff.

> With a foreign camper population of approximately 10%, it is nice to mirror their cultural contributions to our camp family with a similar percentage of international staff. One of our camp's Core Values is Sense of Community. It is wonderful to observe this camaraderie/ awareness develop on the local level of cabins, units and activities and expand/extrapolate/ evolve into a more global perspective of "it takes a village." Over the years we have had counselors from England, Austria, Australia, Sweden, Scotland, Portugal, Ireland, Germany, Japan, Mexico, Canada, Czechoslovakia, Slovenia, New Zealand, Russia, Belgium, France, Italy, Finland, and Iceland. Each individual has added an element of their country's way of life to the fabric of our world at camp. Be it cuisine, humor, tradition, expressions, music, common courtesies, games, political views, language, or expectations, we learn from each other... and we find many more commonalities than differences!"[247]

I also hadn't realized it would be quite the community it was; I expected more of a business, more formal. Needless to say, camp exceeded my expectations. I just thought it was a summer babysitting service, but it's an education and great learning experience."[245] McCarlie, a teacher, also noticed a distinct different between American children and their Scottish counterparts. "Other cultures would consider Americans to be very confident. I can definitely see this comparing my Scottish [students] to the kids I had at camp. I spend so much of my time in school teaching my class to be confident individuals when Americans seem to have that sorted pretty well!"[246]

Campers and staff from France, Australia, and other nations are recognized at a Sunday colors ceremony. *Photo courtesy of Kari Ahern.*

Activity Specialists

Many parents send their children to camp to acquire new skills or to hone those they already have. As a result, superior instruction is essential in summer camp activity areas. Activity specialists are those individuals who have expertise in a specific area. In general, their main responsibility is to provide safe, fun, and age-appropriate activities for the campers and to oversee the staff who teach the activity. These individuals must have extensive knowledge of their activity as well as of the safety procedures and the equipment associated with it. Activity specialists also are often responsible for implementing any relevant awards programs and for tracking campers' progress.

While some activity specialists have cabin responsibilities in addition to those in their activities, many others live separately in staff housing and have other administrative duties such as conducting evening supervision, overseeing special events or mentoring staff. Staff training is a critical aspect of their job; while most counselors already possess highly developed skills in their chosen activities, few have teaching experience. Hence, activity and program specialists provide guidance and assistance to younger staff members who are still developing a teaching style.

Fostering a positive working dynamic among counselors during orientation is critical to creating a cohesive staff. *Photo courtesy of Kari Ahern.*

Camp Pets

Pets can play a very important role in the daily life of a camp. While many early camps had working farms or raised chickens for fresh eggs and milked their own cows, today it is not uncommon to see dogs roaming the grounds with their staff owners or for the office to have a pet cat. Time with pets can be instrumental in consoling a homesick camper or rewarding certain behaviors. Some pets are used to help reinforce the importance of responsibility at camp. A camper who may not be making his bed or helping with cabin clean up might be chosen to help walk or feed the camp's pets to learn accountability.

Pets may be featured in camp talent shows, costume contests, or plays and may often be found lurking around the dining hall or camp store in hopes of a dropped treat. Life as a camp dog is pretty close to perfect: endless opportunities for walks, swims, and playtime, no shortage of pets and lots of treats.

The dog fashion show is a much beloved tradition at Cape Cod Sea Camps. Here, assistant director Jim Flanagan and his dog, Murph, show their stuff. *Photo courtesy of Kari Ahern.*

Though livestock used to be a common presence at some camps, today dogs are much more commonplace.
Photo courtesy of Roy Ballentine.

The life of a camp dog is enviable: an endless supply of pets and treats all summer long!
Photos courtesy of Kari Ahern.

Growing up I went away to summer camps, but only for a week at a time. I didn't even know that other kids went away to camps for a whole summer. It was probably attributed to the fact that I am from California, and going away for a whole summer was not common.

Most of the camps that I went to were through my church, and we would travel to a big campground where we would meet up with other churches from the West Coast. While it was only for a week, they had the traditional summer camp schedule, jamming in as many activities as possible into a day.

My first experiences as a counselor were at day camps through various churches and country clubs. After a few years, I decided that I wanted to become an overnight camp counselor. I looked at Cape Cod Sea Camps in Brewster, Massachusetts, because my mom and aunt had both worked there when they were in college. Even though it was over 3,000 miles away I thought, why not? I had grown up going to the Cape, and this seemed like a great opportunity to branch out and try something new. Turned out to be one of the best decisions I ever made.

To be honest, I was never nervous going into my first summer. When I first found out I was hired, I scoured CCSC's website trying to get a glimpse of what I was getting myself into. But even with my "intense" preparation, I still had no idea what to expect. I spent that first summer getting used to everything around me. Every day I would find myself in a new situation, and would have to rely on the training I did during orientation and my common sense to figure out the proper solution.

I believe the hardest part about being a counselor was maintaining an authoritative role. In some cases like when I first started, I was only three years older than the oldest group at camp, while some counselors only had a year difference. As a counselor you want to be your campers' friends, especially when they are close in age with you. But you are there to be a role model and sometimes you can't always be their friend. I found that everything is about balance. Finding that balance is hard, and even in my third year when I took on more responsibility and became an assistant head counselor, I was still finding myself trying to maintain that balance with my co-counselors. I wanted to have a fun environment, but I also wanted to maintain my authoritative role and have them respect me. While this was certainly challenging at times, it was manageable and did not stop me from enjoying camp.

One of the most rewarding experiences that a counselor can take away from camp and what I took away the most was the relationships that you make. I was fortunate enough to have the same cabin of girls two summers in a row, and the bond that I had already created with them the first summer strengthened so much more. Not only did I establish amazing relationships with my campers, but I did as well with my fellow counselors. Some of the people that I worked with over the past three summers I consider my closest friends. I am even roommates with someone I worked with my first summer, and if it wasn't for camp we would have never met! I also now have friends from all over the world; not many people can say that!

What is one of the best things about camp, and what makes it so special is the bond that you make with your camp friends and campers. I did not expect camp to feel like the second home that it did, and I am so grateful for all of the experiences that I have gained while being a counselor.[248]

—**Justine Darmanian**

Old Campers & New Campers, Happy Campers & Homesick Campers

Opening day brings with it a host of emotions and a wide variety of campers. Certainly there are the veteran campers who have been to camp before, know the routine, and have well-established friendships. There are also the new campers who arrive, often knowing only one or two other campers or none at all. In a 1995 *New York Times* article entitled, "A Summer At Camp: Arriving, Short Sheets, and a Long Way From Home," one camp administrator explained, "You have to understand that the old campers have been waiting all winter to see their friends…It's not that they're excluding, but they have to be reminded to include. After a few days of catching up it will be fine."[249] It is the job of the counselors to meld these individuals from varying backgrounds into a homogenous group over the duration of the session through games, activities, and cabin time.

There are, of course, those campers who have been to camp before and who love camp more than anything. These campers truly know the meaning of "10-4-2," a saying common at Camp Wah-Nee that was highlighted in a 2010 *New York Times* article: "We live 10 months of the year for the two we spend at camp."[250] They have been counting the days and weeks since they last left camp, having set a countdown on their phone as they pulled out of the driveway on closing day. These campers have barely been able to sleep for the days leading up to opening day, as they are giddy with anticipation. They have demanded that their parents leave home at an ungodly hour so that they can be among the first to arrive at camp. Being among the first to arrive ensures the best selection of beds and shelf space, as well as ample time to assess the counselors, returning campers, and new campers. These campers quickly dismiss their parents once they have unpacked and deposited money in the canteen or camp store account. They then eagerly anticipate the arrival of old friends. Renee Tucknott attended Gold Arrow Camp for seven summers. She explains the emotions she experienced on opening day: "I looked forward to seeing all my camp friends each summer. It was like opening presents on Christmas day when I would get off the bus and see all my friends from summers before."[251]

Even among the returning campers there are many who are nervous about the summer ahead. Jessica Werlin, a longtime camper at Gold Arrow Camp, explains, "I was an awkward and shy kind of kid. For me, getting ready for camp meant bracing for a whole new set of social tensions and the discomfort of meeting new people. Being with my friends from home was easy; making new ones was always hard. I never felt like I fit in exactly with the kids who came to GAC, and the minor dread of having to be in that awkward situation was always on my mind when I came to camp."[252] But once ensconced in the daily routines of camp, Werlin felt at home.

A group of friends reunite on the porch of their cabin on opening day. *Photo courtesy of Kari Ahern.*

> *For some…[camp] is better than home. They escape parents' fighting or a school where they are maybe not so popular and return to a place where they are valued.*[253]

While the returning campers have already set up their beds and areas, sized up the counselors, and assessed how winter treated the members of the opposite sex, new campers tend to arrive a bit later in the day, not realizing the importance of an early arrival. The new campers are easy to spot in a sea of people; they look a bit nervous, mistake the dining hall for the infirmary, and have yet to master the lingo. New campers often appear a bit shell-shocked by the ease with which returning campers have settled in. For most, the transition into camp, though sometimes rocky at first, is generally seamless after a few days. New campers who are truly ready for camp embrace traditions, work hard to understand the unique lexicon and develop friendships. However, there are always those who may not be quite ready for a summer away from home.

Homesickness

Without fail, each summer at every camp there are those campers who experience homesickness. There are many factors that can contribute to this. Among the more common causes of homesickness are being away from home for the first time and not knowing anyone; even simply seeing others who are homesick can cause a pandemic outbreak of tears and tummy aches among those who were perfectly well-adjusted only moments before. Homesickness is a normal response to being away from home; even counselors experience it.

Author Leslie Paris explains, "the problem of homesickness offers a unique lens through which to consider the intergenerational production of children's culture and experience: that is, adults' attempts to create cohesive communities for their young charges and the process through which children came to understand themselves as members of new communities."[254] In an article entitled, "Please Let Me Come Home," Paris explains "because homesickness was, in part, a response to the particular conditions of camp life, it tended to abate when children felt a connection to caring and capable adults. Conversely, those campers who had encounters with inexperienced or uncaring counselors were more likely to experience homesickness."[255]

Paris goes on to cite a 1927 edition of the Surprise Lake Camp newspaper that offered sage advice for homesick campers: "'if you find you are becoming homesick it means that you are not active enough and you are not a good mixer. The remedy is simple, play more games with other boys and mix with them and you will be just like the other campers."[256]

The goal, of course, is to help campers through the rough patch of homesickness so that they may enjoy all that camp offers, while developing a sense of independence and a feeling of success. "Children's successful acclimatization to camp life signaled their growing independence, necessary and exciting but somewhat bittersweet for loving parents."[257] Some homesick campers are fairly easy to cure. Once they get over the initial separation from their parents and allow themselves to integrate into the camp community, they find themselves wholly engaged and happy. However, as anyone who has ever been a camp counselor can attest, there are some campers who are completely inconsolable, crying to the point of hyperventilation. Meal times and bed times prove to be exceedingly difficult for these children who can't stop thinking about mom and dad long enough to engage in any of the fun around them. Some campers assume the role of "the homesick one" and even after they are feeling better, they have self-segregated to the point that they don't know how to behave differently. After all, they've become accustomed to being checked on by lots of different people, receiving extra treats, and getting special treatment like golf cart rides or time with the camp dogs. Once cured, all of that would disappear so, in some extreme cases, the tears (now forced) continue.

Paris explains, "Homesickness was emblematic of the difficulty that many experienced in moving from one model of life to another, and the limits of the 'camp family' ideal."[258]

Diane Falanga, author of *P.S. I Hate It Here!: Kids' Letters From Camp* and of *P.S. I Still Hate It Here!: More Kids' Letters From Camp* explains,

> I have a child who always started off camp with a few nights of homesickness. By year three I smartened up and told her ahead of time that the feeling at night she might get as soon as she arrives at camp has an actual name—a label—and that many campers suffer from it. It's called homesickness and it will dissipate. By telling her about this in advance and reminding her that this feeling may be there but will quickly leave, really put her at ease. Misery loves company. She was also relieved to understand that other kids suffer from this, too—and have for the last 100+ years camps have been part of our landscape.[259]

So is there a cure for homesickness? The best medicine is to stay busy and engaged; it is impossible to make friends if you're crying all the time and attached to the hip of a counselor.

"Lifers" (people who spend virtually their whole lives at camp)

> The final category is people who *really, really, really enjoy camp*. These are the *camp cultists*. You probably expect me to say that these campers grow up to be utterly incapable of functioning in a non-camp environment, and end up sleeping on the streets in cardboard boxes. In fact, the opposite is true. Camp cultists grow up to be chief executive officers of major corporations, name partners in Wall Street banking firms, Cabinet secretaries, governors, and presidents of prestigious foundations. Their universities invite them to serve on their boards. Their

> home towns name schools after them. They are the Establishment… For camp cultists, summer camp is an experience that lasts a lifetime. When they're too old to be campers, they come back as counselors. When they're too old to be counselors, they send their children in their stead.[260]
>
> —Timothy Noah

Some might say that lifers suffer from a Peter Pan complex. And to some extent, they may be right. However, a good number of "camp cultists" are teachers in "real life" and, as such, have summers free to return to camp year after year. It is this group that is living testament to the value of camp. It is the lifers who know how to combat homesickness quickly and effectively, who keep camp traditions alive, and who serve as the best advertisement for the importance of the summer camp experience. Lifers are a camp's best marketing tool; they are living proof that a fun-filled, safe, and enjoyable summer will be had by all. Blogger Michael Rosenzweig explains his life-long affinity for camp. "For me, summer camp, especially sleep-away camp, is both an escape from reality as well as a microcosm for the real world. During a few weeks over the summer you can win the Olympics, act in musicals, perform in rock concerts, and make lifelong friends."[261]

Lifers are often the envy of their friends and family, having found a way to preserve a way of life that is unsustainable to most others; it is as though they are drinking from the fountain of youth. Lifers have watched their campers become counselors and counselors become administrators. Lifers have endured the lean years when enrollments were down and the booms when camp was so full that friends were on wait lists to return. Lifers see the world through a unique lens: one that lacks a social hierarchy, cut-throat competition, and any sense of drudgery. Lifers simply seek to ensure that campers and staff make the most of every day at camp.

Friendships form among campers and staff of all ages and from all backgrounds.
Photo courtesy of Kari Ahern.

5
A Summer at Camp

Preparing for Camp

Campers who truly love camp are in a constant state of camp preparation. Once they arrive home from one summer at camp, they begin preparing for the next. One happy camper was quoted on *This American Life* as saying, "Camp is all I talk about during the year. My friends get so mad at me; they're like, 'we don't want to hear about camp anymore.' Because everything that goes on at home, you can always think of something that relates to something that happened at camp. And so then you tell that, and they'll be like, 'camp? We've heard about camp way too much.'"[262]

The psychological preparation for camp is one thing, but physically preparing and packing for camp is another beast altogether. Packing for camp is a Herculean task. How much is too much? How little is problematic in terms of laundry? What if the camper runs out of something? Does one dare risk trying to smuggle in contraband items? The ACA's Bette Bussel emphasizes the importance of packing together. "If campers are to manage their belongings while at camp (for the day or for weeks at a time), they need to pack them. Camp experiences teach children valuable life lessons in how to keep track of and to take care of their belongings. If adults do the packing for and not with campers, children don't know what they have or where to find it."[263] Although Bussel also encourages families to stick closely to the camp's recommended packing list, new camp families will make the rookie mistake of adhering to the list exactly. This could have dire consequences for the camper-to-be. Not only is the camp laundry is bound to lose a few socks and t-shirts, but no one wants to be the only one without the requisite costume/accessory/gear.

As any girl who has even packed for any length of time at sleepaway camp will tell you, it is critical to have everything with you just in case you might need it. After all, you might need leopard print spandex tights, a day-glo wig, or six-inch platform shoes. The amount of product that girls bring to camp for the summer is astounding. There are products for the hair, products for the body, make-up, and sunblock. There are perfumes. There is temporary hair color. Bug repellant. Aloe. There are bottles of back-up products and potions. And there is likely contraband (like aspirin, which should be stored safely in the infirmary). And increasingly, boys, too, are packing anything from home that isn't nailed down. Portable stereos, flags, and sports equipment are often competing for space with musical instruments and fishing gear. Many families have taken to simply boxing all of these necessary accoutrements and shipping them to the camp a week before the camper is to arrive so that it doesn't take up precious space in the car.

Mental preparation for camp is critical. Perhaps the biggest concern for today's campers is being "unplugged" for several weeks. Stripped of the ability to text, email, chat, and Skype, campers are completely out of the loop with their friends from home. Relegated to letter writing, campers may experience a sense of withdrawal until they are fully immersed in the daily life of camp. They must prepare to be away from their friends and relatives and even the family pet for a prolonged period of time. Perhaps they will miss out on annual family traditions like Fourth of July family picnics or camping trips. Of course, what they will gain by being at camp is immeasurable.

Campers bring extraordinary amounts of clothing and personal effects to camp. Keeping their area and bed neat is a challenge for many campers.

Tripp Lake campers arrive via horse and buggy in the camp's early years. *Photo courtesy of Tripp Lake Camp.*

Getting to Camp

Another time-honored tradition is taking the bus to camp (though generally most campers arrive by car). However, unlike the campers of days gone by who rode in school buses, today's campers ride in luxury: air-conditioned coach buses with bathrooms and videos playing. Campers spend their last moments frantically texting, emailing, and posting to Facebook before having to turn in their cell phones at check in. Generally staffed by one or two counselors, the bus to camp generally transports a mix of new and returning campers. As the destination approaches, the excitement mounts and the energy becomes palpable. Campers leap off the bus and into the arms of their friends who have already arrived. This is, of course, a significant departure from the days when campers took a train. In a July 1, 1935, *New York Times* article, the headline read, "Day's Exodus Complicated by Tearful Mothers, Harried Fathers, and Vexed Counselors."[264] The first paragraph of the article stated, "swarms of children shepherded by fluttery mothers and perspiring fathers kept the echoes rumbling in Grand Central Terminal last night in the greatest exodus that railroad officials have handled since 1931."[265] To further contribute to the chaos, "little boys who refused to part with their dogs caused a bedlam. Mothers pounding instructions into inattentive ears, fathers laying down manly precepts and station attendants bawling announcements added to the din."[266] That day, 5,000 children headed to 63 camps, primarily located throughout New England.

Although most campers arrive by car or by bus, there is a small but growing number who arrive by plane. In July 2011, *The New York Times* ran an article entitled, "To Reach Simple Life of Summer Camp, Lining Up for Private Jets." The article pointed out that, "The popularity of private-plane travel is forcing many high-priced camps, where seven-week sessions can easily cost more than $10,000, to balance the habits of their parents against the ethos of simplicity the camps spend the summer promoting."[267] While this may seem convenient and perfectly reasonable to some, to others it represents the antithesis of what camp is all about. Ten days after the aforementioned article ran, a letter to the editor was printed that stated, "Flying children to summer camp in private planes reflects another sad trend in our society: choosing personal convenience over shared experience. For those fortunate enough to attend camp in the first place, that long bus ride—surely still the mode of travel for most campers—provides hours to make friends, comfort teary new kids, and share candy soon to become contraband. The life lessons learned in those hours are worth far more than a quicker trip and a catered lunch."[268] Clearly, planes and trains are the exception to the rule today as most campers arrive by car with their parents.

Camp is magical—a real Disneyland without the Mickey Mouse-shaped pancakes. It's a place removed from the stresses and distractions of the real world, where staff members and campers alike discover a new kind of independence and responsibility. Camp is a place of positive transformation—where you dance to '90s music between bites of cereal in the morning, clean up your dishes and make your bed with no complaints, and meet undoubtedly the coolest people in the world: your 19-year-old counselors.[269]

—Talya Minsberg

Opening Day

For those who have never experienced opening day at a camp, it is an intense and often overwhelming scene. The line to check in begins to form before the staff is even awake in many cases. Parents nervously sip coffee while campers practically levitate with excitement. Squeals can be heard as friends reunite after ten long months apart. Hugs and handshakes abound while pleasantries are exchanged as more and more friends join the line. New campers may be taken aback by the scene and some begin to rethink their decision to attend camp in the first place. Some teeter on the brink of uncertainty as they begin to realize that they will soon be separated from their parents for an extended period of time; tears hover precariously on eyelashes.

The check in process begins, and campers and their parents are greeted enthusiastically by well-scrubbed counselors in their staff-shirts. Children are assigned a cabin or a bunk, new campers are given tours (usually by one of the junior counselors or veteran campers) and the campgrounds become at once enlivened, taking on an entirely different feeling. Whereas, during staff orientation, a few counselors might have kicked around a soccer ball on the field, suddenly there are droves of campers of all shapes and sizes clamoring for the ball. The dining hall, of which only a fraction has been used during orientation, is now bursting at the seams with people and noise. And the cabins, which seemed empty and quiet, are bustling with energy and all manner of possessions. Counselors are suddenly outnumbered (and the neophytes begin to get nervous about this).

All campers must make a stop in the health center (a.k.a. the infirmary) where they are expected to turn over any medications, review any health issues with the nursing staff and, of course, have their heads checked. Naturally, a few parents occupy a good deal of the nurses' time trying to prepare them for every sneeze, sniffle, and hiccup that their child might experience while in their care. Camp nurses, who have seen and heard it all before, are wonderful at assuaging parents' concerns and fears. After the health screens, it's finally time to settle in to the cabin.

The sign says it all: Welcome to Camp!

Unable to contain their excitement and in pursuit of the best bed, campers and their parents arrive before reveille on opening day.

Campers and their parents check in on opening day. *Photo courtesy of Kari Ahern.*

Campers wait with their parents to check in through the health center on opening day at Cape Cod Sea Camps.

Moving In

An early arrival is critical, as there is much at stake, especially for full session campers. Being able to select the bed of your choice is almost as important as who is in your bunk or cabin. Is it better to have a bunk near the door or not? Near a window or in a corner? Close to the bathroom or on the other side of the cabin? And then there is the issue of whether a top or bottom bunk is preferable. Both have their pros and cons. Don't like other people sitting on your bed? Then a top bunk is right for you. Need some additional storage space under the bed? A bottom bunk is your best bet. And of course there is the issue of one's bunkmate. Some of the most enduring camp friendships are those made between bunkmates who insist on bunking together summer after summer. They may coordinate everything from who will bring which posters to how many extension cords they each need prior to their arrival at camp.

> *I distinctly remember the night before I first departed for camp. I was very worried about not knowing anybody and I was specifically worried that nobody was going to help me carry my trunk (campers each were supposed to bring a trunk with their belongings) to my platform tent. I almost didn't go—I was that nervous about the whole trunk carrying. At the end of camp, as I headed home with a lifetime of memories tucked in my pocket, I thought back to that night before camp and all of the experiences I would have missed out on had I given in to my anxiety and not gone to camp.*[270]
>
> —Elizabeth Donnan Kintz

Parents' role in helping their campers settle in can be either relatively complex or quick and simple. Parents' reaction to watching their child's peers unpack is often priceless. This is especially the case for the parents of new campers. These parents, many of whom abided by the suggested packing list sent by the camp, are positively shocked as they watch the other parents—some of whom have arrived with an arsenal of power tools to make any necessary adjustments to the cabin, the bed, or the shelving—take orders from their children about where to hang things, how to unpack the trunk and in what fashion their possessions ought to be organized. Novice parents begin to worry because they didn't know that their child needed a special pair of flip flops earmarked for the shower in addition to a shower caddy. They worry because they only packed ten t-shirts instead of one for every day of the session. New parents will often take aside the cabin counselor to ask if this is normal. The counselor's answer will depend on whether he or she has been to camp before;

A cabin awaits the arrival of campers on opening day. It is unlikely that at any other point in the summer that any cabin is ever as clean as it is on opening day (with the exception, perhaps, of visiting day). *Photo courtesy of Kari Ahern.*

new counselors are generally just as surprised as the new parents by the amount of "stuff" veteran campers bring. Returning staff just smile and laugh, reassuring the rookie parents that their child will be able to borrow whatever he or she needs from the other campers. After seeing their child's cabinmates unpack, some parents have been known to rush out to the nearest store and purchase additional clothing or to overnight more items from home as soon as they get back.

Once the last of the trunks and duffle bags has been unpacked, it's time for the parents to say goodbye. There are a number of different scenarios that unfold. For some, this is a well-established routine. The parents have served their purpose as far as the child is concerned; the tuition has been paid, the car has been unpacked, and the camper is ready to be on his or her own for a few weeks. There is a hug, a kiss and a "see you on visiting day" before the camper dismisses the parents. The parents climb back into the car and return home or head off on their own vacation, child-free. However, there are also parents who have a much harder time saying good-bye. Some parents have been known to lurk in the bushes to keep an eye on their child until they are found by the counselors or the camp director and asked to leave. Some parents require consoling from the staff and a great deal of reassurance that their child will be just fine. Still other parents call to check on their child before they have reached the end of the driveway. Eventually, however, these parents have to entrust their child to the camp; most are able to do so successfully even if it takes a few days.

However, for every camper who has no trouble saying goodbye to his or her parents, there are plenty of campers who struggle to do so. There are those who wrap themselves around their parents so tightly that it is difficult to extricate them from the tangle of arms and legs that they have created. There are others who sob uncontrollably, sitting through lunch staring at a full tray of food with crocodile tears rolling down their cheeks. And there are others who are rendered speechless at the thought of being separated from their parents. For the vast majority of campers who struggle to say goodbye at first, camp proves to be a happy and fulfilling experience (see *Homesickness, page 94*).

The First Night

> *The first night in a summer camp: excitement, anxiety, apprehension, disquiet. Strangers in bunk beds. Cold clear night air. Cicadas and frogs: the mysterious pulsing of the earth. Then, finally, the fall into deep sleep. And awake early to the birds and the dawn. Ground mist on the grass and in the woods. Silent ghostly trees. A lowing cow somewhere in the distance. Blades of grass jeweled with crystalline beads of dew glistening in the first rays of the sun. A city child gazing through a cabin window on his first wondrous morning in a summer camp.*
>
> —Chaim Potok271

After the first night's meal (often "comfort food" like pasta to help ease in the new campers), some name games and ice breakers are played in groups or units, depending on the camp's organization. Cabin meetings are held to help establish rules and guidelines for the summer. Perhaps a campfire is held and s'mores made, but eventually, with a long day behind them, campers and staff settle in for the night as the first day of activities looms large.

6

A Typical Day at Summer Camp

Generally around seven o'clock in the morning, cheerful camp directors all over the country turn on the public address system and play reveille. Though originally this well-known tune was likely played on a real bugle to rouse the campers, today it is generally played on a CD or an iPod. If you listen closely, you can hear drowsy campers stretching in the beds and beginning to rise for another day of fun. Counselors (usually college students, few of whom are morning people) struggle to rouse their campers, though more often it is the campers struggling to wake their counselors, many of whom had no idea how exhausting camp could be when they took the job.

Meanwhile, the dining hall staff has been awake for hours already, preparing to feed the masses. Camp food has come a long way over the years and is, today, a far cry from the bug juice and mystery meat served decades ago. Most camps today offer peanut- and gluten-free meals, vegetarian entrees, and a wide variety of options including salad bars and the like. Breakfast generally consists of an assortment of cereals and juices, a hot option like pancakes or scrambled eggs, fruits, and pastries. Campers, some as young as seven or eight, are wide-eyed as they proceed through the service lines realizing that there is no parent to guide or inform their choices. When they realize that they can eat all the sugar cereal, French toast, and Pop-tarts they want, some campers become positively giddy with excitement. Counselors who neglect to intervene and supervise selections in the dining hall tend to pay the price later in the morning, when the sugar kicks in and the campers are running around the cabin or activity area like they are being fast forwarded; staff members soon learn the importance of enforcing healthy eating choices so as to avoid such melees.

The green tray is an iconic staple of many camp dining halls. With small, differently shaped compartments, it is designed solely for institutional use yet it somehow conjures countless fond memories for anyone who has ever attended camp. While the tray may hold enough food for the average ten-year-old, one group the tray seems not to have been designed for is hungry college-age students. Counselors are often seen making several return trips to the service lines in search of more food.

After breakfast, most campers return to their cabins for cabin clean up. Though campers do not always understand or appreciate the importance of this activity, it is absolutely necessary when living with a group and sharing bathrooms and showers. Today, many counselors fashion a "duty chart" that outlines the jobs assigned to each camper on a rotating basis. The least popular duties include cleaning the toilets, sinks, and showers, as well as emptying the trash, while the less objectionable jobs are sweeping, straightening the clothesline, and supervising one's bunkmates to ensure that they are

The flag is raised at Camp Dudley, signaling the start of another day of summer fun. *Photo courtesy of Camp Dudley.*

Creating a duty chart ensures an equal distribution of responsibility among campers and counselors.

completing their assigned tasks. Cabin inspections are conducted and sometimes the winning bunk is rewarded at the end of a week or a session with a pizza or sundae party, or an extra visit to the canteen or camp store. Losing cabins are sometimes forced to miss out on special activities in order to clean up their cabins. After ensuring that the cabins can no longer be considered bio-hazards, counselors lead their campers to a morning assembly or general gathering where they will receive directions about the day to come.

Many camps include such an assembly as part of their morning ritual. It is during this time that awards are handed out, announcements are made, and the news and sports scores are delivered to a captive audience, which is, for all intents and purposes, cut off from the outside world. At many camps, a formal flag raising ceremony is held each morning before everyone goes to activities and becomes preoccupied. It is at this point, that campers and counselors set out for a busy day of fun in the sun and a myriad of activities.

Campers stand at attention for inspection by Grant Koch, the director, at Camp Monomoy in the 1950s. *Photo courtesy of Cape Cod Sea Camps.*

Campers assemble for colors at Camp Greystone in Tuxedo, North Carolina. *Photo courtesy of Camp Greystone.*

Morning Activities

In the early years of summer camps, most campers enjoyed a virtually unplanned and unstructured day after completing their morning cleaning duties. Most of the activities offered were those with which campers were already familiar, like baseball. Author Abigail Van Slyck points out, "perhaps more surprising than the presence of these familiar games is the absence of other activities that later became synonymous with summer camp, particularly those that encouraged campers to engage directly with the natural environment."[272] A lack of structure characterized many camps until the early twentieth century when it seems that camp directors sought to more formally organize the campers' day. A number of camps chose to offer individualized activities in the morning, then an all-camp swim before lunch, a variety of athletic activities and sports in the afternoon, and games following dinner.[273] It seems logical that the early camps lacked activities that required specialized materials or equipment. This began to change, however, in the early twentieth century when activities such as woodworking and various other crafts were introduced at many camps.

Camp also exposes children and teens to new activities and skills that they may not have the opportunity to develop in school. For example, many camps offer sailing programs, tennis instruction, pottery classes, and drama. In short, camp offers access to new and different activities while also providing instruction at different levels for more traditional interests such as swimming.

> *Archery and canoeing, for instance, were commonly taught at camps, but rarely practiced elsewhere. Horseback riding, mostly the privilege of private campers due to its cost, suggested old-fashioned transportation. So, too, woodwork and crafts activities were held to be quintessentially "campy."*[274]
>
> —Leslie Paris

Boys learn the skills needed for woodworking. *Photo courtesy of Camp Dudley.*

Campers have the opportunity to learn many new skills, such as weaving, while at camp. *Photo courtesy of Roy Ballentine.*

Wind Racers is inspired by the artist's almost two decades at Cape Cod Sea Camps. *Painting by Deborah Fowler Greenwood.*

Sailing

There is a great range of sailing programs and experiences offered by summer camps today. Many offer the opportunity to sail Sunfish on ponds, Optis and Lasers in open water, and 420s and Hobies on lakes. Sailing is certainly one of the most expensive activities for a camp to offer, so many programs are limited in terms of how much they can spend on purchasing and maintaining boats. Campers arrive with varied sailing experience and range from complete novices to experienced racers. Counselors are equipped to work with a range of abilities and strive to teach campers everything from sailing nomenclature to advanced racing tactics.

Some of the earliest sailing camps were located on Cape Cod and, of those, many were in the town of Orleans. Quanset Sailing Camp for girls was established in 1905 by Mrs. E.A.W. Hammatt, and the Reverend Gibson Bell founded Portanimicut Sailing Camp for boys, both on Little Pleasant Bay.[275] In the early 20th century, it was relatively easy for camps like these to establish a sailing program like this; all that was needed was a place to sail and some boats in which to do so. Today, however, camps must meet rigorous criteria before their program can be considered viable. Staff must receive training and certification in CPR, first aid, water safety, and sailing instruction. Extreme safety precautions must be in place and campers must be taught what to do in the event of an emergency. PFDs are no longer optional and equipment must be in exemplary working order before campers are allowed access to it. Nevertheless, sailing remains a staple of many camp programs nationwide.

Kevin Nicolai has attended several Broadreach summer programs. He reflects on his evolution as a sailor.

> I went into Broadreach thinking that I knew a lot about sailing. I did know quite a bit about small boat sailing, but came to find out I knew almost nothing about yacht sailing. Between the two trips, I learned a lot about mapping, all of the different computers and navigational tools, how to more efficiently steer the boat in relation to the wind, and the inner workings of the boat in general. The biggest fear that I had going into the trip was the fear of the unknown. It quickly dissipated when I got onto the boat and got comfortable, which only took a few days. The biggest skill that I learned from the trips was being able to live and work with people that I may not have been very friendly with in a normal school environment. This skill so far has helped me with group work in school where I do not get to choose my partners. I expect this skill to help me interact with people whether it be working on a little project in school, or working with people at a job when I am older.[276]

Campers and staff compete in an annual race held in the evening
Photo courtesy of Kali Parmley Photography.

Richard "Frosty" Frost sails with his children, Dana and Jackson, in an annual sailing race at Cape Cod Sea Camps. Frosty met his wife, Emily, at CCSC in the 1970s, and his children are now staff members at the camp having spent many summers there as campers. *Photo courtesy of Kari Ahern.*

Jim Fay, Cape Cod Sea Camps' Assistant Sailmaster and a science teacher during the school year, explains the learning process at camp vis-à-vis sailing.

> In the classroom or on the water, students go through the process of discrete "eureka" moments, tackling specific skills or concepts. Progressively, units of comprehension and ability are achieved as multiple skills align to enable higher order execution: making a mooring, flying a spinnaker, putting the boat to bed. In the classroom, the instructor then passes the student on to the next year, the next instructor, and the next subject. In the sailing program, the student returns to the instructor, the eureka moments continue, the skill sets evolve, and the student's capabilities broaden. By the time a student graduates from the program they have stared down fear more than once, they have mastered what they had once considered impossible, they have developed an independence and self-confidence not shared by those left onshore, and they have turned to those younger sailors, shared their knowledge, lifted them through their moments of doubt, and encouraged them to aspire for the same daunting goals. That rarely happens in a classroom, but on the water it happens every day.[277]

While many camps offer wonderful learn-to-sail programs with some competition, generally more serious sailors attend camps at local yacht clubs or specialty camps. However, regardless of where campers learn to sail, they are developing life-long skills that are universal and will allow them to enjoy the sport anytime, anywhere. Andy Stern, a highly competitive sailor and coach, looks back on his experience sailing at camp.

> There is definitely something to be said for learning something in an environment where you are free to choose what it is you want to learn. More specifically, learning to sail while at camp represents an opportunity to pursue something free from outside influences. After working with a number of different sailing programs and educational constructs, I always found that it was my experience at camp that was the most unique and rewarding. I largely attribute this to the fact that I chose sailing, or moreover, we found each other. It is for this reason that sailing and I have stuck together for so long. I was never pressured by a parent or system.
>
> While I am now an avid racer and have taught and coached sailing on every level from eight year olds to collegiate racing, I found my experience at camp taught me to be a sailor first and then a racer, rather than forcing racing on me at a very young age. It is because of this that I feel I am a much better overall yachtsman and possess actual seamanship skills. I can recall learning about tides and currents by spending countless hours on the flats observing, learning about celestial navigation with my friends from a British counselor on the tennis courts at night just like in the old days, and learning to race Sunfish, then Mercuries and finally moving into 420s. While I think other programs offer a terrific education in both sailing and racing, it was my experience at camp that gave me a strong foundation.[278]

Swimming

Swimming is, perhaps, the most quintessential of camp activities. Campers and counselors look forward to cooling off in pools, streams, lakes, ponds, and even the ocean, as temperatures rise during the day. Today, swimming is not only an activity in which campers may participate, but it is also a requirement. Many laws have been passed to ensure the safety of swimmers of all levels and at all types of waterfronts.

In her 1914 article entitled, "Life in a Girls' Camp," Anna Worthington Coale wrote, "The swimming at girls' camps has been carefully standardized. The different tests for advancement are based on self-control in the water, confidence, and good head-work, rather than on any exercise that greatly taxes heart or lungs. One of these is the 'canoe test'—fifteen minutes above water. You may float or swim, as you like, and a boat keeps near you all the while. A girl may not go out in a canoe until she has passed this test."[279] Although the description may seem a bit esoteric, the skills are not entirely different from those emphasized in today's swim lessons.

It was during the postwar period of the 1920s and 1930s that swimming programs at camps became more and more structured. "A Red Cross innovation of the 1920s, the buddy system required campers to swim within easy reach of their assigned swimming buddies—close enough, in fact, to be able to grasp hands over head during buddy drills."[280] The need for safety and structure amidst fun became of paramount importance on the waterfront, which proved to be a microcosm of camp. "While early waterfront activities had encouraged campers to look within themselves to find the courage and strength required to test their physical and emotional limits, the safe waterfront required campers to look to others for an external sign that they were ready to take the next step."[281]

While most campers prefer free swim to lessons, swim instruction is absolutely critical to their safety and well-being at camp. Christie Peterson, one of the assistant directors at Cape Cod Sea Camps and a former head of instructional swim says:

> Camp provides an ideal opportunity for children to learn to swim in an atmosphere that encourages safety, structure and enjoyment. At most camps, children of all ages and skill levels are assessed and assigned to swimming levels. They are then given the opportunity to cultivate safe habits in and around the water that include basic stroke development, endurance training, safety lessons and emergency techniques. Camps that offer both free swim and daily lessons allow all children to develop valuable skills that they will be able to use outside of the camp setting too.[282]

Counselors teach campers how to be safe while having fun in the water.

Photographed in 1914, the same year that Anna Worthington Coale published *Life in a Girls' Camp*, young women at Camp Kehonka enjoy swimming in Lake Winnipesaukee. *Photo courtesy of Roy Ballentine.*

Girls at Kehonka refine their diving skills, circa 1920. *Photo courtesy of Roy Ballentine.*

Campers compete in an intercamp swim meet. *Photo courtesy of Kari Ahern.*

Peterson continues:

> It's vital that children feel confident in a variety of aquatic environments and camp is a great place to experience swimming in a pool, lake, pond, or open water while being supervised. At camp many of the activities that children choose to participate in on a daily basis are water-based and require that children have a strong foundation in swimming. Activities including canoeing, kayaking, sailing, waterskiing, windsurfing, surfing, water polo, and swim team all necessitate that a camper has had extensive swimming and water safety lessons. Just like camp, learning to swim is an experience that will stay with you for the rest of your life.[283]

Leslie Paris cites the role of swimming in the evolution of camps. "In [the 1920s], when many children arrived at camp unable to swim, and others rarely swam during the school year, this sport made the transformative promise of camp life particularly tangible. Swimming displayed the unique opportunities available in the natural world, symbolizing the liberty and physicality of camp life."[284] Furthermore, Paris continues, "swimming introduced children to an important vacationing custom, and it was the starting point for other important leisure activities such as boating, water pageants, and aquatic competitions."[285] Henry Wack, author of *The Camping Ideal*, explained that swimming "is truly 'campy' [and] may be participated in by old and young with any degree of exercise desired from swimming long, strenuous races to floating leisurely in the water."[286]

Counselors show off their skills between activity periods. *Photo courtesy of Kari Ahern.*

Campers take the plunge at Camp Wekeela. *Photo courtesy of Camp Wekeela.*

Waterskiing, Kayaking, Canoeing, & Windsurfing

Watersports, like waterskiing, wakeboarding, windsurfing, kayaking, canoeing, and tubing, have been a vital part of many summer camps since their inception; some camps have added fun attractions like water trampolines, aqua climbing walls, and paddle-boating to their waterfronts in recent years. In fact, from June 16 to 26, 1924, there was a Swimming, Canoe, and Campcraft Conference at Camp Quinibeck in Vermont. Such conferences were organized beginning in 1918 and were intended as important training opportunities for staff. Each of the three activities had a separate sub-conference and stringent tests were given to those participants wishing to become certified instructors in those activities.[287] Henry Wack attended the conference and reflected that "We were struck by the fact that in actual lifesaving efforts less real difficulty and danger would be encountered in average cases than the counselors successfully met and overcame in the tests to which the experts had subjected them. In other words, these tests were such as to qualify the successful candidate to meet all average conditions in lifesaving cases."[288] Wack described the counselors in attendance as "the country's best of the athletic counselor type" and made a point of commenting on the spectacle of the canoe training.[289] "Canoe tests afford observers a lot of fun, especially when a camper, clothed in a camp costume, goes as bow paddler with a counselor, is tipped out unexpectedly in twenty feet of water, bobs up, grasps canoe, helps right if overturned, then leisurely undresses in the water, tucks her land clothes safely into the canoe, then tows the canoe ashore or bales out and paddles it."[290]

Former camper Corrinne Loder recalls the challenge of learning to waterski. "Some of my other unforgettable memories include moments when I've had to challenge myself and push myself out of my comfort zone. My first time getting up on waterskis was unreal! I remember how scared I was at the time because the water was cold (I even pretended to see a giant fish swimming around below me so they would let me out) but the counselors in the boat made me give it a shot, and I'll never forget that feeling of first getting up."[291]

Kali Parmley, a former counselor, reflects on the experiences she had teaching campers to waterski.

> Teaching someone to waterski is almost like teaching someone to walk. You watch them struggle to stay upright in the water with these big, overbearing pieces of wood attached to their feet, all while trying to hold onto the ski rope and listen to people yelling directions from the boat. It's a very overwhelming experience for both counselor and new skier. You wish that you could transfer your knowledge directly to their brains to reassure them that they are not going to drown and that in a few minutes they will find their balance in the water, despite thinking that holding onto the rope and flailing their other arm is the only thing that will keep their heads above water. The look on the face of the new skier as they come out of the water instead of face planting and drinking half the lake is priceless. You see a look of surprise, triumph, and fear all at once. A look of "I did it! Look at me! What do I do now!?" It is honestly one of the most fulfilling feelings in the world as a counselor when the boat stops and you see the big smiling face of the skier and you say, "I told you that you could do it!"[292]

Campers enjoy a beautiful day on the water at Camp Towanda in Pennsylvania's Poconos Mountains. *Photo courtesy of Camp Towanda.*

Kayaking allows campers to develop a life-long skill and interest. *Photo courtesy of Kari Ahern.*

Staff members help steady a canoe as campers prepare to shove off. *Photo courtesy of Camp Wa Wa Segowea.*

Windsurfing is a popular activity that most campers don't have the opportunity to try anyplace but at camp. *Photo courtesy of Kari Ahern.*

A camper practices windsurfing upwind. *Photo courtesy of Kari Ahern.*

Girls warm up before receiving lacrosse instruction.

Boys compete for the ball in the annual Monomoy Cup soccer game at Cape Cod Sea Camps. *Photo courtesy of Kari Ahern.*

Land Sports (Soccer, Baseball, etc.)

For many campers, the opportunity to play the sports they love in a less competitive environment than they might experience at home reminds them why they love the sports that they do. There are no parents yelling on the sidelines, no strict training regimens, no peer pressure to score a goal, and no consequences for missing. In short, sports at camp provide campers with a chance to play for fun while honing their skills. Learning from their counselors, many of whom are college athletes, is a wonderful opportunity for mentoring and coaching in an atmosphere that doesn't stress the outcome of a game and where an entire season doesn't hang in the balance when an individual is up at bat. Kelly Flanagan, a college athlete and counselor, explains the value of sports at camp. "I think the ability to learn how to play different sports in a camp setting is so valuable. Kids are able to learn how to play in a fun and supportive setting. No one cares if you miss a pass and there is no pressure on the kids to perform at a high level. The campers simply get to be kids and learn the rules and skills of a new sport. As a counselor, it is fun to watch a lacrosse class when you have experienced players teaching their inexperienced friends how to play and everyone is laughing and having fun!"[293]

General activity camps tend to offer a wide range of land sports including baseball, soccer, field hockey, lacrosse, softball, volleyball, golf and others.

> *Our counselors provide an opportunity for our campers to learn skill development, key concepts, playing strategies, and social behaviors. Campers learn to value physical activity and its contributions to a healthy lifestyle. Campers will appreciate the relationships with others that result from participation in physical activity. Campers will learn the knowledge and skills to select and participate in physical activity safely, competently, and with personal satisfaction. We hope our campers develop a positive attitude about physical activity and respect the role physical activity plays in their pursuit of lifelong health and physically active lifestyle. Our motto is "play safe, play fair, play hard.*[294]
>
> —Jim Flanagan, Assistant Director,
> Cape Cod Sea Camps

Campers compete for ribbons in an annual track meet. *Photo courtesy of Kari Ahern.*

Anna Worthington Coale wrote about the importance of sports at girls' camps in 1914. She stated, "In camp a girl learns, like her brother, to be a 'good sport.' One way is to take defeat cheerfully and to honor your successful competitor. Another way to be a 'good sport' in a girls' camp which some brave girls have learned is to refrain from doing things which you are not able to do."[295]

Baseball, in particular, is one of the most beloved of camp activities. The twentieth century was the era in which baseball officially became America's pastime and, it can be argued, the most popular pastime at summer camps too. "From the earliest camps onward, the other most important athletic event at boys' camps was baseball."[296] Baseball provided the perfect opportunity for camp organizers to foster a sense of camaraderie. "By minimizing the kind of individual competition that might undermine group solidarity, baseball emerged in this period as the team game par excellence."[297] Camp is a place where high school students can play alongside ten year-olds and impart some of their own wisdom while being coached by counselors who are on college baseball teams and may even have some minor league experience.

Campers compete in track meets against their peers and, sometimes, against other camps.

Games: Gaga, Tetherball, and Dodgeball

One thing camps offer that schools are doing less and less of is affording campers the opportunity to simply play.

> Playing develops essential life skills like cooperation, compromise and teamwork. It encourages social-emotional learning. And playing prepares the developing brain for future challenges of all types—cognitive, social, emotional and physical. Summer camps provide unparalleled opportunities for play and at camp, play is a priority. In fact, play, in a variety of forms, dominates the camp day. The fun experiential educational settings of day and overnight camp, where children learn by doing, are full of opportunities for both unstructured free play and play guided by adults. And these opportunities are woven around times of specific instruction and formal learning.[298]

Purposeful play, as many refer to it, is an important part of child development, especially in a society that devotes so much time to screens. Whereas children used to meet up with the other kids in the neighborhood after school to ride bikes, play foursquare or simply explore and build forts, today's children are more inclined to text, play video games, or chat online. Playing games at camp is an essential part of the experience.

As they say, everything old is new again and this is the case with gaga. Meaning "touch, touch" in Hebrew, this dodgeball-like game has enjoyed a tremendous resurgence in recent years. Played in a "gaga pit," players try to hit their opponents below the waist in an effort to get them out. However, if the ball is caught or goes over the pit wall the person who threw it is out. Gaga has become so ubiquitous that *The New York Times* ran a story on it in July, 2012. "It is also appealing because the game is easy to learn, and unlike many playground sports, gaga is not typically dominated by children with natural athletic ability."[299] Another reason it is appealing is the fast-paced nature of the game; players don't find themselves waiting for long periods of time without getting a turn.

According to an article penned by Dr. Douglas Mann, gaga was most likely created by John Crosley at a camp in the 1950s. The Israeli counselors enjoyed the game so much that they took it back to Israel with them and introduced it there. Mann generated what is believed to be the closest thing to an official set of rules. In the past decade, summer camps have scrambled to build enough gaga pits to keep their campers entertained. And though campers appear as though they have just left a pig pen and there is a dust cloud as far as the eye can see after a game, everyone emerges happy and satisfied.

Campers enjoy a game of gaga. *Photo courtesy of Camp Wa Wa Segowea.*

Gaga has enjoyed a tremendous resurgence at camps in the past decade. *Photo courtesy of Kari Ahern.*

Tetherball is a popular activity during free time.

Campers enjoy a lively game of dodgeball. *Photo courtesy of Kari Ahern.*

The following rules have been generated by Dr. Douglas Mann and appeared in his article, "Going Gaga Over Gaga Ball" in *Camp Business* magazine in 2008.

- A player cannot be "out" on the serve.
- The ball must be punched with an open or closed hand.
- Players cannot hit the ball with two hands and cannot touch the ball a second time without it hitting a wall first.
- Players can hit the ball repeatedly, provided that between hits they rebound it off the wall.
- If the ball contacts a player below the waist, that player is out and must leave the gaga pit.
- If the ball contacts a player above the waist, that player is still in, and play continues.
- If the ball leaves the gaga pit, the last player to touch it, whether it was above or below the waist or on a rebound, is out.
- The game is over when there is one player remaining. If the game is taking an extended period of time, a 10-second countdown is used, and there are multiple winners.
- The game can be self-judged; however, due to the pace of the game, an outside referee is recommended to avoid conflict.
- A ball that has some weight to it but is soft is best. Various companies make a foam-filled ball that works well.[300]

Dodgeball, though it tends to conjure images of being pinned against a wall with bigger kids hurling hard playground balls at a small, defenseless child, is enjoying a safe resurgence. Special, Nerf-like smaller dodgeballs allow campers to play the game with little risk of injury (physical or emotional). In order to have a successful dodgeball game, however, it is imperative that staff understand and enforce the rules of fair play. It is an important lesson for campers to learn that some games must be modified in order to ensure everyone's safety and that despite these adjustments, fun can still be had by all.

Tennis

Parents who truly want their children to become competitive tennis players are more likely to send them to tennis academies or specialized tennis camps (much like parents are inclined to do for specialized sailing instruction). For campers who simply enjoy playing tennis or want to learn the basics, tennis instruction at summer camp is a great introduction. Playing tennis at camp, much like sailing or playing sports, is done in a pressure-free way that fosters a life-long love of the sport and while it offers some degree of competition there is significantly less pressure than they might while taking lessons or playing on a school team. Many camps offer tennis ladders, camper-counselor tournaments and mixed doubles events along with traditional instruction.

Tennis is among the oldest camp activities offered. *Photo courtesy of Roy Ballentine.*

Tennis is among the most popular activities at Camp Wekeela. *Photo courtesy of Camp Wekeela.*

Arts & Crafts, Woodworking

Once upon a time, camp arts and crafts programs used to offer only macramé, tie-dye, and gimp. Now, many camps offer ceramics, jewelry making, and digital photography. Campers are given a selection of age-appropriate projects to work on, which allow them to master skills while expressing themselves creatively.

The visual arts are a vitally important aspect of the summer camp experience. In her 2003 article, "Art Matters: The Creative Side of the Summer Camp Experience," Eden Foster explains, "after all, art is a fundamental and traditional camp activity, and the visual arts are experiential learning at its very best."[301] With so many schools cutting arts programs in favor of test preparation, summer camp may be the only opportunity children have to gain exposure to the arts.[302]

Richard Frost has run the woodworking program at Cape Cod Sea Camps for a number of summers. He explains the importance of campers having access to the arts at camp.

> For many of the hundreds of kids coming through the shop every summer, this is their one chance before adulthood to find out that they have some ability to create a fun or useful object. Often they surprise themselves, and their parents, with their success. Many find out they have a love and maybe a skill for visualizing three-dimensional forms, manipulating tools, and patiently attending to the details that make their project high quality. Some learn to creatively solve problems, not to panic when they make a mistake, and not to quit before that last finishing touch.
>
> So many activities at camp reward physical prowess; for many kids without those natural gifts, the arts are where they can excel, and be recognized by peers and adult leaders. This is especially true at camp, where those activities are celebrated. There are qualities (core values) that find unique expression in the shop. I am thinking of the kids whose first priority is to make gifts for people—very often for their parents, as a thank you for sending them to camp. And lots of kids are just as happy helping their friends with projects as they are working on their own. They take great pleasure in their friends' successes.
>
> I love that the shop is devoid of horseplay, and everyone who comes in is expected to take their work, and that of others, seriously. They learn to value quality tools, to take care of them, and to take safety to heart. Who knows what seeds are planted? Sophie still talks about how her father couldn't believe she had the wherewithal to make a

dovetailed box. Ina won the woodworking spirit award one week, and wrote home, "Guess who won the award for being careful and aware of the details? I DID!" Like they would never believe it. And this year, after two years of spending as much time as possible in the shop, Alberto A. wrote to ask me for advice on what tools to buy. Now he sends me pictures of his very own shop, made from his old play house, with a few shiny new tools, including a scroll saw, and his first box, made from the instructions in a book. That's what gets my heart going.[303]

An artist's impression of woodworking projects drying in the sun. *Photo and painting courtesy of Deborah Fowler Greenwood.*

Campers enjoy the opportunity to try new activities like ceramics which is generally something not available in schools. *Photo courtesy of Kari Ahern.*

A camper poses with a project she made in the wood shop. *Photo courtesy of Kari Ahern.*

Lloyd Batchelder instructs campers on ceramics techniques. *Photo courtesy of Camp Dudley.*

Many camps have incorporated ceramics into their arts programs in recent years.

Drama and the Performing Arts

Drama programs at camp provide a safe and supportive environment in which campers can develop their public speaking and performing skills. Many camps offer talent shows and weekly opportunities to showcase the talents of campers and staff alike. Other camps simply give campers a chance to play or hone their skills. Drama enhances the camp community and overall experience for everyone. More importantly, camp drama programs provide an opportunity for some who might be reluctant to participate at school where they don't want the pressure of competing with the more experienced actors and actresses or the "better" singers. Camp stages have created many legends. In fact, the outdoor theater at Cape Cod Sea Camps was once home to the well-known Max Drummey of Chester French and Adam Gardner of Guster (though the two were not contemporaries). On a more serious note, musical greats Rodgers and Hammerstein were campers in the early twentieth century. Richard Rodgers acknowledged that he was significantly influenced by Arthur Loesser, a concert pianist, and his counselor Robert Lippmann.

Generally, most camps put on a final camp show at the end of the summer, which is often a traditional musical or play. Many camps also offer singing, guitar, and dance allowing campers to try something new or hone specific skills. Some camps even offer courses in improvisation, stand up, costume making, set design, and circus art.

Campers' batik projects dry in the summer sun. Batik is a process in which wax is painted onto fabric which is then dyed. *Photo courtesy of Kari Ahern.*

Campers learn that "it's not what you look at but what you see." This principle applies not only to art but also to life in general. *Photo courtesy of Deborah Fowler Greenwood.*

Our camp has many great programs—sailing, archery, swimming, tennis, land sports—and our art program is a strong part of what makes our camp great too! There are arts camps and then there are arts programs at summer camps—and both offer the opportunity for children to explore, express, excel, expand and enjoy!

I have been running what I consider to be an outstanding art program at a multi-activity camp for several years and look forward to each summer and the chance to be part of the magic in the art center at camp. Warm sunlight and cool breezes flow throughout a veritable beehive of activity as campers busily knot, sculpt, draw, print, stamp, carve, and paint their way through mountains of colored yarn, beads, paint, ink, and clay from early morning until dinnertime. Time dissolves and soon it is time to go to the next activity....but not before a quick clean-up and a cheerful wave that tells me my campers are satisfied with their accomplishments, that they thoroughly enjoyed being creative and look forward to the next "Art Mod."

Art at summer camp is different from art at school for me and for my campers in so many ways! Campers can choose the art medium they would like to work in and begin to create alongside other campers from ages seven to seventeen. I often find younger campers inspiring older campers and the energy of this mix ignites creativity and self-confidence for all ages. Many campers find time at summer camp to try new art processes that they would not have the chance to experiment with in school. The worry about grades does not exist at summer camp and the inhibitions dissolve as a result! Art activities at camp offer all ages the opportunity to experience creative problem solving and play with possibilities: an important skill to learn in this ever-changing world.

Art at my summer camp is less intense than it might be at an arts camp, yet the chance to express with a brush and paint what you just experienced on the archery range is probably closer to what a "real artist" needs to create what is personal and true! Our camp art activities also include what I would consider the "meditative" handcrafts such as friendship bracelets, knotting, weaving, basketry, and pottery. These and many other traditional crafts offer campers ways to experience the joy of accomplishing something tangible through the efforts of their own hands. Campers gain self-esteem and confidence from creating their own work and helping others create in a collaborative workshop setting. All campers are invited to exhibit their art in the annual art show and the entire camp community gets the chance to appreciate the creative efforts of their fellow campers.

The performing arts are also an important part of programs offered at many camps. Campers can act, sing, dance, create sets and costumes, direct, and accompany with music when participating in our all-camp productions or even our weekly talent shows. The entire camp community applauds these artistic efforts and encourages fellow campers in ways that boost self-confidence and spark interests that can last a lifetime!

I watched a recent PBS documentary about the tradition of musical theater and was not surprised to learn that many of the "legendary greats"—Rogers and Hammerstein, Leonard Bernstein, Adolf Green, and others—all met at summer camp and shared their excitement for the performing arts with fellow campers as they participated in productions like those of Shakespeare or Gilbert and Sullivan. Who knows what legendary Broadway shows might never have happened had these artistic children never met and collaborated at summer camp!

The chance to be inspired by those who share your love of art, and the opportunity to collaborate with them gives young people a unique experience unlike any other. Our campers take with them a greater capacity for creative vision, a greater appreciation for all the arts and an awareness of the endless possibilities of what could be and where their own imagination could take them![304]

—Deborah Fowler Greenwood, Art Director,
Cape Cod Sea Camps

Archery

Although archery has become a more mainstream activity in recent years, it is yet another quintessential camp experience that many campers are unlikely to find any place but camp. Campers enjoy the opportunity to master a unique skill set that their friends at home are unlikely to have. Many counselors are certified National Archery Association instructors and emphasize both safety and skill development. Many camps adhere to the Junior Olympic Archery Development program (JOAD), which provides some helpful structure for archery programs.

The Easton Foundation, an organization dedicated to promoting the availability of archery programs, cites several reasons why trying archery at camp is an effective introduction to the sport. First, "new archers begin in a friendly low stress environment. [Second,] camp venue provides range space, bow, arrows, target and other equipment [and third,] instead of range fees, the price for lessons is usually included in overall camp fees."[305]

Novices are generally given a "dry lesson" during which they are taught about the proper safety equipment, stance, positioning, and aim. Next, equipped with a size-appropriate bow (either recurve or compound) and arrows, campers may begin shooting at the target. Campers generally advance through a series of awards and may compete in archery tournaments. A number of camps offer "Bullseye Clubs" to which campers are admitted after scoring a certain number of bullseyes. Many campers enjoy the solitude offered by time on the archery range, especially when the rest of their day is so full of team sports, group activities and cabinmates.

Instructors help campers score a round of shooting on the archery range.

Arrows are organized by size as are bows to facilitate distribution to campers. *Photo courtesy of Kari Ahern.*

Generally, youth at summer camps have always loved archery. For many years, it's ranked in the top three most popular camp activities. Why? Because it's fun, youth don't have to join a team, or have any pre-skills to learn it quickly and be successful, and there's no thrill better than seeing your own arrow hit the gold center of a target.

Learning archery adapts to learning other sports. Archery teaches what it feels like to achieve. This feeling follows other sports as well. It teaches self-confidence, following rules, and cause-and-effect (if I do this correctly I will get predicable results).

Camp archery programs generally begin fairly modestly…with a few bales of hay for targets and simple fiberglass bows. Once a camps sees the benefit, they invest in standard targets, clear some land for a dedicated range, invest in program-grade equipment and invest in getting their staff trained and certified as archery instructors under USA Archery, the National Governing Body for archery. These camps then go on to use USA Archery teaching materials in the camps, which gives the youth a better understanding of the sport and a link to archery activities outside of camp.[306]

—Doug Engh, Outreach Director, Easton Foundations

A camper focuses as she aims for the target. *Photo courtesy of Kari Ahern.*

Learning to shoot a rifle takes concentration. *Photo courtesy of Kari Ahern.*

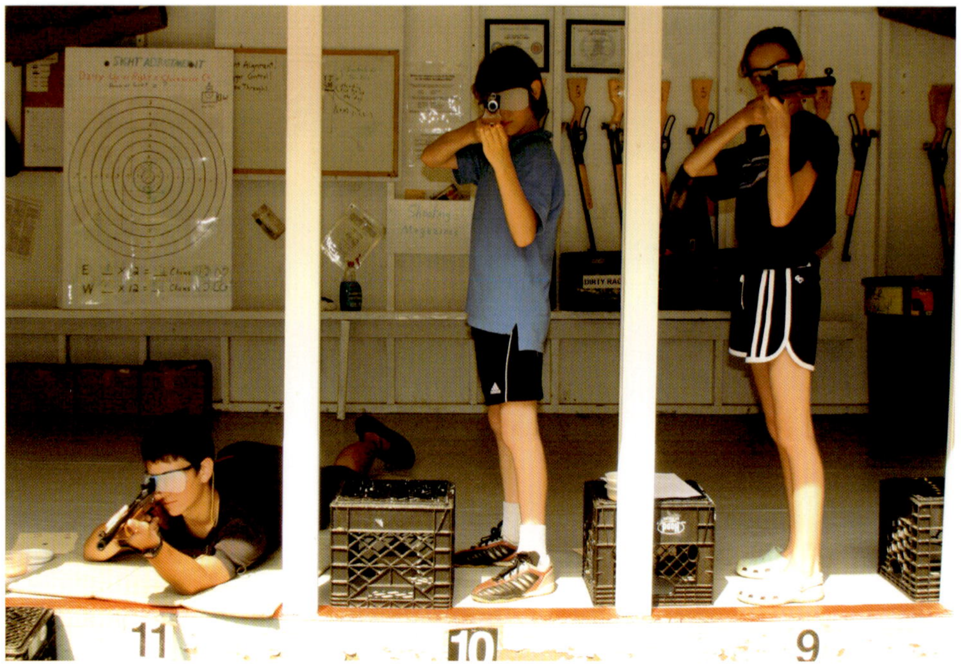

Learning to shoot using one's dominant eye is an important skill for beginners to master. *Photo courtesy of Kari Ahern.*

Riflery

Many camps utilize the Civilian Marksmanship Program (CMP), which has developed a specific program for camps. The program emphasizes instruction in BB guns, air rifles, and smallbore rifles. Superior rifle programs are staffed by certified Civilian Marksmanship Instructors, who teaches shooters the safety, proper shooting techniques, and self-discipline necessary to achieve different award levels. Many camps have kept their riflery programs to help foster an interest in shooting, which is both an NCAA and Olympic sport.[307] Riflery instructor Ben Bertolino explains that "one of the most fundamental aspects of the rifle program is establishing and sticking to a strict routine for every round that is fired. This helps develop the kids' subconscious shooting skills and teaches them that a strong routine is a key to consistent success."[308]

> *The most important lesson I have learned at camp is from [my riflery instructor]: the most important shot is the next. Although he means BB's, it applies to everything.*
>
> —Camper, age 14

Although some parents have concerns about their child being exposed to guns and shooting, others welcome the opportunity for their child to engage in a highly structured activity that encourages focus, patience and responsibility. After all, shooting is an Olympic sport and, when proper safety precautions are taken and campers are taught the necessary respect for firearms, they have the opportunity to develop an interest in an activity they can participate in for a lifetime.

Campers practice shooting from a kneeling position. *Photo courtesy of Kari Ahern.*

Lunch

After a busy morning on the water, hiking, and playing sports, campers and staff descend on the dining hall with voracious appetites. These days, however, a simple PB&J won't do (not just because most camps are nut-free, but also because campers expect more). Though items like grilled cheese and chicken nuggets remain staples of camp lunch offerings, many camps offer extensive salad bars, a multitude of sandwich options, and an array of tasty desserts.

Lunch is often followed by a visit to the camp store or canteen where more sugary treats can be purchased. Candy bars and ice cream make up the usual fare sold at the store, but campers can also purchase other items like sweatshirts, water bottles, flashlights and toothpaste, much of which often goes missing a few weeks into the summer. And once the campers are sufficiently full of food and sugar, the counselors expect them to settle down for rest hour.

The camp store is a place where campers can purchase sweet treats, a cold drink and camp items like t-shirts, blankets, and sweatshirts.

Campers enjoy breakfast in the dining hall as a group of older campers prepares to perform a flash mob.

Rest Hour

Any adult who ever spent any amount of time at camp will tell you that they wish their "real world" jobs included rest hour and any child will tell you the same about school. Rest hour is, perhaps, one of the most time-honored traditions at camp. After a morning full of activity in the hot summer sun and lunch topped off by a trip to the camp store for some candy or ice cream, who doesn't need a nap? While the youngest campers often vehemently resist the idea of lying on their beds and writing letters or reading, the older campers and counselors are grateful for a chance to snooze or simply relax with their friends, listen to music, or play cards.

Rest hour, ironically, is a time when some of the best memories are made and friendships are cemented. Longtime camper Tommy Cusano expounds on the difficulties he has in explaining his camp experience to his friends at home in New Jersey. "After I describe what camp is objectively (a place where a group of young adults gradually become counselors while having a lot of fun along the way), I usually have to add a more personal explanation in response to my friends' looks of confusion: Camp is where some of my best friends are. My fondest memories are not at an archery or swimming mod, but back at the cabin, where I can socialize and build relationships in a unique atmosphere of young leaders. It is a place that I truly cherish, and that is why I keep coming back every year."[309]

From the errant water balloon ambush to the arrival of an unexpected care package, rest hour is often a time when memories are made. It is a delightfully unstructured, yet completely safe opportunity to bond with one's cabinmates, chat with counselors about a vexing dilemma, or to take a moment to reflect on the tremendous opportunities afforded simply by being at summer camp. There is, perhaps, no greater luxury in the world than rest hour on a rainy day. Snuggling under the covers while listening to the rain fall on the cabin roof induces a calm that is rare at camp. Such simplicity and contentedness is rarely experienced outside of camp.

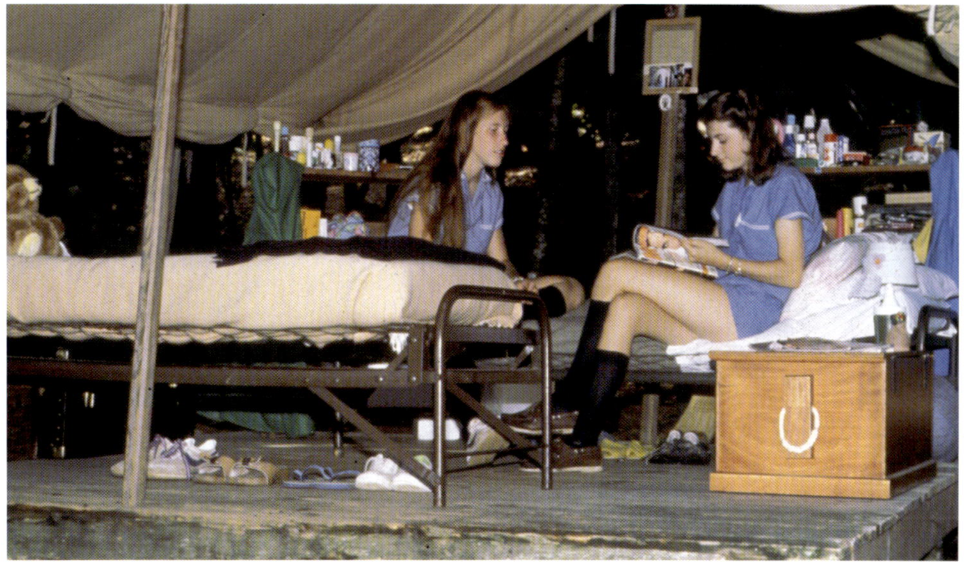

Girls enjoy relaxing in their tent at Camp Kehonka. *Photo courtesy of Roy Ballentine.*

Music has always been a vitally important part of the camp experience. *Photo courtesy of Kari Ahern.*

Mail Call! Letters & Care Packages

Writing and receiving letters is a critical link with the outside world while at camp. In this era of instantaneous electronic communication, campers are still encouraged to write letters home, though, today, many arrive having never addressed an envelope or written a letter by hand. Whereas international campers used to send air mail, which might or might not have arrived home before they did, today many camps scan and e-mail letters to the families of these campers. In a *USA Today* article, reporter Olivia Barker explored how camps today must help campers write the obligatory letter home. Most cabins, she explains, have a sample envelope posted to model how campers should address a letter. However, this strategy doesn't always work. "Stamps—dogs and cats and *Simpsons* characters—are rotated 90 degrees. Last names are missing. The campers' attempts at engaging in an activity that to them is more novelty than necessity are 'so funny,' … 'Grandma,' that's all it says on the envelope. Or 'Grandma, Rye, N.Y.'" The office staff then must determine who has a grandmother in Rye and properly address the envelope before sending it on its way.[310]

While this somewhat romantic return to simpler days of putting pen to paper is appealing to some, "none of this means that communication will ever really go back to the days before cellphones. The letters, which kids fill with LOLs and other Internet-speak rather than full sentences, travel mostly in one direction, because parents don't seem inclined to return to pen and paper, either. Camps now have elaborate systems for parents to send e-mail messages that are printed out and given to campers at mail call."[311]

In the 1930s, the Lawrence Company issued a series of cheap postcards that were designed to be mailed home from camp. "Scoutoons" were geared towards Boy Scouts and later gave way to "Camptoons," which were more general in nature and could be sent home by any camper. Today, camp stationery features everything from generic "camp news" paper to fill-in-the blank postcards that can be written in mere seconds, allowing the author entrance to the next meal in some cases.

For many, writing home is a way to combat homesickness. However, parents should remember that, often, by the time they receive a letter begging for them to come pick up their camper, that the homesickness has subsided and said camper has adjusted to camp life. Author Diane Falanga says,

> After reading through thousands of camp letters for my *P.S. I Hate It Here: Kids' Letters From Camp* books, I firmly believe that letter writing is a cure-all. There's absolutely nothing like taking pen to paper, getting the emotions out, connecting with mom and dad (albeit from the bunk

Care packages arrive on the second day of camp at Cape Cod Sea Camps' 2013 season.

A camper reads a letter from home on her bunk.

at camp) and opining. Often, kids do not have a chance to send the letters straightaway—so they can look back on their words the next day, let it all marinate a bit, scratch out some things that got better over the day. Looking back over our written words and working it out on paper can often be a 'magic trick' for most of us.[312]

Consider, too, the parents in this scenario. Some pen letters almost daily, chronicling every minute of life at home, while others may send a postcard from their own vacation. Many parents eagerly head to the mailbox each day that their child is away at camp, hoping for a glimpse into junior's camp experience, while some families know that no news is good news. Blogger Ayun Halliday offers some sage advice for parents wanting to write their children at camp. First, she advises, "loosen the leash. You have an entire school year to hector your child about practicing his musical instrument, washing hands after using the washroom, and eating vegetables...Resist the urge to micromanage until he comes home sunburned to a crisp, teeth rotting out of his head, wearing a pair of underpants that's gone three weeks without changing."[313] She also recommends that parents not use pet names when writing to their children, "unless you want your fourteen-year-old son's bunk mates calling him Precious Angel-Mouse for the rest of the summer."[314] And for the parents whose campers have yet to set pen to paper? Halliday advises, "To all of you whose children have yet to drop so much as one measly line home. Keep a stiff upper lip. Vouchsafe that they must be having too much fun to write."[315]

While receiving a letter is exciting, the ultimate highlight of any camper's day is receiving a care package. Few recipients, however, are likely aware of the venerable origins of the care package. "The original 'care packages' began as badly needed hunger relief in the aftermath of war. The first care packages were created in 1946 when twenty-two American organizations worked together to arrange for packages to be sent to the starving survivors of World War II."[316] These packages had quite a different appearance from those delivered to camps today. Most of the original care packages were encased in a great deal of wrapping, secured with metal bands or wax seals, since they had to endure being dropped from a plane and landing on the ground. "The acronym, CARE, originally stood for Cooperative for American Remittances to Europe and now stands for Cooperative for Assistance and Relief Everywhere."[317] Today, this acronym might stand for "Camp Always Requires Everything," "Cookies And Real Entertainment," "Camp Accoutrements Required for Everyone," or "Contraband Articles [which are] Really Essential."

It used to be that care packages contained a batch of mom's homemade chocolate chip cookies (many of which had broken en route) with a note in her familiar script reminding the recipient to share with his or her bunkmates. Today, however, care packages have taken on a life of their own. Sealed with

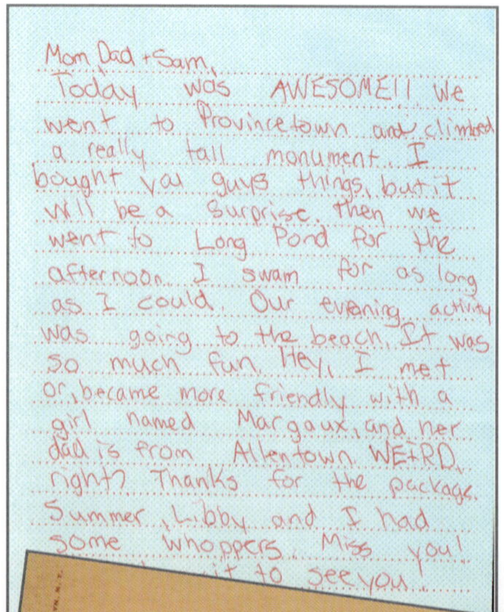

A letter revealing one camper's thoughts about her times at camp. *Photo courtesy of Kathie Wachs.*

The Cost of Writing Home

Year	Cost of a Stamp
1863	3¢
1883	2¢
1917	3¢
1919	2¢
1932	3¢
1958	4¢
1963	5¢
1968	6¢
1971	8¢
1974	10¢
1978	15¢
1981	20¢
1985	22¢
1988	25¢
1991	29¢
1995	32¢
1999	33¢
2001	34¢
2002	37¢
2006	39¢
2007	41¢
2008	42¢
2009	44¢
2012	45¢

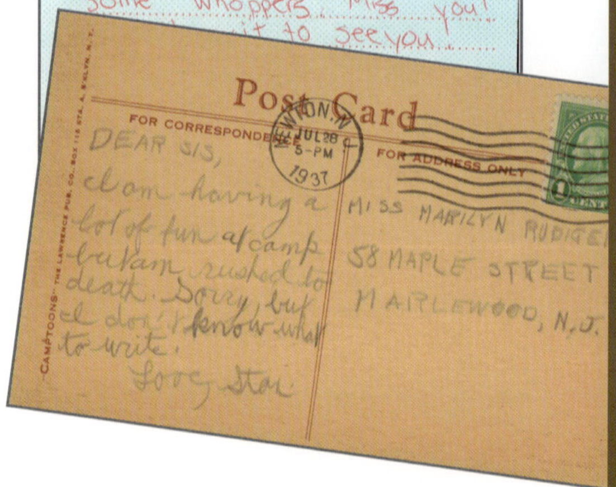

A camper named Stan writes home to his sister, Marilyn, about being "rushed to death." Aside from that, he apologizes for not knowing what to write.

Camptoons and *Scoutoons* were produced by the Lawrence Company in New York in the 1930s and 1940s.

a Kiss, a company specializing in care packages, sent its first packages in June 1984.[318] This family-owned business now boasts more than 700 items for possible inclusion in either custom-made or ready-made packages, which can be shipped to campers at virtually any camp in the United States. The company's web site even offers an online database of camps with various restrictions so that the packages won't be confiscated upon arrival.

Today, many camps place limitations on the number and/or the contents of care packages. With so many allergies and dietary restrictions, it is often dangerous to have "unsafe" food in the cabins. In addition, counselors and camp directors will attest to the fact that it is also unwise to allow campers unlimited, unsupervised access to so much sugar at all times of the day. There are still plenty of options for parents, though. Care packages may include small personal fans, whoopee cushions, water guns, Mad Libs, or (heaven forbid) books. Twenty-first century care packages also have been known to include the occasional illicit piece of technology (e.g.: cell phones, iPods, and laptops) which is quickly confiscated once it starts ringing or beeping. Sealed with a Kiss even offers packages by theme including "Cool & Unusual," "Super Stretchy," "Brainy & Creative," and "That's Just Gross." There are also the more traditional themes such as "Plush Animals," "Summer Camp Essentials," and "Outdoor Games."[319]

Once the packages have been opened and ransacked, the letters have been read and re-read and the campers have finally settled in for rest hour, the bugle sounds, and it's time for afternoon activities.

Girls look forward to receiving mail by boat at Camp Kehonka. *Photo courtesy of Roy Ballentine.*

Afternoon Activities

Camps have made a lot of changes to their programs and what campers *don't* have these days is much free time while they're at camp. In a 2008 *New York Times* article reflecting on her reunion at Camp Walt Whitman, reporter Susan Dominus mused on the changes to the camp's program since her days as a camper.

> None of those changes speak so much to the transformation of childhood, however, as the loss of those two hours of free, unscheduled time from 4 to 6. Campers who would have once spent that time rearranging their sticker collection, working on the crawl stroke, or heading with vague ambitions of a blueberry binge to Priestley's farm, now choose defined electives, escorted from their previous group activity to the next—maybe sailing or dance or gymnastics or sketching by the lake. What could be bad? Nothing, of course—except the absence of nothing. A certain kind of kid suffers from a deficit of nothing all year long, and now, it seems, even summer camps don't supply it... Sometimes nothing at all came out of those two hours, and that was exactly the point. Camp brochures often love to talk about how much kids grow when they rise to meet new challenges, but they also grow in those interstitial moments, the unobserved lulls when a body (or soul, or both), can simply drift.[320]

At most camps, afternoons look similar to the mornings in terms of activities though some camps add a free swim option to the afternoon's offerings. Additionally, some activities that might take place off campus or might require more time are held in the afternoon.

Learning about one's natural surroundings is an important part of the camp experience. *Photo courtesy of Kari Ahern.*

Horseback Riding

In a 2004 article for *Camping,* Kathy Thurber explains, "children need activities that foster empathy and compassion, responsibility and self-control. Skill-based riding programs provide for the development of a set of competencies that contribute to self-esteem and physical fitness. And achieving a working 'friendship' with a horse remains a particularly empowering experience for both boys and girls."[321] Her article goes on to explain that learning to ride a horse requires a completely different skill set than many children and teens are accustomed to using today. Riding a horse is not like playing a video game; the animal will not respond like a controller does to quick reflexes Thurber quips. "It may not be easy to entice children to do something that requires them to slow down and pay attention before they can ask horses to jump fences or canter. Safety and success depend on awareness, patience, and respect for another being—the horse."[322]

Horseback riding requires communication skills, patience, and self-discipline, all of which are fostered by being at camp. Caring for and tending to the needs of a horse, however, does offer campers a wonderful sense of purpose and responsibility. The relationship that a rider can develop with a horse can be critical to the fostering of self-esteem and, in some cases, can be therapeutic as well. Extroverted campers may learn to temper their nature a bit around horses while quiet, shy campers may become a bit more outgoing as they grow more comfortable around their horse.

Sue Ballentine, owner, trainer and instructor at High Meadows Farms, explains the value of caring for horses in a summer camp setting.

> Attending summer camp as a kid is probably one of the best experiences you can give your child, and when you couple it together with horseback riding, it makes it the absolute best experience possible! Horseback riding is more than just a "sport." It is a partnership, it is an understanding, and it is a responsibility. Through horseback riding you learn about patience, trust, leadership, and love. With it you gain self-confidence, a sense of belonging, and a friendship like no other. In a horseback riding camp you achieve all of these things plus the fun and social interactions between you and your peers. At horse camp you are completely immersed in the life of the barn. It is more than just coming for an hour lesson and leaving. It is the feeding, the cleaning, the grooming, and the constant care that the horses require. Learning how to ride is more than just sitting on the horse's back—it is about the daily interactions and responsibility that these animals have placed in our hands for their care. Horses change lives. Summer camp changes lives. Put the two together and you have one happy camper![323]

The bond between horse and human is a special one, as these campers learn. Campers assume a great responsibility for the horses they ride at camp. *Photo courtesy of Sue Ballentine, High Meadows Farms.*

Horseback riding is a popular activity offered by many camps. Here, a camper at Cheley Colorado Camps feels the exhilaration of riding. *Photo courtesy of Cheley Colorado Camps.*

Nature

Of course, an integral part of the camp experience is communing with nature; simply being outside is a welcome break from the world of computers, video games, and classrooms that typically define kids' school year. Some camps emphasize their relationship with nature more than others, which is evident in their program and, also, largely a factor of their location. For some, spending an afternoon identifying the local flora and fauna provides a great sense of satisfaction, while for others taking part in a challenging hike up a nearby mountain is the ideal.

Depending on the location of the camp, nature as an activity may mean any number of different things. For some, it might mean collecting hermit crabs and snails for an aquarium, while for others it might mean identifying flora and fauna native to the area. In *The Summer Camp Memory Book,* authors Richard and Kellie Gutman point out that, "the sedentary life of bug and leaf collecting was no match for tennis, baseball, riflery and water-skiing."[324] However, for aspiring naturalists, an activity period spent communing with nature was exactly what they'd hoped for when signing up for a summer at camp. Some early camps (and far fewer today) had their own bees, chickens, or goats that needed tending to; campers may have collected eggs or milk when necessary as part of their time in the nature program. Other nature programs may have been a bit craftier, creating keepsakes out of twigs, sand, and shells found on the camp's grounds.

Campers enjoy rowing a dinghy on a pond. *Photo courtesy of Kari Ahern.*

Campers explore tidal pools while looking for marine life.

Campers are all smiles before setting out on a challenging hike at Gold Arrow Camp. *Photo courtesy of Gold Arrow Camp*

Wilderness Adventure: Hiking, Climbing, Orienteering

Thanks to the invention of smartphones and GPS, few of us actually need to know how to read a map and use a compass. However, one of the oldest skills needed by campers and counselors alike is the ability to orient oneself using only these tools. Many camps still offer orienteering whether it's for a single activity period or as part of a longer trip. Wilderness adventure activities take campers outside of their comfort zones and force them to engage with others face to face. This is especially important today as so many kids, teens, and young adults spend so much time gazing at computer screens, cell phones, and televisions.

Rock climbing is an exciting opportunity for many campers; it provides a challenge for many that may require individuals to overcome fears and to rely on others. Campers are taught the basics of bouldering and rapelling in addition to how to set anchors and lead climbs. The sense of achievement and success one feels after completing his or her first climb is nothing short of exhilarating. For others, hiking to the summit of a nearby mountain, preparing a meal and camping out overnight is a tremendous accomplishment. Significant bonds are formed among the group as they can collectively report back to their peers that they succeeded. White water rafting, like so many other camp activities, promotes teamwork among campers, while orienteering allows campers to become more self-reliant. In short, adventure in the wilderness promotes skills and values that are often overlooked during the school year in favor of curriculum and content mastery; ironically, it is the skills acquired in such wilderness situations that often prove to be most significant in life.

Many camps offer overnight trips that may include all of the aforementioned skills; in some cases such trips are important rites of passage for specific bunks or age groups. Sometimes, the successful completion of such a trip results in the awarding of a special plaque, pin, or patch, or simply the opportunity to carve one's name in a special spot.

The list of activities offered by camps goes on and on. Many camps offer ropes courses, zip lines, and cycling to name a few additional activities. Depending on the location and resources of a camp, some may offer ranch work or SCUBA diving. Ropes courses are also popular, as is fishing. Perhaps the most important lesson learned from a hiking, climbing, or backpacking experience at camp is how to survive with just the essentials. Kids today are accustomed to having everything they could possibly need (and more) at their disposal. Spending time in the wilderness teaches campers that they can get by and make do with the bare minimum: an important lesson in a society of excess.

Campers appreciate the John Muir Wilderness in the Sierra Nevadas, home to Gold Arrow Camp. *Photo courtesy of Gold Arrow Camp.*

Campers cool off in the Leaf River at Camp Kupugani. *Photo courtesy of Camp Kupugani.*

Campers enjoy tubing on Camp Wekeela's Little Bear Pond. *Photo courtesy of Camp Wekeela.*

Camp Echo's annual Blob Competition is a highlight of the summer for many. Children from every division are chosen to represent their Olympic team to be blobbed in front of the entire camp. Judges score on everything from height to technique and splash! *Photo courtesy of Camp Echo.*

A typical day of boating at Camp Echo on the lake with the 500-foot zip-line overhead. *Photo courtesy of Camp Echo.*

Campers prepare for an overnight hike at Gold Arrow Camp. *Photo courtesy of Gold Arrow Camp*

Trips and Excursions

Many camps offer trips as well. For some camps, these may be day trips to nearby cities while for others, rafting, biking or camping trips might be offered. These excursions offer exciting opportunities for campers, especially those who might come from far away, to see a different part of the country or participate in something that they might not have the chance to do at home. The focus of these trips is generally promoting teamwork, building self-reliance and developing a healthy respect for nature and the environment.

Wilderness adventure trips are considered a rite of passage at many camps. In *Campingly Yours*, Thomas Adler writes about the legendary canoe trip he and his cabin took. After two days of canoeing, Adler's group reached their campsite. "It was called River Rats...the site was very old and full of interesting history...the building looked like it had been around forever. There were all sorts of names and dates on the walls...[my friend] and I found a pen and scribbled our names in a low corner, thus officially incorporating us into the lore of River Rats."[325] Such trips are intended to promote close bonds among a small group of campers and to instill a sense of accomplishment in the participants. Often, these trips are used to teach outdoor living skills such as setting up camp, making a fire, and using it to cook, skills today's youth are unlikely to learn elsewhere.

A camper flies high on Camp Echo's trapeze. *Photo courtesy of Camp Echo.*

Many camps organize excursions to water parks or amusement parks, often as a special treat for older campers or those staying for a longer session. New England camps often take campers to Boston for the day where they might explore Quincy Market and the New England Aquarium or see a show. Campers (especially the older ones) love the opportunity to reconnect with "civilization" and eat "real food," but they are always thrilled to return to the cocoon of camp at the end of the day.

Dinner and Evening Activity

Dinner is usually welcomed by campers and staff alike, providing an opportunity to unwind after a long day. There is often a blessing said before campers and staff dig in and many meals are ended with songs before evening activities begin. The pace of this meal is generally a bit more relaxed than lunch and offers a chance for people to catch up with each other about the day's activities. Many camps serve dinner family style which means campers must use proper manners and etiquette. At some camps, campers dine with their cabinmates while other camps assign campers to tables so that they have an opportunity to interact with campers of different ages. Many camps opt for a more traditional cafeteria style service, allowing campers to choose from a wide variety of options, which often include a salad bar and a pasta bar in addition to the main course.

At camp, children don't finish eating dinner and head for the television set, computer, or video games. Instead, dinner is generally followed by an age-appropriate evening activity, which is most often organized by cabin or unit. While past campers and counselors might fondly recall spending a lot of time around the campfire in the evening, these days evening activities are significantly more elaborate.

Among girls' favorite evening activities are lip synch contests, fashion shows, and paper bag skits. These activities are easy to organize and require little planning and few supplies. For lip synchs, campers select their favorite song, choose costumes and then mouth the words to the song in front of their peers. Some routines can be quite elaborate while others are less complex, but hilarity always ensues. Fashion shows are a tried and true evening activity. Some fashion shows may center around a theme such as a red, white, and blue fashion show for the Fourth of July, while others may be a bit more of a challenge. For example, "trashion shows" require the participants to design fabulous outfits out of trash bags. Paper bag skits are another favorite evening activity especially among the younger campers. Counselors fill paper bags with random items, divide up the campers into small groups and then give them time to create a skit using all of the items in the bag. Another perennial favorite evening activity among the girls is counselor makeovers. Counselors are forced into their campers' clothes (which are often preferable to their own), subjected to heaps of make-up and hair products and then made to walk "the runway" all in the name of fun. The beauty of these activities is that they have stood the test of time and they can be organized at a moment's notice, which makes them a good alternative for rainy days as well.

Boys are often content with less elaborate evening activities. Some other favorite evening activities include reverse scavenger hunts in which campers

Boys alert their fellow campers that it's dinner time at Camp Nathan Hale.
Photo courtesy of the Library of Congress.

Girls enjoy a meal together at Wyonegonic Camp in Denmark, Maine. *Photo courtesy of Wyonegonic Camp for Girls.*

Girls from Camp Kehonka enjoy a social with the boys from a nearby camp. *Photo courtesy of Roy Ballentine.*

Campers enjoy a dance jamboree at Camp Interlochen in Michigan. *Photo courtesy of the Library of Congress.*

Staff members help campers perfect the art of roasting marshmallows. *Photo courtesy of Camp Towanda.*

Counselors perform a song from *The Sound of Music. Photo courtesy of Philipp Luerzer.*

Campers enjoy a sunset beach walk. *Photo courtesy of Kari Ahern.*

Abby Berman sports a custom creation in a "trashion show" in which campers' outfits were made from trash bags and duct tape. *Photo courtesy of Philipp Luerzer.*

Campers celebrate a sunset victory during an intracamp athletic event. *Photo courtesy of Camp Towanda.*

Campers enjoy seeing their counselors dress up in silly outfits.

have to run to their cabins and come back with as many random items as they can wear or carry while the counselors make a list of items (e.g.: lacrosse stick, toothbrush, envelope, etc.). The camper or team with the most items on the list wins. Two-minute dress-up is another favorite activity. The counselors call out someone's name (such as a camp director or celebrity) and the campers have two minutes to run back to their cabins and dress like the person. A variation of this is counselor impressions. It is always fun to see how accurately the campers can portray their counselors down to the hairstyle, outfit choice, and favorite phrases. Boys often enjoy playing various sports in the evenings (especially if they don't play them during the day because they are busy sailing or playing tennis), as well as having the chance to try an activity like riflery, which they might not have as part of their daily schedule. And of course, pool parties or a dip in the lake are always welcome, especially on the oppressively hot evenings where the air is thick and heavy. And from time to time, it's nice to simply sit around a campfire and tell stories. Some campers are routinely surprised by how much fun they can have without electronics.

Tomas Ayala explains the challenges of planning a fun and engaging evening activity for a large group of boys.

> One of the hardest parts of planning an activity for a group of campers is the diversity in their interests and backgrounds. I like to ask campers what type of activities they would like to do throughout a summer so I can get a general idea of where the group as a whole stands activity and interest wise. With this, two things are achieved. First, they feel like they are a part of the decision-making process, which in turn will garner you respect from them, and second, it makes it easier to plan your activities with a foundation of common interests among the campers themselves. Campers love to feel included in decisions, especially at camp where a lot of their day is already scheduled and regimented down to the minute. Giving them a little decision making power in their summer will make it more fun for them and the respect you will earn will make the summer more fun for you as well. After all, camping is meant to be fun for both the campers and counselors.[326]

Veteran counselor Kelly Flanagan explains that there are challenges when trying to plan evening activities that will engage everyone. "It is important to switch up the evening activities so that they appeal to everyone. Sometimes girls don't like participating in active sports and others don't like partaking in lip syncs. It is important to rotate the evening activities during the week because the girls have different interests and, as a counselor, you want to make sure everyone is having fun. I found it helpful to assign different counselors each week to be in charge of planning that week's evening activities; this allows for different ideas to be created and it will make sure that the kids will continue to be engaged."[327]

Some evening activities involve the entire camp community. Talent shows featuring campers and staff or plays put on by the campers in the drama activity that week might provide some entertainment for the night. Other all-camp evening activities might include more active options like a counselor hunt which, in theory, sounds like a great idea until whomever is in charge realizes that there is no supervision of the campers. It may be stating the obvious, but to effectively run a counselor hunt, not everyone can hide. Boundaries must be set for both campers and counselors and limitations established (i.e.: can counselors hide in dumpsters or up in trees?) and then supervisors and as many other staff as are available must help supervise as campers run—quite literally—all over the place in search of their counselors. Prizes may be awarded to the counselors who were never found or to the campers who found the most counselors. Regardless of the outcome, this is a great activity to tire out the entire community and ensure a good night's rest!

The possibilities for evening activities are endless. Gold rush event is also extremely popular. Silver- and gold-painted rocks are hidden all over camp. Campers are divided up into teams and counselors, dressed as bandits, are armed with water guns. Campers try to collect as much "gold" and "silver" as they can without getting caught (sprayed by a counselor). The camp store is often used as the "bank" where teams try to deposit their rocks before getting caught.

Scavenger hunts can be great fun and can be quite varied. Sometimes, it is information (like camp trivia) being sought while other times campers are in search of specific objects that might be hidden around the camp. In today's digital age, photo scavenger hunts are also great fun and allow campers to capture memories while engaging in a fun competition. For example, campers must photograph the entire group with the camp's owner or corral as many camp dogs into a photo as possible. Casino Nights are often popular among older campers who enjoy the opportunity to dress up and play cards and roulette, and even "get married" in a Las Vegas-inspired wedding chapel.

There is, however, one evening activity that exhilarates many while simultaneously striking fear in many others. That activity is none other than the camp dance, where romance begins for some and young hearts are broken for others. Legends are made at the camp dance, whether it's the result of one's outfit, unique dance moves, or admirable tenacity with regard to the object of desire. Truth be told, in order to do justice to the camp dance, an entire chapter or even a book must be devoted to this institution. However, that would lead to the embarrassment of thousands of otherwise successful and well-adjusted individuals of all ages.

Camp dances have evolved significantly over the years, just like all other aspects of summer camp. In the early years of camping, boys were taken over to the girls' camp (also known as the "sister camp") for socials, which were a much more formal affair. This still holds true for single-sex camps today (minus the formal part). Today, many camp dances are glorified costume parties, with campers and counselors dressing up thematically or simply putting together an array of strange items like tutus, goggles, and cowboy hats. Some camps might hire a DJ, complete with lights and smoke machines, while others might simply use an equally effective iPod. One longtime camper recalls that "going to the camp dance as a younger camper meant dressing up and having your counselors do your hair and help you put on your first ounce of makeup. It meant giggling with your friends and as the night goes on, dancing like no one is watching."[328]

As camp is a place of firsts for many who attend, many of these firsts take place at camp dances; campers often experience their first slow dance and even their first kiss in this setting. Once campers return to their cabins (or respective camps) for the night, the rumor mill begins to churn away at lightning speed. Detailed debriefings take place long after lights out, while weighty decisions are made about whether to go through with plans to sneak out and meet the object of one's affection.

Camp dances are sometimes even more memorable than one's own prom; they are devoid of stress, there is no dress to be purchased, no limo to be rented, and no pressure to make the event memorable. "Dressing up" for a dance at camp often means simply finding a clean pair of shorts and a t-shirt while transportation is a non-issue. Camp dances are the very essence of summer camp: good, clean, honest fun.

Campers share their talents during "Wa Wa's Got Talent." *Photo courtesy of Camp Wa Wa Segowea.*

Campers admire a beautiful sunset before retiring to their cabins for the night. *Photo courtesy of Roy Ballentine.*

A camper plays the bugle at Camp Nathan Hale, Southfields, New York. *Photo courtesy of the Library of Congress.*

"Taps" (Lights Out)

After a busy day of activities and time shared with friends, it is eventually necessary to get ready for bed and go to sleep in preparation for the next busy day ahead. Campers brush their teeth and settle into bed, where they snuggle with a favorite stuffed animal from home. Some counselors may choose to read aloud to their campers, while others may allow their campers some flashlight time so that they can read on their own. A hush settles over the camp as "Taps" is played.

The playing of "Taps" at camp can be traced back to camps' military roots. According to bugle historian Jari Villanueva, "the music for 'Taps' was adapted by Union General Daniel Butterfield for his brigade in July, 1862...As the story goes, General Butterfield was not pleased with the call for Extinguish Lights, feeling that the call was too formal to signal the days end and with the help of the brigade bugler, Oliver Willcox Norton, wrote 'Taps'" to honor his men while in camp at Harrison's Landing, Virginia, following the Seven Day's battle...The call, sounded that night in July, 1862, soon spread to other units of the Union Army and was even used by the Confederates. 'Taps' was made an official bugle call after the war."[330]

Hearing "Taps" played is, perhaps, one of the most visceral memories for campers of all ages. If nothing else, it provides a brief time for introspective reflection on the day's accomplishments or a moment to look towards the next day's goals. For most of the younger campers, "Taps" means lights out, though the older campers may get to stay up a bit later. Counselors of younger campers often look forward to their nights on duty when they can go to bed early with their campers while staff working with older campers might enjoy playing cards after "Taps." Teenage campers sometimes enjoy "mingling" after "Taps," when they have a chance to socialize with the opposite sex under the watchful eye of the counselors. Regardless of when campers and counselors finally drift off, sleep at summer camp is virtually guaranteed to be sound after such a busy day of fun.

Each summer on the night before the last night of camp at Cape Cod Sea Camps, the following poem is read by Rick Francis, the camp's program director. The poem, entitled "Thoughts at Bedtime," was written by one of his counselors, Albion G. Hart.

Boys at Camp Nathan Hale gather around the campfire to sing. *Photo courtesy of the Library of Congress.*

Oh, heck, now I gotta go to bed,
But Mom said to do what the counselor said.
And I guess I'm tired and I'll probably sleep.
Now what did he say? Not another peep.

Gee, what did I forget to do?
I brushed my teeth, and I washed—that's true.
And I hung my clothes on the proper hook.
Now, where's my bunkmate? I think I'll look.

He's there, but he shouldn't be shining that light.
Maybe the counselor won't read tonight.

Gosh, wasn't it fun at the shop today!
I'm making a boat in the proper way.
I've scraped her, and sanded, and used not a nail.
She's really a beauty. I hope she'll sail.

And I swam my fifty. And wasn't I proud!
I felt so tickled, I yelled out loud.
I did it! I did it! I gotta write Dad.
He said if I didn't, he'd be right mad.

Mom sent a postcard and said she missed me.
It's been a long time, since last she kissed me.
But I've grown an inch, and I've gained two pounds.
Why I've almost forgotten the way she sounds
When she comes to cover me up each night.
Gee, I hope tomorrow the sun shines bright.
For then I'm sure we'll be going fishing.
That's just the thing I've been wishing.

Isn't it quiet on the Cape at night,
And isn't it pretty when the moon is bright.
Gosh, I'm lucky to be down here!
Somebody's coming—awfully near.

It's only the counselor...yes, I'm all right.
I'm almost asleep...Good night, good night.
I shot a forty on my Bar One.
Gee, using a rifle is surely fun!

If I stretch way out, it feels real good.
I'll go to sleep now. I know I should.
I'm just too sleepy to even pray,
But I'll say "Our Father" and call it a day,

And God bless Mommy, and God bless Dad.
I hope they know the fun I've had.
Gee, I hope tomorrow the sun shines bright,
And we'll go fishing...Good night...Good night.[331]

Sundays

And then, after a busy week of activities, comes Sunday. Early camp leaders saw to it that the Sunday schedule was more contemplative in nature than the rest of the week. Religious services were held at many camps and there was plenty of time for writing letters home or reading. Even today, Sunday is typically the day that finds campers wearing a camp uniform of some sort or at least their cleanest clothes. Van Slyck remarks that on Sundays, "at most camps, youngsters donned more formal attire—at boys' camps, long white trousers and white shirts—to discourage active forms of recreation."[332] A number of camps constructed outdoor chapels to provide a sacrosanct space for worship amidst the pristine peace and quiet offered by nature. Some camps went so far as to include a Sunday school curriculum into their observance of the Sabbath.

Members of the upper staff (some of whom are dressed in costume for the Fourth of July) await the parade of campers. *Photo courtesy of Cape Cod Sea Camps.*

Sunday schedules vary widely from camp to camp. Some camps allow campers to sleep in and attend breakfast in their pajamas. Religiously affiliated camps usually offer opportunities for prayer and introspection. Many camps offer more relaxing activities on Sunday, with plenty of down time to rest up for the busy week ahead. Silly or unconventional activities might be offered, which allow staff members to showcase their unusual skills like juggling or to teach campers a new game. Often, free swim provides some relief from the heat and a break from lessons. Some camps offer special hikes or fishing trips that aren't part of the daily routine. There is no shortage of things to do on a Sunday at camp.

Some camps offer a vespers service either in the morning or afternoon, sometimes in conjunction with flag raising or lowering. Most common among camps on Sundays, however, is the emphasis placed on reflection, the opportunity to discuss important topics like friendship and community and a chance to give thanks for one's camp experience.

Allan Peterson explains Sundays at Cape Cod Sea Camps:

> Sundays are the days that everyone at camp takes a breath. Campers still have activities, counselors and department heads are still running said activities. Sunday is the day to do dog grooming for all the camp dogs. Sunday is the day to go to the beach and play at the bay. Sunday is the day for sail races and enjoying all the Cape has to offer. Sunday is where you hear the song and wear your whites for colors. Sundays is when the cannon is blasted and it always still takes you by surprise. Sundays is wondering what buffet will be at dinner? Sundays is vespers and truly thinking and reflecting on the past week. Did I do enough? Did the kids have fun? What else could I do to help the campers' experiences? Sunday is singing along at vespers, but not out loud. Sunday is the early show...Sunday is almost over. Sunday is seeing campfires, hearing campers laugh, hearing the ocean, seeing the smiles. Sunday is the playing of "Taps" and its lights out. Tomorrow is Monday and a new week begins and ends...until next Sunday.[333]

Every morning and evening the entire camp gathers to raise and lower the flag. This is an opportunity each day to either talk about the coming day or to reflect on the day past at Camp Echo. *Photo courtesy of Camp Echo.*

Campers and counselors relax on the beach on Sundays at Cape Cod Sea Camps.

Katy Jack Goerke explains a different kind of Sunday at another camp:

> At Tomahawk Scout Reservation, Sundays are the first day of the week. A majority of staff just got back from their day off on Saturday, there is a fresh energy buzzing around the staff table. New week, new scouts, clean clothes, the opportunities are endless. At the flag ceremony the scouts are teeming with energy for the new week, most are decked out in their Class A uniforms just for the occasion. The new scouts eagerly explore every inch of the parade field, as if to find the source of the magic that makes summer camp so great. As the day progresses the scouts break up and go to merit badge classes or their activities. Each one is new and exciting. Staff scramble to memorize names with faces and get their classes started off on the right foot. The afternoon mellows out into chapel right before dinner. The dinner crowd is just as excited as the breakfast crowd because the best part of Sunday is yet to come. The CAMPFIRE!!! In just a few short hours staff members will be getting pied in the face, attacked by foam noodles, cracking fart and poop jokes, and if everything goes well, someone will get thrown in the lake. This sacred ritual of camp shenanigans will of course end on a solem note a reflection of what the week will mean for the scouts. As the scouts "silently" disperse back to their sites with their leaders, the staff gather to get psyched up for the next week. The smell of thrilled testosterone now fills the woods and all of its inhabitants are set on edge in the anticipation of the coming week's adventures.[334]

The flag is raised to begin the day at Camp Wa Wa Segowea. *Photo courtesy of Camp Wa Wa Segowea.*

The camp community gathers as the flag is lowered at the end of a day. *Photo courtesy of Camp Wa Wa Segowea.*

Visiting Day

Visiting Day generally arrives midway through the summer or a session. Campers are instructed to shower, put on the cleanest clothes they have, brush their hair, and clean the cabin. Counselors dig up their staff shirts once more (many for the first time since opening day) and prepare to sing their campers' praises to the steady stream of parents that come through the cabin. The dining hall generally prepares an exceptionally good meal or two that day, and activity specialists brace themselves for the parents who think they can sail, shoot an arrow, or handle a band saw without their assistance.

Campers are smart enough to take advantage of their parents while they are visiting. Local grocery stores and restaurants tend to experience an exceptionally high volume of customers as campers insist on stocking up on "real food" for their cabins and eating lunch out. However, in many cases, visiting day is more for the adults than for the children; parents need visual confirmation that their progeny are safe, clean, and happy. Oftentimes, special activities are planned like all-camp dances or performances and parents are disappointed that their children would rather participate in these events than spend time as a family. Columnist Frank Rich writes about his experience as a parent on visiting day:

> On visiting day, my sons will behave the same way I did to my parents 30-odd years ago. They will show off their independence half the time, exchanging indecipherable in-jokes with their counselors, only later filling me in on their exploits on lake, mountain, and playing field; then they will act as if they barely know me, because true independence means pretending your parents no longer exist and are to be tolerated only to the extent that they airlift bags of salt-and-vinegar potato chips and Snickers into your junk-food-free zone.[335]

Though penned in 1981, Susan Gordon wrote a "Parents' Guide to Visiting Day at Camp" for *The New York Times* which still offers some sound advice. She encouraged parents to do the following:

> Be prepared for some changes in your child's appearance... Remember, you are at camp only for one day. Control the urge to speak your mind. Lay off the scolding... When you visit your child's cabin, studiously avoid any close examination of his or her toilet kit. The toothpaste, soap, and shampoo you assiduously purchased in June may still be unwrapped... At departure time, don't be surprised if, having seen what all the other parents brought their children, your child has made a new list of "must-haves" for you to send by mail... Make your goodbyes short.[336]

With the disruption to the well-established daily routine, many campers experience a difficult time saying good bye to their parents at the end of the day or weekend, sometimes reverting back to homesickness. It takes a well-trained and compassionate staff to restore order to the camp after the last parent has finally left the grounds.

Jessica Benjamin drops off her youngest child, Faye, for ten days at camp. While her older sister and brothers have attended the same camp for many years, 2012 was Faye's first year. It was a very positive experience for her.

7 Creating a Camp Community

Campers enjoy a moment of levity after cleaning the stables at High Meadows Farms. *Photo courtesy of Sue Ballentine, High Meadows Farms.*

While history and customs are significant aspects of camp and should be honored, each summer is a little bit different. The cast of characters changes and new traditions are started. The start of each summer brings with it an opportunity to create a unique camp community that will never be replicated. This is both exciting and a little bit scary (especially for veterans who typically cling nostalgically to the way things have been done in the past) while presenting camp administrators with a tremendous responsibility.

In a 2002 article entitled, "The Camp Community and the World Community," Tom Schweinhart validates the importance of the construction of such communities.

> In our fast-paced world of technology, camps expose young people to a different kind of environment—a community-based atmosphere in which campers learn about living, working, and playing together. In addition, campers typically learn a healthy respect for nature. The life skills that many youth experience at camp help to form thinking patterns that impact the type of adults they will become. Living in a camp community helps prepare youth to be positive contributors to their communities.... Adolescence is a particularly important time to focus on community. As young people establish their individual identities and achieve increasing independence from their families, they begin to reach out to peer groups as a major source of friendship, support, and influence.[338]

The creation of a cohesive camp community starts with staff orientation. Staff, particularly those new to a camp or their position, must be welcomed enthusiastically. Information must be presented in a clear and concise fashion, and the tone and expectations for the summer must be set early. Much of staff orientation is often spent certifying counselors in CPR, lifeguarding, and a variety of other important areas which, while important, are not especially fun due to their serious nature. Staff must get acquainted with the activities they will be teaching, the others with whom they will be working, and the philosophy of the camp that employs them. If done well, staff orientation creates an unparalleled cohesiveness among counselors that will help set the tone for the campers when they arrive. It is also critical to identify barriers to creating communities such as bullying and to train staff in how to identify and overcome these hurdles so as to ensure the safety and well-being of each and every camper.

At camp, you're never left to fend for yourself. No matter what's going on—an acute bout of homesickness, a heartbreak, or just getting frustrated about not being able to make a basket in basketball—your fellow campers and counselors are always there to offer help, or at least a shoulder to cry on or to help make the situation better. Camp is about building each other up and creating a community, so no matter how you feel the rest of the year, it's almost impossible to feel utterly alone and misunderstood at camp, surrounded by so many supportive people. Camp is basically designed to create new shared experience and to foster bonding, which makes the friendships you make there extra special, and long-lasting. I rarely talk to anyone from elementary, middle, or high school, but the camp friends I made during that same period are still some of my favorite people in the world, and I will keep in touch with them for the rest of my life. We still quote inside jokes we came up with when we were 12. There's just something about camp friends.[337]

Staff members work together to plan activities for the summer. *Photo courtesy of Kari Ahern.*

Staff members get to know one another during orientation at Cape Cod Sea Camps.
Photo courtesy of Kari Ahern.

Campers and staff gather for an all-camp assembly. These gatherings are critical to building a strong community.
Photo courtesy of Roy Ballentine.

Many camps emphasize core values such as friendship, integrity, independence, teamwork, and sportsmanship. These values should be evident in the camp's day-to-day operation and embedded in all activities offered to campers. Camp administrators and counselors often reference such guiding principles at camp assemblies or gatherings, in council rings or vespers services. Having core values is an important step in helping campers gain an appreciation of others, respecting differences and being part of a caring and compassionate community.

Jeff Cheley, director of Cheley Colorado Camps, explains the importance of creating a sense of community early in the summer.

> As a 92-year-old summer camp, we have many cherished traditions. The one we are most proud of (and is integral to our success) is the Code of Living. The second night of the term, the campers in each unit get together and brainstorm a list of traits they want to strive to uphold throughout the summer. As 60 boys or girls living and playing together, they need to have something to strive to live up to. The campers have the full say in the list of five to ten traits for that unit for that summer. Some of the most common traits are honesty, integrity, cleanliness, supportiveness, empathy, sense of humor. We have also seen Carpe Diem and Hakuna Matata or other trendy words. The campers really buy into the Code of Living. They strive to uphold it during the summer and many of them keep a copy in their wallet or post it on their wall at home. We have a blue kerchief that each camper receives on the fourth night of camp that symbolizes their commitment to the Code of Living.[339]

Many camps choose to honor members of the community in a number of different ways. One popular practice is to give out spirit awards in units and activities. Often, campers are praised for their positive attitude, perseverance, generosity, and willingness to try new things. This is a wonderful way to recognize members of the camp community, especially those campers who don't always win swim races or score soccer goals. It provides positive reinforcement and encourages campers to continue taking risks by trying new things in a safe environment. Some camps also give campers and staff an opportunity to recognize one another for going out of their way to help others. At Cape Cod Sea Camps, for example, every member of the community has the opportunity to give a wampum to another individual. The wampum is a quahog shell (frequently found on the camp's beach) that is polished in a rock tumbler until it is shiny. The wampum was used by the Native Americans who inhabited Cape Cod as a form of currency, but at camp, the wampum has great emotional significance. It is considered an honor to be awarded a wampum and to be recognized in front of the whole camp. Acknowledgment of such qualities also serves as an exemplar for the rest of the campers in terms of what type of behavior is desired in the community.

All-camp activities, be they assemblies, games, meals, or special events, are also critical to the creation of a tight-knit community. In order to truly be invested in the camp experience, it is essential that campers know and interact with children and staff in other groups. Such relationships are fostered through activities like art and drama, where participation and instruction are usually not based on skill level, and through all-camp celebrations like July 4th games and cookouts. Many camps assign campers to tables for meals so that they are given a more structured opportunity to meet other campers and staff. Finally, some camps have big brother or big sister programs, where older campers are assigned to a younger camper. This is especially helpful for new campers so that they feel welcome and have an immediate connection to another community member.

Another important way camps honor the contributions of campers and staff to the community is by recognizing longevity and commitment to camp. Some camps award a special badge or patch, while others honor longtime campers and counselors with special dinners and celebrations. Many camps have ceremonies where feathers or other items of significance are given, each one representing a summer spent at camp. Recognizing and celebrating campers' contributions to the camp community is an important way to establish loyalty and to ensure that individuals feel that they are valued members of the community.

Campers at Cape Cod Sea Camps have the opportunity to present a wampum to a camper or counselor who has had a positive impact on them.

Unit Life

At most camps, campers are divided up into units that include several cabins in which campers of the same age live; each unit generally has its own identity within the camp community. Although it is wonderful for younger campers to have older campers as role models and for older campers to mentor those who are younger, it is vitally important for campers to have a peer group both in their cabin and beyond. Age-appropriate activities foster a sense of unity and purpose that cannot always be achieved with bigger multi-age groups; what is considered "fun" to a twelve-year-old girl is most likely considered horribly dull to a nine-year-old boy. Camps and their staff must be attuned to this and must work hard to ensure that activities are differentiated.

Camp Wyonegonic unit leader Barbie Cobb explains how cabins come together as a unit.

> We do several things at Wyo to foster camaraderie among the campers. First, we build cabin communities—each cabin counselor had 3–5 campers of her own, and they develop cabin guidelines, chores schedules, and calendars. The girls learn to work together as a group. Then, we work to create connections between all of the campers in the unit...we do a lot of fun cabin time, "grade level" time, and then unit times when all of the campers play games together. We also have teams, and the girls are picked randomly to be on two different teams, and they remain on these teams throughout their years at camp. This enables them to always have a group of friends who might not be in their cabin or activities.[340]

If there's a more reliable Rorschach than sleep-away camp, I'd like to see it. How you responded to being shipped off (often at an appallingly tender age) to a cluster of cedar cabins beside a mountain lake; to being taught Native American crafts, chants, and songs of dubious authenticity; and to being subjected to various painful hazing rituals—many of them involving underwear—reveals an awful lot about your fundamental character.[341]

Cabin Life

Cabins are where campers and counselors spend the bulk of their free time. For the youngest campers, often the vast majority of cabin members are new to camp so everyone experiences camp life for the first time together. However, as campers get older, they tend to request their friends as bunkmates; an older camper who is new to camp may be a bit intimidated by the fact that all of her cabinmates have spent a number of summers together and already have well-developed friendships. As a home-away-from-home, cabins generally have a different feel depending on who inhabits them for the summer. For example, the cabin of a group of ten-year-old boys is relatively Spartan in comparison to that of a group of fifteen-year-old girls who tend to bring everything from home that isn't nailed down. While the music played, the posters hung, and the fashions worn have changed dramatically over the history of summer camps, one thing has not: cabins promote a sense of unity and belonging. Cabins are where inside jokes are born, rainy days are spent, and lifelong friendships formed.

Forming strong bonds with one's peers is, perhaps, the most significant aspect of the camp experience.
Photo courtesy of Roy Ballentine.

Traditions

A camp without tradition
Is like a game without a team,
Is like a kid without camp spirit
Is like a book without a theme.

A day without some fun had
Is like our lake without a moon,
Is like a trip without a counselor,
Is like a song without a tune.

So it's up to us at Walden
To make tradition last,
To form a stronger tie
With the years gone by,
As it has been in the past.[342]

One of the most comforting aspects of camp is the cyclical nature of events. Each summer has its opening day, visiting day, and closing day rituals along with a host of significant events in between. "Camp traditions have been vital to the ...camp experience, but they are also constantly being invented, recycled, revisited, and sometimes let go."[343] Well-established traditions are an important part of creating a camp community. Having anticipated events, such as Color Wars, mid-season ceremonies, and talent shows, allows campers and staff to feel that they are an important part of something special. Some traditions are quite simple, such as raising and lowering the flag each day; however, participating in something that the earliest campers did and that campers across the country do allows campers to feel a sense of connection between past and present.

Sherry Maxman attended Camp Hochelaga in South Hero, Vermont, from 1973 to 1980. She reflects on the importance of traditions at camp: "I think traditions kept going because it gave you a sense of comfort and belonging and permanence. The 'outside world' changed and got scary, but everything at camp remained the same."[344] Cheley Colorado Camps' Jeff Cheley explains that:

> Our summer camp traditions continue to work because of our commitment to them. We realize that many of our "anchors" are instrumental to the success of our program. We are fortunate to have a strong group of returning staff each year and a core of staff that continue to return. Traditions are what summer camps are about so we work hard to maintain them. We also joke that there is a difference between a tradition and "something that we did last summer." We make sure that we continue the positive and powerful traditions and squash the "but we did it this way last summer" traditions that don't support our mission. We have even distributed surveys on the best and worst traditions at camp to make sure that we are aware of all of the traditions that have been established.[345]

Campers gather for an assembly at Camp Kehonka. Such rituals are an important part of creating a camp community. *Photo courtesy of Roy Ballentine.*

One tradition that transcends time and distance is the campfire, which is, many would argue, the most iconic image of summer camp. Reaching back to Native American roots, "synonymous with the camp experience, there is something both touching and dramatic about the campfire. When combined with an opening or closing ceremony, or a rite of passage, it becomes almost transcendent. Each campfire is unique; each ritual is beautiful and powerful. And each one is remembered for a lifetime."[346]

Traditions are an essential part of our lives—from holiday celebrations, to family gatherings. It is only fitting that camp, where the feeling of family and community is so strong, honors tradition—not only the traditions of the past, but the traditions that are being carried forward into the next generation of camp.[347]

Staff preparing for an annual performance before the camp's owner, A. Cooper "Bally" Ballentine. *Photo courtesy of Roy Ballentine.*

Camps also have many unique traditions that happen year after year. Shelby Bruselof explains a beloved tradition at Camp Kennedy: the Unbirthday Party. "In the middle of the summer everyone would get a camper or counselor's name and would have to make them a gift to give to them on the last night. The more creative you were, the better the gift. Some would knit hats, build boxes, or paint pictures."[348] Camp Wyonegonic has started hosting Wyoween on July 31 each summer for which campers dress in costume and

Halloween activities are held. Carol Sudduth, Wyonegonic's director, explains, "Wyoween is a creative evening program presented to teenage campers in the dark of night by staff—scary, of course. [Campers] dress up [and] a few screams curdling through the pine trees is part of the fun."[349]

In 1998, Ira Glass examined traditions at summer camps for *This American Life*. His report underscores the importance of tradition at camps.

> The special songs and ceremonies are a part of so many American camps and it's not just because they're fun. A camp director in Wisconsin told us as we were putting together today's program that financially, you cannot run a camp without lots of repeat customers. These traditions bring kids back year after year.
>
> You have the kids singing constantly about their loyalty to their cabinmates and their camp. You let them know about all the extra rights and privileges and honors they're going to get if they return as older campers. It is part of making the business run. And in addition, it's part of what makes camp thrilling. It is using all of the stagecraft that all the world's religions have always used. The ceremonies, the chanting, the repeated words, the official honors, and offices, but for an entirely secular purpose—to thrill children, to make them feel part of something big and special."[350]

Campfires are a staple of virtually every summer camp. Their roots can be traced back to the Native American influences on the earliest camps.

Initiations and Pranks

Although the twenty-first century has seen a distinct lack of pranks and initiations (many of which would, in today's climate, be categorized as hazing), summer camps have a long tradition of "welcoming" new campers and counselors into the camp fold by subjecting them to an array of gags and jokes, none of which were ultimately harmful but rather cause for laughter. Back in the day, many campers were tricked into stepping into a bucket of tar that left them both sockless and shoeless. Often someone's bed would be moved to a raft at low tide only to find said bed inaccessible six hours later when the tide was in. A host of other pranks and initiation rites include short-sheeting one's bed, covering the toilet with Saran wrap, water balloon or shaving cream fights, and the hiding of toilet paper or light bulbs. Scary stories and camp legends were often passed down from summer to summer, scaring only the neophytes who didn't know any better. And would it really be camp if no bras or underwear were raised up the flagpole?

In *Children's Nature,* Leslie Paris writes, "campers arrived at camp already conscious of their own differences from one another. Camps' rituals of incorporation did not make all campers equal but provided them a variety of ways successfully to integrate themselves into the community."[351]

Today, gags and "pranks" are no longer done at someone's expense. Instead, they serve as bonding activities intended to bring a cabin or group closer together under the counselors' watchful eye. "Now, there may be 'official' or staged pranks: Instead of sneaking out under a counselor's nose, a counselor may sneak a cabin out for an ice-cream raid on the kitchen after lights out. In places where hiding someone's shoes is still allowed, it's generally because that camp has an established culture of respect that can absorb the prank without it being seen as bullying; having your stuff missing may actually be a badge of honor. As for the 'Ghost of the One-armed Hunter' stalking those who would venture out at night, well, the spooky spirits tend to be friendly ones these days, lest a terrified child stay home next summer."[352]

Campers reveal a prank in which they dismantled a number of split rail fences and built a Lincoln Log-like structure. *Photo courtesy of Kari Ahern.*

Camp Nicknames

Many camps have a tradition of bestowing nicknames on campers and staff alike. In *Children's Nature,* Leslie Paris writes "special camp names testified to new identities and experiences, asserting children's disjunction from ordinary life, while illustrating their active participation in making camps into special spaces of personal transformation. Nicknames also ritualized new ways of thinking about family and kinship outside traditional bounds."[353]

At some camps, this is an informal activity, simply the result of living in close quarters and getting to know one another well. At other camps, receiving a nickname is a highly formalized process that is essentially institutionalized. Audrey Monke, owner and director of Gold Arrow Camp in Lakeshore, California, explains the role of nicknames at GAC.

> At GAC, people get their nicknames when they become a counselor. They usually think them up themselves, but when people can't pick, we help them out. The best ones are somehow related to them (their personality/experiences/likes) or their job. So, our former head cook, who is a Japanese American, was "Sushi." One current staff is "Cubbie" because she's a Cubs fan. Some people go by their favorite food or animal or character. We have just about every Lion King character (Mufasa, Rafiki, Nala, Simba, etc.). One longtime staffer is "Tqoe" (The Queen of Everything). There aren't really any rules, except for we "retire" camp nicknames for people who've worked at camp five or more years so the name can't be used again.[354]

In the autobiographical *Campingly Yours*, Thomas C. Adler recounts his experiences at North Star Camp for Boys. Adler received a letter from his older brother who attended camp a year before him. The last line of the letter read, "P.S. Everyone here calls me The Flash because they say I walk slow, don't tie my shoes, and come from Missoura."[355] The following summer, Adler also attended camp and had a challenging first day. He was given a hard time by the older campers and felt homesick. However, after showcasing his impressive baseball skills, the older campers accepted him. One said to him, "'I just found out that you're Flash's little brother, so I'm gonna call you Kid Flash.'"[356] As such, Adler gains some much-desired credibility and instant camp fame.

In short, camp nicknames allow kids to adopt an alter ego. Perhaps quiet and shy at home, some individuals blossom and become extroverts in the camp setting. Adopting a nickname or a camp name is a practice of many camps. At some camps, only staff have nicknames and never even tell their campers their real names. Other camps award nicknames to campers when they reach a certain age. Regardless of how one attains his or her nickname at camp, it is an important rite of passage that symbolizes one's inclusion and membership in the camp community.

Color Wars

Unrivaled in its intensity is the annual Color War held at many camps. For many, it is the ultimate highlight of the summer.

> Temporarily reconfiguring camp community, Color War drew the youngest and the oldest campers together across lines of age difference, while dividing individual tents or cabins into two. As such, the event dramatized camps' inevitable internal factions, while allowing every child to feel part of a team. Some might succeed at field sports; others helped their team by winning a crucial game of checkers, writing a popular camp song, or simply cheering especially loudly. At many camps, the entire community, including the camp doctor and nurse, participated. New campers looked forward with eagerness to the opening ceremonies, when they found out which team they would be on.[357]

Author Leslie Paris believes that Schroon Lake Camp in New York was among the first to experiment with the notion of Color War in 1916 by hosting "Red and Gray week."[358] Early Color Wars were often simply all-camp games of Capture the Flag or tug-of-war. Today, however, Color Wars often last for several days or a week and become completely all-consuming for the campers and the staff. Paris offers commentary on the experience:

> From the 1920s onward, Color War held a place of honor as the single most important special event at many camps. Blending pageantry and athletics, this competition was possibly an elaboration of a war game, Capture the Flag, popular at many northeastern boys' camps by the 1910s, in which teams named after colors (often blue and gray for the Union and Confederate armies of the American Civil War) tried to enter one another's territory while remaining unseen. By the mid-1910s, Color War had evolved into a large-scale competition comprising of many smaller contests, held near the end of the camp season, when campers had tired of the ordinary routine.[359]

Over the hundred years since the first Color War, society's focus on competition among children has ebbed and flowed. While some in today's world believe that Color War undoes all the good that camp is about by pitting campers against one another and forcing divisions, others assert that Color War does more to unify the community than anything else. It is a quintessential camp experience that transcends age, background, and gender. It fosters

The entire camp community embraces the arrival of Color War! *Photo courtesy of Camp Wekeela.*

Tetherball is a camp favorite. *Photo courtesy of Camp Wekeela.*

The annual Color War at Camp Wekeela pits the Green Team against the White Team. *Photo courtesy of Camp Wekeela.*

friendships that might not have been formed otherwise. It creates memories that last a lifetime. Campers who come up through the ranks aspire to be team leaders (often called Color War generals), while the youngest campers idolize the older campers who shepherd them through the experience.

Camps have become so clever about how they break out (announce the beginning of) Color Wars that it is hard to imagine what could possibly be left for them to do. Newcomers have trouble understanding what all the fuss is about, while the veteran campers, overcome by emotion and excitement, await the breakout at any moment. Some camps have an impressive fireworks display while others, like Tall Pines Day Camp, employ local news anchors to create and air a fake news story. Tyler Hill Camp went so far as to stage a wedding, which was interrupted by a rogue guest to announce Color War. Some camps even stage a "fakeout" to mislead campers into thinking Color War is starting. Many camp directors confess to planning these fakeouts and breakouts all year long and some even spend a substantial amount of their budget on these productions. But it's all worth it, as most campers will attest. Color War is an iconic part of the camp experience.

Richard and Kellie Gutman explain in *The Summer Camp Memory Book* that, "once it had begun, Color War took over every aspect of camp. The goal, simply enough, was to amass more points than your opponents. All life was governed by the awarding of points for victories and the deducting of points for infractions. Athletic competitions were do or die…If you weren't in a competition or practicing for one, you were expected to be in attendance somewhere, cheering your team on."[360] They explain that the final event and announcement of the winner was followed by an emotional scene. "Pure bedlam broke loose and hysteria took over."[361]

Color War is such a transformative experience that many adults find themselves reminiscing about the event later in life. In 2012, former camper and counselor Jennifer Rheuban began a new organization called Adult Color Wars. As a single woman in Los Angeles, she found herself wondering, "'When did we go back to the seventh grade dance where boys were on one side and girls were on another? Have we become so accustomed to only knowing how to socialize by text or email, and of course only with alcohol?'"[362] She explains, "My mind went back to the basics of what I loved as a kid and of course ended up thinking about camp. Shabbat-o-grams, tie-dye shirts, song sessions, and colors wars came to mind. And then a light bulb went off in my head…Color Wars. What if I organized an Adult Color Wars at camp to bring people together to essentially be a kid for a day—no bars, no alcohol, not a 'singles' thing, no pretenses. Just pure fun."[363] Rheuban's organization now raises money to fund camperships so that children who would otherwise be unable to attend camp have the opportunity to do so. Adult Color Wars take place twice a year—in the fall and the spring—pitting former campers against one another in the gaga pits, tossing water balloons to one another and engaging in relay races. The Adult Color Wars Web site also allows individuals to send Shabbat-O-Grams as they did when they were campers. Shabbat-O-Grams provided an opportunity for campers to send a note to friends telling them what their favorite part of the week had been or to recall a special memory. Sending electronic Shabbat-O-Grams lets adults relive their days at Jewish summer camp while reaching out to friends.

One would think that the outcome of the annual Color War would soon be forgotten come the end of the summer. Nothing could be further from the truth. Color War is the stuff of which camp legends are made. Scoring the pivotal run in a baseball game or earning the most points for spirited singing gives campers a sense of contribution to the team and to the camp community in general. Camp alumni return wanting to see the plaque from the summer they won Color War. It is likely that no matter how much camps may change in the future, Color War is a permanent fixture.

Teamwork is an important aspect of Color War.
Photo courtesy of Camp Wekeela.

Songs

Singing is another significant tradition that has also been passed down over the years. Many camps still sing songs that the very first campers sang, even though new songs are being created each summer or lyrics to popular songs are changed to reflect the summer's events.

Visit any camp anywhere and you are likely to hear at least a few groups spontaneously break into song at meals, on the bus, in a sailboat, or in the cabin. But why does the nature of camp lend itself to group singing? Some researchers believe that singing at camps was simply a reflection of what was happening in American society when camps began. "In the late 1800s/early 1900s, the confluence of the wilderness movement and establishment of National and Provincial (State) Parks, produced the drive to get kids out of the city and into the natural environment. And there was the amazing phenomenon of singing in early movie theaters, and, of course, in parlors around the home piano. But more than a mere pastime, song was widely seen as a means, in many different settings, of uniting people in action and inculcating certain values."[364]

Often, campfires are where much singing takes place. It is thought that the tradition of singing at camps began as camp gospel revival meetings.[365] Longtime camp guru Jack Pearse explains, "At camp, we sing songs that are fun, upbeat, harmonious, or inspiring. Most of all, the songs are easy to sing and remember. We sing folk songs; spirituals; patriotic songs; religious songs; fun, nonsense, novelty, action songs; melodious (rounds, partner songs); popular songs that are 'catchy;' songs that we write (or adapt) ourselves."[366] Early campers most likely sang wartime songs of the Civil War and even, perhaps, some spirituals. Folk songs (like the ubiquitous "Kum Bah Yah") and patriotic songs have also been popular at camps over the years. Today, many campers and staff rewrite the lyrics to popular songs making them camp-centric. Of course, most camps have a handful of camp songs that are passed down from generation to generation; knowing the lyrics makes you part of a special group of camp insiders of all ages. Some former campers sing their camp songs with as much fervor as they might sing their alma mater's fight song.

Generally, younger campers often look to the oldest campers to lead them in song, especially at the start of the summer. Sherri Maxman recalls that many Hochelaga traditions were based around singing. "On the first night of each session, the counselors would come marching through the dining hall at dinner, forming a long chain led by the camp director, singing a song called 'Little Red Caboose.'"[367] This was something that returning campers looked forward to and that new campers came to enjoy.

Singing together is an important part of the ritual bonding at camp. You don't have to be particularly skilled or even in tune; it is simply a means by which campers and staff come together, celebrating their common experience. Although many camps have their own unique songs, there are certain songs that anyone who has ever attended camp anywhere will know, thereby giving all campers a strong sense of community from one camp to another (see page 224, *Camp Songs*).

Campfires

A sense of community is, by far, one of the most significant aspects of the camp experience. Most campers and staff will report that the main reason they choose to return to camp is for their friends. The strong relationships built over the course of the summer are the result of very deliberate work by the camp administration to make sure that everyone—campers, counselors, support staff—feels that their contributions are valued and that they are appreciated. The depth of this experience is unlikely to be replicated anywhere else. So finding ways to promote this kind of community building is essential and campfires are an important part of it.

In a 2001 speech to the Tri-State Camping Conference, Michael Eisner, then-CEO of Disney, shared the following reflection.

> Every time I was on fire detail, the situation and challenge was different. But, every time the rich reward was the same as we simply sat and enjoyed our consuming creation. And, there was one aspect in particular that never failed to intrigue me, and that was the process of seeing the single small flame of the match spread to the kindling and then the twigs and then the smaller branches and finally the larger logs. It didn't dawn on me until years later, but this was the perfect metaphor for the creative process. In much the same way, the fragile spark of an idea can spread to become a great work of art or a movie or a political movement or an automobile or a Space Shuttle or a new communications technology. But, these blazing achievements can only happen if the initial idea is cared for, protected, and nurtured until it is ready to spread...But, much of the success I've achieved can be traced to the direct and metaphorical lessons I learned in building those campfires.[368]

Campfires are a significant part of the overall camp experience and are instrumental in bringing together the entire camp. Campfires denote different traditions for different camps. At some camps, they are a time for performances and singing while at others they are a forum for reflection and introspection. S'mores often play a significant role in campfires; younger campers must learn from the older campers and staff how to achieve the perfect roasted marshmallow.

Campfires are an iconic symbol of camp. *Photo courtesy of Gold Arrow Camp*

Aptly described in the Camp Laurel blog, "campfires instantly evoke feelings of togetherness and promote an atmosphere of being together in an intimate setting that is unique to the people who are present."[369] Many camps hold campfires to bookend the camping season, marking its beginning and end, often with special corresponding ceremonies to differentiate these fires from those held throughout the season.

If I lived to be nearly a hundred
And every year one of joy,
I wonder if I should remember
The times when, as a boy,
I sat by the fire at Pemi
With a group of the nation's best
As the moon drifted low o'er the hillside
And finally dropped in the west.
And I wonder if anyone's better
For anything I've done or said,
And whether good will in the heart may
Offset mistakes of the head.
Perhaps when life's mem'ries are gathered
The camp ones will be with the rest
As the moon drifts low o'er the hillside
And finally drops in the west."[370]

Campers and counselors share their experiences around a campfire. *Photo courtesy of Camp Wa Wa Segowea.*

Making Your Mark

Many campers seek innocuous ways to leave their mark in the annals of the camp's history, especially as the summer begins to draw to a close. One of the most popular ways to do this is by writing your name on the walls or ceilings of the cabin in which you spent the summer. As Thomas Adler explains in *Campingly Yours,* while participating in a traditional camp canoeing trip, he and a bunkmate "found a pen and scribbled our names in a low corner, thus officially incorporating us into the lore of River Rats."[371]

Many camp alumni relish returning to their old stomping grounds years later with families in tow. They can recall precisely where they wrote their names and are eager to share this minor act of rebellion and self-preservation with children and grandchildren. It is especially devastating when cabins have been repainted or remodeled, leaving no trace of one's existence for the present generation of campers to wonder about. Nevertheless, former campers know their signature is there, albeit under layers of paint.

Other camps have more legitimate and long-lasting ways of preserving campers' presence and contributions. One way is by creating plaques that list every camper's name, which are often hung in a central location. Another way to leave a trace of one's legacy is by earning the highest award possible in an activity. At Cape Cod Sea Camps, for example, all campers earning their Blue Star Expert award in riflery are recorded on a special plaque at the range.

Only the most legendary of camp figures, having left their mark in a myriad of ways, are lucky enough to have buildings or cabins named after them so that their legacies live on for generations to come. These men and women are the ones who have shaped the camp experience for thousands of campers, who created the traditions decades ago that remain an integral part of the camp experience today; thus, it is wholly appropriate that cabins and other camp buildings bear their names.

At the end of each summer, many camps have a tradition of making plaques with all of the campers' names on them. The plaques are then hung in cabins, dining halls, or other common areas. *Photo courtesy of Kari Ahern.*

Both celebrating and lamenting the last night of camp, final candles are lit at Camp Echo. *Photo courtesy of Camp Echo.*

Closing Ceremonies and Saying Goodbye

> *Sending them to camp as campers, and supporting them as they return as staff members, gives them a gift that they'll keep for the rest of their lives, one you or their non-camp friends might not completely understand. When they get home, after gawking at carpeting and eating their favorite home foods, they'll dump their piles of laundry and collapse in their beds, with funky tan lines from sandals. Soon, they'll tell you all about camp—the canoe trip, their new favorite sport, the huge frog they saw, their favorite Friday picnic lunch and their new best friends from all around the country. Soon. And when they do, let them revel, just a little, in exactly how much you don't "get."*[372]
>
> —Talya Minsberg

There is an overwhelming, nearly paralyzing sadness that pervades the camp community as each camp season comes to a close. Promises are made to keep in touch and to return the following summer. Final moments are savored. It isn't just the realization that school is about to begin again, but the idea that you will no longer share the daily interaction with others to whom you have grown so close in such a short but intense period of time.

Every camp has its own traditions to mark the end of the summer. Camp Hochelaga's most beloved tradition was Candlelight, an event held at mid-summer and at the end of summer, "during which everyone got a lit candle to place in the lake and make a wish as the candles floated out to a giant "H" ablaze in the water. Afterwards, [campers] write a letter to [themselves] that the camp collected and would send out to your home during the winter."[373] Many camps located on lakes or ponds have a special moonlight ceremony on the water in canoes or other boats where candles are set afloat, maudlin songs are sung, and memories shared.

It is hard to explain what is most difficult for campers and staff about saying goodbye at the end of the summer. When asked to reflect on this, responses are varied. One 15-year-old camper said, "The hardest thing about leaving camp at the end of the summer is knowing that I have a tough year of school ahead and leaving my favorite place on earth,"[374] while another 14-year-old explained, "Definitely the hardest thing about leaving camp is knowing when I wake up the next day I won't be woken up by reveille or see my friends or go to activities. I have to wait ten more months until camp starts all over again."[375]

Jackson Bloch and Julia Luerzer are awarded the Service Cup in recognition of their contributions to the Cape Cod Sea Camps community in 2010.

Campers say their tearful goodbyes knowing they won't be reunited for a year. *Photo courtesy of Kari Ahern.*

The ephemeral nature of the camp experience was never clearer than at those moments when campers held one another tightly and promised to be friends forever.[376]

The last full day of camp is an interesting amalgam of experiences ranging from the mundane to the sublime. Generally, early in the day campers are directed to pack up their possessions; however, in order to do so, they must first find them. A scavenger hunt of sorts ensues as campers go in search of missing t-shirts, rogue socks, and long-lost towels. Items that have spent the better part of the summer on the cabin's clothesline go unclaimed despite counselors' insistence that they must belong to *someone*. Packing lists are reconciled with actual possessions and staff members try to corral campers into the general vicinity despite the temptation to wander off in search of friends in other cabins and units.

As the day progresses, emotions take over. Everything is done with such finality: the *last* walk on the beach, the *last* swim in the lake, the *last* meal in the dining hall, the *last* time the camp's song is sung, the *last* time Taps will be played. Tears begin to flow. Boys try to fight them, not wanting to show their emotions and true feelings about camp. Girls become practically hysterical and inconsolable at the prospect of saying good-bye.

After the pins and needles excitement of the awards ceremony, along with a very sappy, tear-jerking speech or two, it was time for the last singing of the good-night song and taps, which signified the end of camp. You ambled back to your cabin in the moonlight and flashlight for that final night, the last cold water wash, and cool night's sleep on the squeaky cot. You whispered in the dark forever that night. The next morning was an anticlimax, getting up at the crack of dawn and leaving to catch buses, trains, and planes. But all thoughts were still with the summer, and many headed off for home saying, 'This was it—the best season ever.' [377]

Campers make a valiant effort to stay up all night, sharing stories and eating the last of the care packages, though many nod off as dawn nears. As rReveille is played on closing day, campers and counselors emerge bleary-eyed from the cabins and wander zombie-like around the grounds saying good-bye to new friends and old friends, to boyfriends and girlfriends, to anyone who crosses their path. Some campers, even those who were the most homesick of all at the start of the summer, try to hide from their parents as they arrive to pick them up, trying in vain to drag out the last day of camp. Author Leslie Paris sums up the final events of the camp season. "End of season rites celebrated personal as well as collective transformation. Camp culture had helped to produce in children self-consciousness about the inevitable transitions they underwent as they moved from one stage of childhood to the next: acquiring new skills, growing bigger and stronger, and adopting new social roles."[378]

Before email, Skype, and Facebook, campers were forced to collect addresses if they wanted to keep in touch with their summer friends. Autograph books were signed, final photos taken, and (in the 1980s) summer mix tapes were made. Clothes were often traded (especially school t-shirts) or mistakenly packed (since one could hardly be expected to remember what mom had packed for him or her eight weeks prior). Arts and crafts projects were not-so-carefully packed and ribbons or awards won placed in the top tray of one's trunk.

Departing from camp, while still melodramatic today, is significantly less so than it was a decade or two ago. Today, campers Skype on their way home, chat online and friend each other on Facebook immediately upon departure. Nevertheless, the ending of one summer means that the next one will be different. Despite promises to the contrary, never again will all the same members of the community be together in the same place. It is hard to accept that people grow up, move on and, for one reason or another, might not return. But it is a safe assumption that a new crop of equally wonderful people will descend upon the camp the following summer eager to have just as much fun and make equally vivid memories.

Chris Thurber and John Malinowski explain that campers react to closing day in a number of different ways. They organize them into categories including Fountain of Youth kids, Poker Face kids, Tearful Campers and Sensationalists.

> Fountain of Youth kids will be very excited about their camp experience and will immediately want to describe everything about camp in two minutes...Parents should just smile and go along for the ride (with a camera, of course!). Poker Face kids probably had a great time at camp, but are oddly quiet on closing day. They don't want to tell their parents much right away, but parents should not assume this is because they disliked camp. It's just that Poker Face kids have an especially hard time leaving...Tearful Campers are visibly moved by the close of camp. Tears are a real testament to the power of the overnight camp experience... Tearful Campers may want to leave quickly to avoid the awkwardness of the moment, or they may wish to linger. Sensationalists immediately tell their parents the single most dramatic thing that happened to them during their camp stay...Don't assume the worst. All campers have a mix of powerful positive and negative experiences at camp.[379]

No time was more nostalgic than the last night of camp, a moment when the community gathered to recall the summer that was coming to an end. Goodbyes, like the initiations that came before them, took place through ritual events designed to secure camp community while acknowledging its endpoint.[380]

Returning Home

The transition from camp to home is a difficult one for many. Marjorie Ingall penned an article entitled, "Home Again" for *Tablet Magazine*'s "Worst-Case Scenario Survival Handbook: Back from Summer Camp Edition." She claimed to provide, "a public service: a guide to negotiating those rocky few weeks between the return of your child from summer camp and the start of school."[381] The third scenario about which she advised parents was how to react when their "child will not stop lying on couch and moaning about missing camp friends." Ingall offered three "survival strategies" for distraught parents:

1. Have child write letters. *(Parent should attempt to keep sarcasm out of voice when pointing out that, in the previous four weeks, child was not nearly so eager to write to her own parents, whom she has known for eight years.)*

2. Have child use telephone. *(Parent should insert earplugs before handing child telephone, lest parent's hearing be permanently damaged by lunatic chanting of [age group] cheer at increasing volume.)*

3. Remind child of future reunion opportunities.

4. When child demands immediate visit with friends or child will never ever come out of room or eat ever again, remind child that we do not negotiate with terrorists.[382]

This is followed by scenario number four in which "child *(still lying on couch and moaning)* refuses to do camp laundry or assist in household chores." Fighting fire with fire, she recommends:

1. Establish…cleanup system similar to that of camp. Give child daily cleanliness score; promise ice cream for non-filth achievement.

2. Tell child it is now Color War and her team will lose to the Blue Team if they do not clean up.[383]

What every parent should remember is that the more "campsick" a child is upon returning home, the more successful the summer was.

Campers wave farewell to their friends as they head for home at the end of a glorious summer. *Photo courtesy of Kari Ahern.*

Summer Camp in Popular Culture

Camp is a popular subject matter for television shows and films (though less so than one might think) and it also provides an excellent backdrop for young adult fiction and literature. A 1981 *New York Times* article mused that "mystery meat, bug juice, making out, poison ivy, sex talk, dances, parents' visiting day, and the silliness of adults in Bermuda shorts have all become handy clichés for authors to use in sketching the texture of summer camp. The result is an idealized view of a long-past experience...Too often summer becomes a backdrop for some moral lesson about independence or ethics, when for many children it is just the opposite—a time of exploration and freedom, of breaking the rules."[384] With a built-in, nostalgic audience, there could be no better fodder for the media.

Movies

Camps have been given the Hollywood treatment many times throughout history. They strive to capitalize on the sense of melancholy felt by anyone who has ever attended camp, but often fail to capture the essence of camp either by creating exaggerated stereotypes or concocting silly story lines.

The very first film about camps was a silent film created by the Girl Scouts in 1918. Entitled *The Golden Eaglet: The Story of a Girl Scout*, the film gave viewers the opportunity to see girls maintaining the camp site and engaged in various activities like learning to tie knots. This film, however, was more of an informational video than it was a form of entertainment.[385] The first use of summer camp as the setting for a film was 1937's *Make a Wish*. The film featured a boy at camp who befriends a composer suffering from writers' block. The composer is inspired by the boy's beautiful mother and he is able to write again.

One of the best-known films set at a camp is *The Parent Trap*. The 1961 original and the 1998 remake told a story of identical twin girls who were separated and raised individually by one of their parents. The girls meet at summer camp and switch places to meet the other parent while planning to reunite their family. The original 1961 film featured Hayley Mills, Maureen O'Hara, and Brian Keith, while the 1998 remake starred a young Lindsay Lohan, Dennis Quaid, and Natasha Richardson.

In 1979's *Meatballs,* Bill Murray stars as a somewhat inept camp counselor whose endless shenanigans lead to the consternation of the camp's director, Morty (played by Harvey Atkin). Murray's character, Tripper, does, however, make a significant connection with one camper who struggles to fit in with the others. *Meatballs* was filmed at Camp White Pine in Ontario and utilized actual campers and counselors as extras. In an effort to capitalize on the film's success, *Meatballs II* was released in 1984. Having nothing to do with the first film, the sequel takes place at the financially failing Camp Sasquatch. The owner, Coach Giddy, tries to save the camp from being acquired by rival Camp Patton. The fate of the camp is settled by an annual end of the summer boxing match between representatives from the two camps. *Meatballs III* (1986) and *Meatballs 4* (1992) were inauspicious sequels, bringing the franchise to an ill-fated halt.

Also in 1979, director Chuck Vincent brought audiences *Summer Camp,* in which the camp's owner recruits past campers to spend the weekend at the camp where they met. However, his ulterior motives include getting the group to fix up the camp and give him money. Old grudges are settled and pranks are played as the group reunites after a decade. Also of this era was *Little Darlings*, released in 1980 and starring Tatum O'Neal and Kristy McNichol as teens in a competition to see who can lose their virginity first while at camp. This coming of age film featured a catchy soundtrack with Blondie, Supertramp, and The Cars.

David Wain directed cult classic *Wet Hot American Summer* in 2001, though the film was set in 1981. The star-studded cast included David Hyde Pierce, Janeane Garofalo, Michael Ian Black, Paul Rudd, Molly Shannon, Amy Poehler, and Bradley Cooper. Set on the final day of the summer at Camp Firewood, the various characters have a great deal to resolve before heading home. The camp's director (Janeane Garofalo) is in love with a local astrophysicist (David Hyde Pierce), who is trying to save the camp from an earth-bound piece of the NASA space station. The rest of the camp staff is concerned with putting on the final camp show, heading home to divorcing parents, or simply obtaining the object of their desire. The film is not only a spoof of life at camp, but also something of a period piece.

> *WHAS* is pitched specifically to Reagan-era latchkey kids who grew up watching these movies on television, and have a certain generalized nostalgia about the fashions, hairstyles, graphical elements, and other minutiae that seeped into their wood-paneled family rooms. Moreover, the film also speaks to a generation of middle-class Jewish boys and girls whose parents shipped them off to summer camp for one or two months at a time. So if you're a middle-class Jew who came of age in

the early '80s, watched a lot of television, and are given to nostalgia for misspent youth, *Wet Hot American Summer* is the movie for you.[386]

The 1980s brought viewers a series of movies about Ernest (Jim Varney's iconic character) including *Ernest Goes to Camp*. Kamp Kikakee is the destination for Ernest and a group of juvenile delinquents who are sentenced to the camp where they are not well received by their peers. This film, like so many others, included yet another side plot about a camp being threatened by a selfish corporation.

Filmed on location at Ontario's Camp Tamakwa, *Indian Summer* opened in 1993. Similar to the premise of other camp-related films, camp owner Lou Handler (portrayed by Alan Arkin) invites a group of former campers (including Diane Lane, Bill Paxton, and Kimberly Williams) back to camp, where he plans to announce his retirement. Christopher Lloyd starred in 1994's *Camp Nowhere* in which Morris "Mud" Himmel and his friends are desperate to avoid going to a boring camp. They hatch a plan, blackmail a former teacher to help them convince their parents that the camp of their creation is, in fact, legitimate, and forbids them to visit. Some lead their parents to believe that it is a weight loss camp while others convince their parents that the camp is a military camp or an acting camp. Without parents, counselors, or rules, the kids create their ideal summer and successfully fool their parents. Later that decade, *Camp Stories* (1997) told the story of a Jewish summer camp and starred Jerry Stiller, Elliot Gould, and Jason Biggs. This film also featured a retiring camp director and the usual conflicts among staff and campers found in films of this genre.

Judd Apatow and Steven Brill brought audiences *Heavyweights* in 1995. The film's main character, Gerry Garner (played by Aaron Schwartz), is sent to Camp Hope, where overweight boys go to lose weight during the long, hot days of summer. Unfortunately, the camp's owners, the Bushkins (played by Jerry Stiller and Anne Meara), file for bankruptcy and are forced to sell the camp to a weight loss fanatic named Tony Perkins (Ben Stiller), who is seeking to produce a top weight loss infomercial featuring the campers. Ultimately, the campers and counselors plot to overthrow Tony. Once they do, the campers vote to put counselor Pat in charge as they train to defeat their rival camp in an annual competition.

Todd Graff's 2003 film *Camp* focused on a musical camp populated by aspiring performers. Each of the campers comes with both literal and figurative baggage; one boy struggles to relate to his family, while another camper has her jaw wired shut to avoid gaining weight. The campers must come together to perform a new show every two weeks, which presents a significant challenge for all involved. *Summercamp* was released in 2006 and was made by Bradley Beesley and Sarah Price. The film, which proclaimed, "there's s'more to growing up," followed campers as young as six and as old as fifteen to camp for the summer as they made friends, struggled with homesickness, and gained a bit of independence. And finally, Wes Anderson's 2012 film, *Moonrise Kingdom,* was set against the backdrop of Camp Ivanhoe in 1965. Two pre-teens decide to form a pact and run away to live in the wilderness. Ed Norton and Bruce Willis play two of the idiosyncratic adults in search of the children. Perhaps the only camp-related film ever to be nominated for an Academy Award, *Moonrise Kingdom* received a nomination for Best Original Screenplay but ultimately lost.

Though camp provides a great setting for a film, it is virtually impossible to capture the essence of the experience without resorting to stereotypes and trite plotlines. Perhaps one day, Hollywood's best will be able to accurately portray the institution and the accompanying rites and rituals that have defined the adolescence of so many generations.

TV Shows

"Salute Your Shorts" aired on Nickelodeon from 1991 to 1993 and was based on a 1986 book of the same title by Thomas Hill and Steve Slavkin. Though filmed in Los Angeles, the show took place at the fictional Camp Anawanna. The show featured seven campers who spent their summer trying to outsmart their counselor, Kevin "Ug" Lee. Fans have even created a Web site for Anawanna and the show continues to air in reruns. Another popular show produced for the Disney Channel, *"Bug Juice"* chronicled a summer at Camp Wayziyatah in Maine in its first season, at Camp Highlander in North Carolina in its second and at New Mexico's Brush Ranch Camp in its third and final season. The show featured middle school-aged campers and their counselors as they navigated a typical summer at camp. Viewers saw campers try new activities, witnessed young romances blossom, and learned about the stress of living in such close quarters for the summer. Today, a number of fans have created "where are they now" pages highlighting the casts' accomplishments since their days at camp for both *"Bug Juice"* and *"Salute Your Shorts."*

In 2013, a number of television networks seemed to recognize what so many have known for so long: that anything with a summer camp theme is highly marketable. The USA network aired a reality competition called *"Summer Camp"* while NBC greenlit *"Camp,"* a 13-episode foray into daily life at Little Hawk Family Camp. Television shows, like films, are also limited in their ability to truly capture life at summer camp and, while it is tempting to try to do so, perhaps the camp experience is best left not to the reality TV genre, but rather to reality itself.

Books

Numerous books have been set at summer camp, many of which enjoy greater success with audiences than their counterparts on film. Young adult authors and sisters-in-law Joanne and Karen Rock (who write under the pseudonym JK Rock) have penned *Camp Boyfriend* and its prequel, *Camp Kiss.* Karen explains why camp is a perfect setting for a novel geared towards teens:

> Summer camp is literally the place of so many firsts... the first time you live away from home...the first time you learn to miss your little brother...the first time you ate something you cooked yourself (over an open fire!)... the first time you confided secrets in four complete strangers...the first boy you crushed on... the first boy you kissed... the first boy who broke your heart...the first time you felt yourself start to grow (inside and out). I adore summer camp and it has so many possibilities for a writer from the unique characters, the gorgeous settings, the one-of-a-kind experiences, and the "camp-only" traditions. Camp is like a speeded up version of life that renews itself every summer and so too do the campers. In this way, we could create a world in which a lot could happen in a short amount of time, then come back to the amazing world of Camp Juniper Point and focus on other characters.[387]

Joanne echoes these sentiments:

> As a teen, summer time offers a unique opportunity to step out of the normal school cliques and meet new people. You might spend a few weeks with a grandparent or go on vacation, but you're changing your routine and often, your perspective. Summer camp is a fantastic setting for this kind of experience—mixing up the norm and connecting with friends in different ways. You have the chance to really be someone else or—best of all—discover who you really are."[388]

There are dozens and dozens of young adult books set at summer camp. From Paula Danziger's 1980 classic *There's a Bat in Bunk Five* to an American Girl title, *Molly Saves the Day,* camp provides a rich and diverse backdrop for many types of literature including young adult, mystery, and thriller. Some authors have found an eager audience for anything camp-related. For example, author Melissa J. Morgan (a pseudonym) has penned, to date, 25 books in the *Camp Confidential* young adult series. Set at Camp Lakeview, the characters are inspired by girls Morgan knew at the United Nations International School in New York City. Morgan also wrote the series *Summer Confidential* and is set to work on a new series entitled *CITs.* Morgan's books, aimed at readers nine and up, emphasize some general summer camp themes such as acceptance and friendship.

While young adult novels are aimed at current campers, there is a whole different type of literature geared towards adults who long for the lazy days of their youth. Disney CEO Michael Eisner began the trend of reflections on summer camp with his 2005 autobiography *Camp.* The book examines the impact Eisner's experience at Camp Keewaydin had on his future and emphasizes themes similar to anyone who has ever been a camper. Thomas C. Adler's *Campingly Yours* chronicles his experience as a camper at North Star Camp for boys and later as co-director of Chippewa Ranch Camp for girls. Told from the perspective of a reluctant first-time camper who eventually becomes a "lifer," this tender tale of growing up and self-exploration perfectly captures the camp experience. The anthology *Sleepaway* compiled by Eric Simonoff is a delightful compendium of short stories about a host of familiar summer camp experiences including offerings by Margaret Atwood and David Sedaris.

For the moments that words simply cannot describe, Roger Bennett and Jules Shell offer *Camp Camp: Where Fantasy Island Meets Lord of the Flies,* a riotous celebration of summer camps through photos and brief anecdotes. Anyone who attended camp in the 1970s and 1980s is bound to have a shoebox full of photos like those featured in *Camp Camp.* So visceral are the memories of camp evoked that the scent of Coppertone, baby oil, and hairspray wafts out from between the pages.

In the same vein but with more sentiment and less sarcasm is Laurie Susan Kahn's *Sleepaway: The Girls of Summer and the Camps They Love.* Published in 2003 in a scrapbook-like format, Kahn seamlessly weaves together the threads of girls' camp experiences from a variety of different camps as well as her own. Kahn claims that "it was not until 1987, when she was named Vice President, Director of Radio and Television Production, at Young & Rubicam in New York, that she overcame her disappointment at never having been Color War captain."[389]

In short, anyone who has ever attended camp in any capacity understands why authors are inclined to set their work at a camp; camps are microcosms of society with a host of character options and enough built-in drama to keep any plot interesting.

Celebrities at Camp

Celebrities who attended summer camp include actors James Pickens, Jr., and Justin Chambers, Blair Underwood, Chevy Chase, Matt Damon, Leonardo DiCaprio, Courteney Cox, Natalie Portman, Dermot Mulroney, Reese Witherspoon, Julia Roberts, and Paul Newman to name a few. Athletes Dorothy Hamill, Drew Brees, and Kerri Strug, and authors J.D. Salinger, Cathy Guisewite, Michael Thompson, and Dave Barry also spent their summers at camp. Musicians Bob Dylan, Lisa Loeb, Neil Diamond, and Norah Jones were campers, and entrepreneurs Michael Eisner, Martha Stewart, Ralph Lauren, and Sherry Lansing were as well. Even Albert Einstein and Sally Ride attended camps as children as did First Lady Michelle Obama, Chief Justices Sandra Day O'Connor and Ruth Bader Ginsberg, former Secretary of State Condoleeza Rice, and Presidents Ford and Bush.[390] Even first daughter Malia Obama attended camp during her father's first term in office. What does this tell us? That camp appeals to a broad range of children from diverse backgrounds and that there is something for everyone each summer.

In fact, many celebrities have taken to sponsoring or funding summer camp programs. In conjunction with the Fresh Air Fund, Camp Mariah hosts 300 teens who are given the opportunity to explore a variety of career paths. Held at the Fresh Air Fund's Sharpe Reservation, Mariah herself visits the camp and meets with campers. Darryl McDaniels of the band Run DMC works with the New York Foundling to give kids a break from urban life and a chance to enjoy themselves at camp. Former *Cosby Show* darling Keshia Knight Pulliam sponsors Kamp Kizzy which, like Camp Mariah, helps girls explore their leadership skills and career options. Pop star Usher funds Camp New Look which gives campers a taste of sports and entertainment career options. Campers have the chance to network with industry pals of Usher and are treated to an all-star celebrity basketball game at some point during their stay.

Other Summer Camp Memorabilia and Media

Books, television shows, and films aren't the only popular culture venues in which summer camp is explored and celebrated. In 1965, Milton Bradley released a board game called "Camp Granada," which was based on the popular 1963 song "Hello Muddah, Hello Fadduh" written by Allan Sherman. The goal of the game is to return home from camp. In 2003, Dead Ant Games released "Summer Camp" the card game. In this game, each player assumes the identity of a camper and "players do their best to persuade the coolest kids at camp to hang out with them, while simultaneously sending the uber-dorks into other player's cabins. One camper might lead a late night toilet paper attack, while another slips off to the lake for some skinny dipping with a summer fling. Watch out for the visit from grandma and grandpa or the surprising prescription of orthopedic shoes! For every cool person, event and item in your cabin, you garner 'cool points,' while un-cool cards take the same points away."[392]

"CampAntics" is another, more recent board game. Each trip around the board represents a day at camp. Campers may draw mischief cards, become "happy campers," and enjoy sunny days (jackpot spots) while gaining or losing acorns (like currency).[393] Campers and their families will enjoy the opportunity to simulate the camp experience through a board game, especially during the winter while camp seems but a distant memory.

There are even soundtracks to summer camp. No, not the mix tapes or playlists made at the end of the summer to capture the essence of daily life at camp but rather a legitimate album. "Oybaby Presents: We Sang That At Camp—Songs Remembered from Jewish Summer Camp" is a mix of Hebrew and English camp standards that provides a trip down memory lane for anyone who went to a Jewish camp.

The urge to reminisce about such a sacred part of childhood is apparent in the entertainment industry and takes many forms. From young adult novels and memoirs to kitschy films and card games, camp is a vivid memory for millions who hold onto it tightly. Reliving these sacred days through film, television, music, and other forms of entertainment is a means by which people can continue to reminisce about their time at camp.

8
The Camp Experience Through the Years

Invariably, no matter how remote the location of a camp, social trends manage to pervade camp culture. Somehow, each summer, everyone shows up with the same fashions and footwear. Summer reading assignments are remarkably similar among campers, though the books often spend much of the summer on the shelf, necessitating a summer reading cram session once the campers return home. Naturally, music has always played an important role at camp. Not only is singing ubiquitous but records, then 8-tracks, tapes, CDs, and now iPods have provided the soundtrack to rainy days spent in cabins, camp dances, late nights and rest hours. Though the pop culture icons have changed over the years, their presence on posters decorating cabin walls has not.

Here is a (woefully incomplete) list of the music, books, fashions, and trends that conjure visceral memories for campers past and present.

1860s

The Civil War dominated life in the 1860s. However, it was also a time of expansion west. Miles and miles of railroad were laid and the transcontinental telegraph line connected the country's two coasts. Urbanization and trade unions flourished. In the wake of the war, Americans began to enjoy their leisure time with the advent of board games and dime novels. Music was characterized largely by Civil War ballads and those with a religious bent. The 1860s witnessed the birth of burlesque and traveling shows. Technology moved ahead with the advent of the camera, the air brake, and the vacuum cleaner.

1860s Summer Reading

Alice in Wonderland by Lewis Carroll
Great Expectations by Charles Dickens
The Innocents Abroad by Mark Twain
Little Women by Louisa May Alcott
Les Miserables by Victor Hugo
Ragged Dick by Horatio Alger, Jr.
War and Peace by Leo Tolstoy

Songs That Defined the Decade

"The Battle Hymn of the Republic"
"Dixie"
"Battle Cry of Freedom"
"When Johnny Comes Marching Home," Louis Lambert, 1863
"Song of All Songs," Stephen Foster, 1866
"The Blue Danube," Johann Strauss, 1867
"Little Brown Jug," R.E. Eastburn, 1869

What We Wore

the Garibaldi shirt
loose-fitting coats and trousers
suspenders
vests
waistcoats
clothing inspired by Civil War soldiers

1870s

American cities continued to grow exponentially during the Gilded Age and life-altering products were invented. The 1870s saw the development of tomato ketchup, toothpaste, department stores, Ivory soap and barbed wire. P.T. Barnum's three-ring circus was dubbed "The Greatest Show on Earth" and burlesque shows took to the road. DNA was discovered and things became a bit brighter with the invention of the lightbulb. Families enjoyed listening to records on their phonographs; spirituals and war songs remained popular despite the phase of Reconstruction.

1870s Summer Reading

The Adventures of Tom Sawyer by Mark Twain
The Age of Innocence by Edith Wharton
Anna Karenina by Leo Tolstoy
Around the World in Eighty Days by Jules Verne
Black Beauty by Anna Seawell
Little Men by Louisa May Alcott

Songs That Defined the Decade

"The Ride of the Valkyries"
"Up from Somerset"
"The Dingle Puck Goat"
"The Little Old Log Cabin in the Lane," William Shakespeare Hays, 1871
"Silver Threads Among the Gold," H.P. Danks, 1873

What We Wore

sack suits
short, flat, oiled hair
colorful, heavily starched shirts
girls' skirt lengths determined by their age
Little Lord Fauntleroy suits for boys

1880s

With the Industrial Revolution in full swing, Americans were on the go more than ever. Immigrants began to flood the United States, the nationwide railway system was completed, and factories were ubiquitous. Most children were educated in one-room schoolhouses. Gilbert and Sullivan operettas became popular while touring the country. Most homes had running water, gas, and electricity. Men wore the sack suit while women still donned dresses and corsets. Tennis and croquet were popular recreational activities, and football was created. Researchers began to explore ways to address public health concerns while sociologists promoted the idea of social Darwinism.

1880s Summer Reading

Adventures of Huck Finn by Mark Twain
The Brothers Karamazov by Fyodor Dostoevsky
A Connecticut Yankee in King Arthur's Court by Mark Twain
Dr. Jekyll & Mr. Hyde by Robert Louis Stevenson
Treasure Island by Robert Louis Stevenson

Songs That Defined the Decade

"My Darling Clementine"
"Sweet Violets"
"In the Evening by the Moonlight"
"The Big Ship Sails"

What We Wore

corsets
ditto suits
Norfolk jackets
narrower skirts
cutaway jackets
sack suits

1890s

Skyscrapers began to dominate urban skylines across America in the 1890s. Immigrants continue to pour into the United States to the point that the federal government opened Ellis Island to accommodate them. So-called "separate but equal" educational facilities were the standard and public education began to take shape. Americans enjoyed their leisure time by riding bicycles, dancing the two-step and watching Buffalo Bill's Wild West Show while basketball became a popular new pastime. The gas-powered automobile allowed Americans great mobility and the ability to explore their ever-expanding nation.

1890s Summer Reading
The Adventures of Sherlock Holmes by Sir Arthur Conan Doyle
The Awakening by Kate Chopin
Dracula by Bram Stoker
Heart of Darkness by Joseph Conrad
The Island of Doctor Moreau by H.G. Wells
The Jungle Book by Rudyard Kipling
The Picture of Dorian Gray by Oscar Wilde
The Red Badge of Courage by Stephen Crane
Tess of the d'Urbervilles by Thomas Hardy
The Turn of the Screw by Henry James
The War of the Worlds by H.G. Wells

Songs That Defined the Decade
"Won't You Be My Sweetheart?" H.C. Verner, 1893
"A Hot Time in the Old Town," Theodore Metz, 1896
"Stars and Stripes Forever," John Philip Sousa, 1898
"Hello! Ma Baby," Joseph E. Howard, 1899
"Original Rags," Scott Joplin, 1899

What We Wore
bicycling dress or tennis dress
walking suits for women
Turkish trousers and "cycling costumes"
bowler and boater hats
Leg-o-mutton (gigot) sleeves

1900s and 1910s

The first decade of the century brought about many possibilities. With the Wright Brothers' 1903 flight and the introduction of Ford's Model T in 1908, Americans were on the move. The first junior high school was established in Columbus, Ohio, indicating that Americans were beginning to recognize and acknowledge the needs of pre-teens and teens. Sadly, however, many boys and girls, even those of school age, were forced to work due to the dire economic situation faced by their families. Teens were often found visiting amusement parks, going to the nickelodeon or the penny arcade. Church groups and the scout movements were popular ways to place limits on teens who might otherwise find trouble. The second decade of the century witnessed significant tragedies including the First World War (1914-1919), the sinking of the *Titanic* (1912), and a flu epidemic (1918-1919). Camp, therefore, was a perfect antidote to this culture.

1900s Summer Reading
Anne of Green Gables by L.M Montgomery
The Call of the Wild by Jack London
The Jungle by Upton Sinclair
Just So Stories by Rudyard Kipling
Rebecca of Sunnybrook Farm by Kate Douglas Wiggin
A Room with a View by E.M. Forster
A Tree Grows in Brooklyn by Betty Smith
The Wind in the Willows by Kenneth Grahame
The Wonderful Wizard of Oz by L. Frank Baum

1910s Summer Reading
Ethan Frome by Edith Wharton
Howard's End by E.M Forster
The Metamorphosis by Franz Kafka
My Antonia by Willa Cather
Penrod by Booth Tarkington
Peter Pan by J.M. Barrie
The Phantom of the Opera by Gaston Leroux
Pollyanna by Eleanor H. Porter
Pygmalion by George Bernard Shaw
The Secret Garden by Frances Hodgson Burnet
Seventeen by Booth Tarkington
Tarzan of the Apes by Edgar Rice Burroughs

Songs That Defined the Decade

"In the Good Old Summertime," George Evans, 1902
"In My Merry Oldsmobile," Gus Edwards, 1905
"Let Me Call You Sweetheart," Peerless Quartet, 1910
" By the Light of the Silvery Moon," Billy Murray & Haydn Quartet, 1910
"For Me and My Gal," Van & Schenk, 1917
Ragtime
Anything that the Turkey Trot, Bunny Hug, Monkey Glide, Possum Trot or the Grizzly Bear could be danced to

What We Wore

"The Gibson Girl look"
sailor-style dresses
high collared dresses
knickers for boys
short hair for boys, very long hair for girls

1920s

Americans in the 1920s were relieved to see an end to World War I, though international tensions still existed. Technology began to boom as vacuums, refrigerators, and processed food became staples of middle class life. Though some teens still held either part- or full-time jobs, many more were able to continue with their education through high school as families became a bit more economically stable (until the stock market crash in 1929, of course). Teens also had greater mobility in response to the growth of the automobile industry. This, along with significant changes in fashion (especially for girls) and racier films, led many parents to worry about what their children were doing in their free time.

Summer camps of the 1920s continued as a response to what was perceived as the threat of urbanization and industrialization. Camps were a healthy alternative to city living and offered children the opportunity to be outside in the fresh air. The idea of camps fit perfectly into the Jazz Age and the enjoyment of leisure that defined the decade.

Summer Reading in the 1920s

The Age of Innocence by Edith Wharton
All Quiet on the Western Front by Erich Maria Remarque
Babbit by Sinclair Lewis
The Boxcar Children by Gertrude Chandler Warner
Gentlemen Prefer Blondes by Anita Loos
The Great Gatsby by F. Scott Fitzgerald
Main Street by Sinclair Lewis
This Side of Paradise by F. Scott Fitzgerald
The Story of Doctor Dolittle by Hugh Lofting
The Sun Also Rises by Ernest Hemingway

Songs That Defined the Decade

"I'll Be With You in Apple Blossom Time," The Andrews Sisters, 1920
"Ain't We Got Fun?" Van & Schenck, 1921
" I'm Just Wild About Harry," Noble Sissle, 1921
"Swanee," Al Jolson, 1920
"It Had to Be You," Isham Jones, 1924
"Sweet Georgia Brown," Ben Bernie, 1925
"Makin' Whoopee," Eddie Cantor, 1925
"My Blue Heaven," Gene Austin, 1927
"Am I Blue?" Ethel Waters, 1929
"When You're Smiling," Louis Armstrong, 1929
"Someone to Watch Over Me," Gertrude Lawrence, 1927
Music from Tin Pan Alley
Anything to which they could do the Tottle, the Black Bottom, the Varsity Drag, or the Charleston

What We Wore

"the Bob" or "the Eton" hairstyles for women
flapper fashion ("shebas")
lower necklines, dropped waistlines, bare knees and ankles
one-piece bathing suits
middies
bloomers
short, loose dresses for girls
sailor suits
short pants for boys
sport clothing (V-neck sweaters, open collared shirts)

1930s

The Great Depression irrefutably affected every aspect of American life. Teens were often forced to drop out of school and find work to help their family through the hard economic times. Some schools even had to close as a result of economic hardships; this gave pre-teens and teens an abundance of unstructured time and caused their parents great worry. Camp, for those who could afford it, was the perfect antidote to such idleness. While at camp, however, children and teens would miss out on whatever movies were in the theaters during the summer and the latest comic books wouldn't be read until they returned home.

Summer Reading in the 1930s

Anthony Adverse by Erle Stanley Gardner
Gone with the Wind by Margaret Mitchell
The Good Earth by Pearl Buck
Goodbye, Mr. Chips by James Hilton
The Grapes of Wrath by John Steinbeck
The Importance of Living by Lin Yutang
Of Mice and Men by John Steinbeck
Rebecca by Daphne du Maurier
The Sword in the Stone by Terence Hanbury White
The Yearling by Marjorie Kinnan Rawlings

Songs That Defined the Decade

"Happy Days Are Here Again," Ben Selvin, 1930
"I've Got Five Dollars," Rodgers and Hart, 1931
"Goodnight Sweetheart," Guy Lombardo, 1931
"Stormy Weather," Ethel Waters, 1933
"Pennies from Heaven," Bing Crosby, 1936
"The Way You Look Tonight," Fred Astaire, 1936
One o'clock Jump," Count Basie, 1937
"In the Mood," Glenn Miller Orchestra, 1939
"Over the Rainbow," Judy Garland, 1939

What We Wore

simple print dresses for girls and women or dresses of varying lengths
neutral colored, one piece swimsuits for women
scarves and fedoras
high waisted pants, sweater vests and hats for men
anything with the newly invented zipper!
butterfly sleeves and banjo sleeves
beach pajamas
halter tops

1940s

The 1940s were ushered in with World War II. School children were preoccupied with the war overseas as older teens watched their friends and relatives go off to fight. Families experienced rations, many women went off to join the work force for the first time, and teens were asserting themselves at home. Campers would, of course, miss the latest television and radio program while at camp; surely updates on *The Lone Ranger* and *The Cisco Kid* were given in letters sent from home. The same went for comic strips; campers, no doubt, wondered what the latest turn of events was in "Popeye" and "Donald Duck." And the drive-in would simply have to wait until the summer was over.

The New York Times published "A Teen-Age Bill of Rights" in 1945, which was intended to help "guide" parents when raising their teens. The article stated that teens had:

1. The right to let childhood be forgotten.
2. The right to a "say" about his own life.
3. The right to make mistakes, and to find out for himself.
4. The right to have rules explained, not imposed.
5. The right to have fun and companions.
6. The right to question ideas.
7. The right to be at the Romantic Age.
8. The right to a fair chance and opportunity.
9. The right to struggle toward his own philosophy of life.
10. The right to professional help when necessary.[394]

Summer camp, then, provided a perfect environment in which to exercise these rights. The federal government even sponsored some camps with nationalistic fervor; the Civilian Conservation Core (CCC) and the National Youth Administration (NYA) sponsored camps that emphasized "better physical condition [and] a better mental attitude."[395]

Summer Reading in the 1940s

All the King's Men by Robert Penn Warren
Animal Farm by George Orwell
The Big Fisherman by Lloyd C. Douglas
The Doll's House by Rumer Godden
For Whom the Bell Tolls by Ernest Hemingway
Going on Sixteen by Betty Cavana
The Hardy Boys series by Franklin W. Dixon
The Keys to the Kingdom by A.J. Cronin
The Miracle of the Bells by Russell Jancy
Mrs. Miniver by Jan Struther
Nancy Drew books by Carolyn Keene
Native Son by Richard Wright
Seventeenth Summer by Maureen Daly

Songs That Defined the Decade

"I'll Never Smile Again," Frank Sinatra and the Tommy Dorsey Orchestra, 1940
"Only Forever," Bing Crosby, 1940
"I Don't Want to Set the World on Fire," The Ink Spots, 1941
"Amapola"Jimmy Dorsey, 1941
"Boogie Woogie Bugle Boy of Company B," Andrews Sisters, 1941
"Chattanooga Choo Choo," Glenn Miller Orchestra, 1941
"String of Pearls," Glenn Miller Orchestra, 1942
"Paper Dolls," The Mills Brothers, 1943
" I'm Making Believe," Ella Fitzgerald and the Ink Spots, 1943
"Sentimental Journey," Doris Day and the Les Brown Orchestra, 1945
"It's Been a Long Long Time," Harry James and Helen Forest, 1945
"Lover Man," Billie Holiday, 1945
"I Love You for Sentimental Reasons," Nat King Cole, 1946
"Some Enchanted Evening," Perry Como, 1949
Anything that kids could Jitterbug to

What We Wore

rolled up jeans
halter tops
cork-soled shoes
Hawaiian shirts
Eisenhower jackets
overalls
pin curls and long bob hairstyles for girls and "boogie cuts" for boys
pleated, plaid skirts
bobby sox

1950s

Despite the beginning of the Cold War and the rise of McCarthyism, the 1950s were a relatively stable era. Life in the suburbs was booming and teens enjoyed new freedoms and influences like television. School sports and cheerleading were popular as were teen clubs and sock hops. But all of that school-year activity was put on hold when children and teens left for the summer to attend camp; no doubt a number of *MAD* magazines and perhaps even the contraband issue of *Playboy* were smuggled in duffle bags to camp. Families had more economic stability, which meant that more children and teens were able to attend camps. The wholesome fun offered by camps was perfectly in keeping with the cultural values and norms of the 1950s.

Summer Reading in the 1950s

Atlas Shrugged by Ayn Rand
The Catcher in the Rye by J.D. Salinger
Charlotte's Web by E.B. White
Crypt of Terror, The Haunt of Fear and *Crime Does Not Pay* comics
Doctor Zhivago by Boris Pasternak
East of Eden by John Steinbeck
Eloise by Kay Thompson
Exodus by Leon Uris
The Family Under the Bridge by Natalie Savage Carlson
From Here to Eternity by James Jones
MAD magazine
Marjorie Morningstar by Herman Wouk
The Old Man and the Sea by Ernest Hemingway
Peyton Place by Grace Metalious
Seventeen magazine
Street Rod by Henry Gregor Felsen
The Wheel on the School by Meindert DeJong

Songs That Defined the Decade

"Rock Around the Clock," Bill Haley & His Comets, 1953
" Blue Suede Shoes," Carl Perkins, 1955
"Only You," The Platters, 1955
"Unchained Melody," The Platters, 1955
"In the Still of the Night," Five Satins, 1956
"Goodnight My Love," The McGuire Sisters, 1956
"Hound Dog," Elvis Presley, 1956
"Blueberry Hill," Fats Domino, 1957
"Wake Up Little Susie," The Everly Brothers, 1957
"Jailhouse Rock," Elvis Presley, 1957
"Whole Lot of Shakin' Going On," Jerry Lee Lewis, 1957
"La Bamba," Ritchie Valens, 1958
"Johnny B. Goode," Chuck Berry, 1958
"I Only Have Eyes for You," The Flamingos, 1959

What We Wore

the bobby-soxer look
sleeveless dresses
Ray Ban Wayfarers
pedal pushers
crew cuts, flat tops and pompadours
the DA (duck's ass hair style)
Bermuda shorts
chinos
madras plaid
poodle skirts
saddle shoes
jeans
penny loafers
leather jackets
anything pink and black

1960s

The hope and optimism that were ushered in with John F. Kennedy's election were soon dashed as the conflict in Vietnam escalated. A number of high-profile assassinations and racial conflicts put the country on edge. Parents, especially those worried about the influence of hippie culture, were only too glad to send their children off to camp for a few weeks or months.

Summer camps provided an important escape for children of the 1960s; coming of age in an era of war, protests and violence took its toll on the younger generation. At home, campers may have experienced their mothers grappling with the new concept of feminism or older siblings being drafted so arriving at camp was a much-needed break from a tense society. It was, no doubt, a challenge for girls to maintain their bouffant hairstyles and for boys to keep their Nehru jackets clean and wrinkle-free while at camp. Although campers would miss watching *American Bandstand* while away, at least they were able to keep up with new music by listening to FM radio, a new invention.

Summer Reading in the 1960s

The Andromeda Strain by Michael Chriton
Charlotte Sometimes by Penelope Farmer
The Chosen by Chaim Potok
The Contender by Robert Lipsyte
The Egypt Game by Zilpha Keatley Snyder
Franny and Zooey by J.D. Salinger
Glamour, *Mademoiselle,* and *Rolling Stone* magazines
The Godfather by Mario Puzo
Island of the Blue Dolphins by Scott O'Dell
To Kill a Mockingbird by Harper Lee
Legion of Super Heroes comics
The Outsiders by S.E. Hinton
Tropic of Cancer by Henry Miller
Valley of the Dolls by Jacqueline Susann

Songs That Defined the Decade

"This Magic Moment," Jay & the Americans, 1960
"Stand By Me," Ben E. King, 1961
"Will You Love Me Tomorrow," Shirelles, 1961
"The Locomotion," Little Eva, 1962
"Surfin Safari," The Beach Boys, 1962
"Louie Louie," Kingsmen, 1963
"Blue Velvet," Bobby Vinton, 1963
"Surfin' USA," The Beach Boys, 1963
"Wipe Out," Surfaris, 1963
"I Feel Good," James Brown, 1964
"Dancing in the Street," Martha & the Vandellas, 1964
"You Really Got Me," The Kinks, 1964
"Don't Worry Baby," The Beach Boys, 1964
"In My Life," The Beatles, 1965
"Good Vibrations," The Beach Boys, 1966
"I'm a Believer," The Monkees, 1966
"The Monkees," The Monkees, 1966
"Respect," Aretha Franklin, 1967
"Soul Man," Sam & Dave, 1967
"Nights in White Satin," The Moody Blues, 1967
"Hey Jude," The Beatles, 1968
"Born To Be Wild," Steppenwolf, 1968
"Mony Mony," Tommy James & the Shondells, 1968
Anything teens could do the Twist, the Mashed Potato, the Frug or the Watusi to

What We Wore

bell bottoms
fringed vests
mini-skirts
go-go boots
peace signs
tie-dye
Indian print dresses
patchwork skirts
love beads
granny glasses
preppy or Ivy League look
Madras and Bermuda shorts
bouffant or cropped hair for girls

1970s

The United States entered the 1970s with a sigh of relief that the tumultuous 1960s were over in spite of the continued conflict in Vietnam. While some campers may have adopted pet rocks while at camp, their Sea-Monkeys and lava lamps had to be left at home for safe keeping. Those who followed television may have been disappointed to miss new episodes of *Happy Days, The Wonderful World of Walt Disney, The Brady Bunch,* and *The Sonny and Cher Show* while away from home. Girls may have found it difficult to make their way around the grounds in clogs and platform shoes and fortunately, most boys opted to leave their leisure suits at home. Lines from *Star Wars, Rocky, The Godfather,* and *Jaws* were regularly quoted and often made their way into camp skits. Campers lay on their beds reading *Mrs. Frisby and the Rats of NIMH, Bridge to Terabithia,* and *Roll of Thunder, Hear My Cry* during rest hours and rainy days.

Summer Reading in the 1970s

A Hero Ain't Nothing but a Sandwich by Alice Childress
Anastasia Krupnik by Lois Lowry
Are You There God? It's Me, Margaret by Judy Blume
Blubber by Judy Blume
Carrie by Stephen King
The Chocolate War by Robert Cormier
The Exorcist by William Blatty
Forever by Judy Blume
Go Ask Alice by Anonymous
I Am the Cheese by Robert Cormier
Jaws by Peter Benchley
Jonathan Livingston Seagull by Richard Bach
Love Story by Erich Segal
Otherwise Known as Sheila the Great by Judy Blume
Rabbit Redux by John Updike
Rich Man, Poor Man by Irwin Shaw
Roll of Thunder, Hear My Cry by Mildred D. Taylor
Rumble Fish by S.E. Hinton
Summer of My German Soldier by Bette Greene
Tales of a Fourth Grade Nothing by Judy Blume
Tinker, Tailor, Soldier, Spy by John le Carre
Watership Down by Richard Adams
The Winds of War by Herman Wouk

Songs That Defined the Decade

"Your Song," Elton John, 1970
"Stairway to Heaven," Led Zeppelin, 1971
"If You Don't Know Me by Now," Harold Melvin & the Blue Notes, 1972
"Angie," The Rolling Stones, 1973
"Let's Get It On," Marvin Gaye, 1973
"Lady Marmalade," LaBelle, 1974
"Can't Get Enough of Your Love, Babe," Barry White, 1974
"The Hustle," Van McCoy, 1975
"Bohemian Rhapsody," Queen, 1975
"Play That Funky Music," Wild Cherry, 1976
"Hotel California," The Eagles, 1976
"Disco Inferno," The Trammps, 1976
"Stayin' Alive," The Bee Gees, 1977
"I Will Survive," Gloria Gaynor, 1978
"Heart of Glass," Blondie, 1978
"Old Time Rock and Roll," Bob Seeger, 1978
"I Wanna Be Sedated," The Ramones, 1978
"Le Freak," Chic, 1978
"Good Times," Chic, 1979
"Rapper's Delight," The Sugar Hill Gang, 1979

What We Wore

anything made of denim
leotards
bell bottoms
mini-skirts and dresses
hot pants
cut-off jeans shorts
ironed hair
the hag hairstyle
cloche hats
wide-collared, tight-fitting shirts for boys
leisure suits

1980s

Campers of the 1980s left behind MTV, Atari, and Rubik's Cubes when they came to camp. They did, however, make sure to pack their leg warmers, parachute pants and Members Only jackets lest they not be fashionable. No doubt there were more than a few disagreements between the Preps and the Punks. It is likely that more than a few Cabbage Patch dolls spent summers adorning the beds of campers nationwide, while posters of Kirk Cameron hung from cabin walls everywhere.

Countless rest hours were spent playing M.A.S.H., which was certain to tell everyone's future in terms of where they would live, whom they would marry, what kind of car they would drive and how many children they would have. The camp store stocked Skittles, Nerds, Runts, Five Alive, gummy bears, and SweeTarts. Care packages may have included Rubik's Cubes and graphic novels. VCRs at home were set to record *The Cosby Show, Family Ties,* and *Miami Vice* while campers were away. Gimp and macramé remained staples of arts and crafts programs. Girls read *Jacob Have I Loved, Dicey's Song,* and *Sarah, Plain and Tall* until flashlights had to be turned off. Scenes from *Dirty Dancing* were re-enacted over and over at camp dances.

Was camp in the '80s totally radical? No duh.

Summer Reading in the 1980s

Beyond the Chocolate War by Robert Cormier
The Castle in the Attic by Elizabeth Winthrop
Contact by Carl Sagan
The Firm by John Grisham
Homecoming by Cynthia Voigt
Lake Wobegon Days by Garrison Keillor
Masquerade by Kit Williams
Sassy and *Young Miss* magazines
The *Sweet Valley High* series by Francine Pascal
The Sum of All Fears by Tom Clancy
Tiger Eyes by Judy Blume

Songs That Defined the Decade

"Keep On Loving You," REO Speedwagon, 1980
"What I Like About You," The Romantics, 1980
"Shook Me," AC/DC, 1980
"Mickey," Tony Basil, 1981
"Super Freak," Rick James, 1981
"Tempted," Squeeze, 1981
"In the Air Tonight," Phil Collins, 1981
"Don't Stop Believing," Journey, 1981
"Jenny/867-5309," Tommy Tutone, 1981
"Jessie's Girl," Rick Springfield, 1981
"Beat It," Michael Jackson, 1982
"Come on Eileen," Dexy's Midnight Runners, 1982
"Down Under," Men at Work, 1982
"Thriller," Michael Jackson, 1982
"Walking on Sunshine," Katrina and the Waves, 1983
"99 Luftballoons," Nena, 1983
"Total Eclipse of the Heart," Bonnie Tyler, 1983
"Sister Christian," Night Ranger, 1983
"Jump," Van Halen, 1984
"Girls Just Want to Have Fun," Cyndi Lauper, 1984
"Like a Virgin," Madonna, 1984
"Wake Me Up Before You Go-Go," Wham!, 1984
"We're Not Gonna Take It," Twisted Sister, 1984
"Material Girl," Madonna, 1984
"I Want to Know What Love Is," Foreigner, 1984
"Purple Rain," Prince, 1984
"Time After Time," Cyndi Lauper, 1984
"Born in the USA," Bruce Springsteen, 1984
"Take on Me," A-Ha, 1985
"Fight for Your Right," Beastie Boys, 1986
"Walk Like an Egyptian," The Bangles, 1986
"Walk This Way," Run DMC, 1986
"Push It," Salt-n-Pepa, 1986
"With or Without You," U2, 1987
"Bust a Move," Young MC, 1989

"Love Shack," The B-52s, 1989
"Wild Thing," Tone Loc, 1989
Music you could "mosh" to or do line dances to

What We Wore
neon colors
shoulder pads
leggings
penny loafers
lace
Fair Isle sweaters
Quiksilver and OP shorts
polo shirts with popped collars
Ray Ban Aviators
designer labels (Izod, Liz Claiborne, Gucci, Sassoon, etc.)
parachute pants
bandanas
leg warmers
Mohawks, permed hair, side pony tails, teased hair
lots of jewelry

Camp Granada

Written by Allan Sherman

Hello Muddah, hello Fadduh,
Here I am at Camp Granada.
Camp is very entertaining,
And they say we'll have some fun if it stops raining.

I went hiking with Joe Spivey.
He developed poison ivy.
You remember Leonard Skinner.
He got ptomaine poisoning last night after dinner.

All the counselors hate the waiters,
And the lake has alligators.
And the head coach wants no sissies,
So he reads to us from something called Ulysses.

Now I don't want this should scare ya,
But my bunk mate has malaria.
You remember Jeffrey Hardy.
They're about to organize a searching party.

Take me home, oh Muddah, Fadduh,
Take me home, I hate Granada,
Don't leave me out here in the forest, where
I might get eaten by a bear.

Take me home, I promise I will not make noise,
Or mess the house with other boys.
Oh please don't make me stay,
I've been here one whole day.

Dearest Fadduh, darling Muddah,
How's my precious little Bruddah?
Let me come home if you miss me.
I would even let Aunt Bertha hug and kis me.

Wait a minute, it stopped hailing.
Guys are swimming, guys are sailing.
Playing baseball, gee that's better.
Muddah, Fadduh, kindly disregard this letter![391]

1990s

Emerging from a decade of blinding neon, campers of the 1990s seemed to have matured into young adults with little warning. Perhaps the result of increasing amounts of technology, this new societal norm was relaxed upon one's arrival at camp. Summer reading selections included *Holes, The Giver, Maniac Magee,* and the *Chicken Soup for the Soul* books. Campers had to turn off their enormous cell phones and Nintendos at home though the portable CD player most likely made the cut when packing. Younger campers may have had to limit the number of Beanie Babies they packed while parents were left strict instructions for tending to the Tamagotchi pets left in their care.

Summer Reading in 1990s

Catherine, Called Birdy by Karen Cushman
Divine Secrets of the Ya-Ya Sisterhood by Rebecca Wells
The *Goosebumps* series by R.L. Stine
The *Harry Potter* series by J.K. Rowling
Into the Wild by Jon Krakauer
Into Thin Air by Jon Krakauer
The Giver by Lois Lowry
The Golden Compass Philip Pullman
Holes by Louis Sachar
Maniac Magee by Jerry Spinelli
The Perks of Being a Wallflower by Stephen Chbosky
Tuesdays With Morrie by Mitch Albom
The Watsons Go to Birmingham by Christopher Paul Curtis
Wicked: The Life and Times of the Wicked Witch of the West by Gregory Maguire

Songs That Defined the Decade

"The Humpty Dance," Digital Underground, 1990
"Ice Ice Baby," Vanilla Ice, 1990
"Vogue," Madonna, 1990
"U Can't Touch This," MC Hammer, 1990
"Groove Is in the Heart," Deee-Lite, 1990
"Nothing Compares to You," Sinead O'Connor, 1990
"One," U2, 1991
"Gonna Make You Sweat," C+C Music Factory, 1991
"I'm Too Sexy," Right Said Fred, 1992
"Jump Around," House of Pain, 1992
"Baby Got Back," Sir Mix-A-Lot, 1992
"I Will Always Love You," Whitney Houston, 1992
"Damn I Wish I Was Your Lover," Sophie B. Hawkins, 1992
"I Don't Want to Wait," Paula Cole, 1992
"Poison," Bell Biv DeVoe, 1993
"Linger," The Cranberries, 1993
"Wonderwall," Oasis, 1995
"Killing Me Softly With His Song," The Fugees, 1996
"My Heart Will Go On*Celine Dion, 1997
"MMMBop," Hanson, 1997
"Wannabe," Spice Girls, 1997
"You're Still the One," Shania Twain, 1998
"I'll Be," Edwin McCain, 1998
"Gettin' Jiggy With It," Will Smith, 1998
"Baby One More Time," Britney Spears, 1999
"Livin' La Vida Loca," Ricky Martin, 1999

What We Wore

overall shorts
floral dresses
flannel shirts
parachute pants
Doc Marten shoes
Converse sneakers
hair scrunchies
Umbro shorts
bodysuits
Champion sweatshirts
jeans
sneakers of all shapes, colors and sizes
"The Rachel" hairstyle for girls
hair extensions, braids, temporary hair color
baseball caps

2000s

In the wake of a hotly contested election, George Bush assumed the presidency and months later, America suffered the worst terrorist attack on its soil to date; the following summer in 2002, summer camps played an important part in the healing process for victims' families and their children. Technology seemed to explode with the invention of the iPod and, later, the iPad, the creation of YouTube, MySpace, and Facebook as well as the Wii gaming system. And while what's old is new again, campers and counselors arrived at camp looking much like their 1980s preppy counterparts with trunks full of madras shorts, Lilly Pulitzer dresses, and Vineyard Vines polo shirts.

Summer Reading in 2000s

The Da Vinci Code by Dan Brown
The *Divergent* series by Veronica Roth
The *Harry Potter* series by J.K. Rowling
The Hunger Games trilogy
The Lovely Bones by Alice Sebold
The *Percy Jackson* series by Rick Riordan
The Perks of Being a Wallflower by Stephen Chbosky
Sisterhood of the Traveling Pants by Ann Brashares
The *Twilight* series by Stephenie Meyer

Songs That Defined the Decade

"Oops! I Did It Again," Britney Spears, 2000
"Drops of Jupiter," Train, 2001
"I Hope You Dance," LeAnn Womack, 2001
"Fallin'," Alicia Keys, 2001
"Get the Party Started," Pink, 2001
"Crazy In Love," Beyonce, 2003
"Hey Ya!" OutKast, 2003
"Since U Been Gone," Kelly Clarkson, 2004
"Hollaback Girl," Gwen Stefani, 2005
"You're Beautiful," James Blunt, 2005
"SexyBack," Justin Timberlake, 2006
"Single Ladies," Beyonce, 2008
"Chasing Pavements," Adele, 2008
"I Gotta Feeling," Black Eyed Peas, 2009
"Bad Romance," Lady Gaga, 2009
"Call Me Maybe," Carly Rae Jepsen, 2012
"What Makes You Beautiful," One Direction, 2012
"We Found Love," Rhianna, 2012
"Sexy and I Know It," LMFAO, 2012

What We Wore

Lacrosse pinneys
Soffee shorts
UGGs
Crocs
skinny jeans
flip flops
Lilly Pulitzer dresses
Vineyard Vines clothing
hoodies

Learning to function independently and mastering the art of teamwork are essential lessons learned at camp.
Photo courtesy of Camp Wekeela.

Summer Camps in the 21st Century

In the June/July 2012 issue of *Town & Country*, a feature entitled "Camp Tales" ran, which highlighted a variety of different summer camps and the common themes they share: "Mosquito bites. Homesickness. Merit Badges. Capsized canoes. Great stories (and friends) for life. Camp remains an American rite of passage preserved in the glow of perpetual summer—impervious to iPads, brimming with nostalgia, and, it seems, as popular as ever."[396]

As previously stated, one of the main reasons so many campers and counselors return to their camps summer after summer is the sense of tradition and the annual activities and events that take place without fail. Perhaps most important is that the values camps seek to instill have gone largely unchanged. Independence, self-confidence, leadership, resourcefulness, and a sense of community are just some of the qualities camps strive to promote. In spite of the abundance of technology available to children and adults today, most camp directors are working hard to keep their camps free of electronic distractions; after all, camps are "people places" where the focus is on developing interpersonal relationships.

The American Camp Association cites the operation of approximately 12,000 camps in the United States. Of these, 7000 are dedicated overnight camps and 5000 are day camps. The ACA also states that "88% of ACA-accredited camps offer swimming, 48% offer horseback riding, 22% offer wilderness programs, 12% travel/tour programs, 57% teambuilding, and 21% community service."[397] This indicates that many summer camp activities remain, at their core, the same as those that characterized the earliest camps. And although families seek some modern amenities, for the most part they also desire the authentic camp experience for their children. Scholar Leslie Paris explains that "no camp culture is frozen in time...camps have always run a middle course between continuity and change. While they promise old-fashioned pleasures, they have also continually adapted to new ideas in children's recreation and in American culture at large."[398]

Jeff Cheley explains, "It is definitely a different world. Parents are more protective of their children and want them to have every advantage they can have. The idea of unplugging and experiencing unstructured play can be difficult to understand. They are used to having full access to teachers, coaches and other people involved in their child's life."[399] Hence, the summer camp experience is important for both the child attending camp and for the parents sending the child to camp. Parents begin to realize that their children are perhaps more self-reliant and independent than they give them credit for at home, and children realize that taking responsibility for themselves and working through a challenging situation on their own feels good. A recent article by Marla Coleman refers to psychologist Madeline Levine's theory that camp is the antidote to overparenting.[400] Coleman suggests that "a counselor is not invested in the same way as a parent who, understandably, finds it hard to endorse a 'successful failure,' which provides the traction for mastery. And yet successful failure is exactly what we encourage at camp, along with an invitation for exploration and collaboration and manageable risk taking."[401] Further, she asserts, "if every child had a camp experience, we might just be able to stem the tide of overzealous parenting—because then all children would benefit from the 'try something new' environment of camp and the inevitable outcomes of believing in their own abilities to achieve their goals and picture their successes."[402]

> *Camp and school are the yin and yang of education: If school is the science of learning, then camp is the art of navigating the sometimes choppy waters of learning and life.*[403]

A camper enjoys a makeshift waterslide to beat the heat on a hot summer day. *Photo courtesy of Kari Ahern.*

According to www.therightcamp.com, some of the most "exciting summer camp trends" include healthier food options, community service projects, going green, rookie days or weekends, and "cutting edge fun."[404] One instance of an exemplary service project is the Cape Cod Sea Camps' involvement with and dedication to the Pan-Mass Challenge. An annual two-day, 192-mile bike ride across Massachusetts, the PMC is a fundraiser for the Dana-Farber Cancer Institute. Each year, the entire CCSC community participates in a week of fundraisers to sponsor the camp's team. Events include a pie toss, pizza and bake sales, staff car washes, and a Zumba-thon to raise money. Staff members volunteer to work the overnight and early morning shifts, making breakfast for the riders at the Massachusetts Maritime Academy and helping riders load luggage into trailers. The resident camp wakes up extra-early on the Sunday morning of the event and lines up along "Da Hedge" (the edge of the camp that borders Route 6A along which bikers ride) to cheer on riders while the oldest campers serve breakfast on the field. This service project is personal to the entire CCSC community, many members of which have family members who have been touched by cancer; to date, the camp's PMC team has raised over one million dollars. Campers and staff enjoy the opportunity to come together as a community and help others. Often, they are motivated to return to their hometowns and communities and participate in other service activities.

The Cape Cod Sea Camps team rides in the Pan-Mass Challenge every year to benefit the Dana Farber Cancer Institute. The team stops at "Da Hedge" where the entire camp community is stationed to cheer on riders. *Photo courtesy of Kari Ahern.*

Campers enjoying themselves, even without technology!
Photo courtesy of Gold Arrow Camp.

21st Century Challenges

Today's summer camps are working hard to keep up with the needs and demands of twenty-first century campers and their families. Some camps have started offering shorter stays rather than expecting families to commit to one- or two-month sessions. These week-long, ten day or two-week sessions are perfect for novice campers who want to try out a brief stay or sample several different camps or for those who have other commitments like family trips or required sports camps.

> *For most, given the choice between Angry Birds and Color War, it's really no choice at all.*
>
> —Ash Carter [405]

Today, the very notion of summer camp is threatened by the push by some for year-round schools and increased time on learning. What many policymakers fail to see is that school is no substitute for the lessons learned at summer camp. Although camps do not offer direct instruction in content areas like math and English, they do offer an opportunity to improve one's self-esteem and resiliency and to meet other developmental needs like creative expression. American Camp Association CEO Peg Smith explains, "It's just possible that our children are beginning to lag behind other nations in academic achievement because we are focusing on the wrong things. Teaching children to pass standardized tests doesn't necessarily teach them to think for themselves. Education is about more than teaching answers; it's about equipping our kids with the ability to develop the art of seeing the possibilities."[406] Smith adds, "Perhaps the answer lies beyond the classroom in much more natural, developmental settings that promote experiential learning, improve social skills and physical fitness, teach kids to take calculated risks in a safe environment, and expand the creative mind. With the current trend in our education system, we are leaving little room for innovation. What's more, institutionalizing children endangers the ages and stages of childhood development and threatens the maturation process that produces healthy, productive adults."[407]

Camps provide a sense of community that is not often experienced in today's world. Whereas twenty years ago neighborhood pals would ride bikes and play in the woods, today's kids are more likely to be in front of a computer or television with minimal interpersonal interaction and physical activity. Set in a natural environment where self-reliance is critical, children must solve real-world problems and negotiate personal relationships in ways that they do not experience at school. As alluded to above, camp truly is the antidote to what ails society.

Here are some things kids are still doing at sleep-away summer camp: learning woodworking, taking swimming lessons, making bracelets out of colored strings and letter beads that spell EMILY or ALLIE, trudging back to a hunter green cabin after an endless sunstroke kickball game, running to the canteen for water ice on moonlit, cricket-serenade nights, writing letters home begging for gum, getting the nickname "Chunks," zip-lining, co-opting Indian words, obsessing over the girls/boys in the other bunks, dodging bees, collecting splinters, fighting homesickness, and trying to look cool despite everything.[408]

While the goal of camp is to help kids enjoy the simple life and unplug, their parents, on the other hand, struggle to do so for themselves. As a result, a number of "high-end sleep-away camps in the Northeast now employ full-time parent liaisons...[the job can be described] as 'almost like a hotel concierge listening to a client's needs.' The liaisons are emblematic of what sleep-away camp experts say is an increasing emphasis on catering to increasingly high-maintenance parents, including those who make unsolicited bunk placement requests, flagrantly flout a camp's ban on cellphones and junk food, and consider summer an ideal time to give their offspring a secret vacation from Ritalin."[409] While this may seem counterproductive to fostering children's independence and self-reliance, camp owners recognize the importance of assuaging parents' fears and concerns; "accommodating parents makes sense, since without happy parents, there would be no campers at all, happy or otherwise."[410] In her article, "Years of Adventures and Challenges," Connie Coutellier writes, "parents' expectations have changed in the past ten years. They are more anxious and more aware of best practices, health and behavior concerns, healthy foods, and what their child is feeling on a daily basis."[411] This awareness, coupled with the fact that parents are used to having unbridled, around-the-clock access to their children and those who work with them, has created a new set of needs and challenges for camp administrators.

Another significant change to the landscape of camps is in the types of camps offered. William Hageman, a columnist for the *Chicago Tribune* reflected on the diversity that characterizes today's summer camps. "Summer camps used to be fairly homogenous. Boating, sports, ghost stories around the campfire, noogies, Saran-wrapped toilets. Many camps still feature those fun and character-building activities. But now kids can also study Shakespeare or polish their banjo skills."[412] So in addition to general activity camps, religious camps, sports camps, and arts camps, a multitude of specialty camps have sprung up in recent years. Twenty-first-century children can attend lumberjack camp in the Adirondacks, bluegrass camp in Nashville, firefighter camp in New Hampshire, etiquette camp in Charleston, forensics camp in New Jersey, archaeology camp in Colorado, surf camp in Hawaii, or clown camp in California. And these, of course, are just a sampling of quirky camp offerings.

Yet another significant difference, however, is the way campers arrive at and depart from camp. Gone are the days of taking a train or even a bus to camp. Today, some families go so far as to charter private planes instead of packing up the family car/station wagon/SUV. "Last July [2011] was the busiest month ever at the airport in Augusta, Maine, as private jets full of kids en route to the state's many camps crowded the runways."[413] Another significant difference? "In our litigious times, health and safety are Job 1. Staff training, for example, includes discussions about how to avoid body contact—never initiate a hug with a camper—and how to recognize an eating disorder."[414]

Perhaps the greatest change in camps is the fight against modern telecommunications; it is a challenge to bridge the gap between tradition and technology. "While parents, educators, and Middle Eastern autocrats keep losing ground in the war on wireless technology, summer camp directors have so far managed to hold the line...Like Walkmen and boomboxes before them, iPods and other MP3 players are permitted at many camps, but later-generation touchscreen models—digital Swiss Army knives that play a lot more than music—are often banned."[415] Cell phones are generally not allowed and most camps have taken to confiscating them or allowing them to be used at specific times while under supervision. Unfortunately, parents are sometimes part of the problem with helping camps manage technology. Some go so far as to encourage their children to hand over decoy phones while others have been known to mail their children phones in a care package. And often, the push to have a cell phone at camp for unlimited access is from the parents; after all, their children are too busy having fun at camp.

The secret to a successful camp, one that understands parental needs, is making the kids want to come back again next summer...That's partly about the friendships, which campers forge in shared moments of independence and maintain off-season via texting and Facebook and Skype. But it's also the world-of-its-own that a great camp creates with its rituals and legends and secret words that outsiders don't get. It's about the rising status and privilege a camper gains by returning year after year.[416]

Aspiring archaeologists excavate a site in Colorado at Crow Canyon Archaeological Center. *Photo courtesy of Crow Canyon Archaeological Center.*

The benefits of allowing today's children and teens a chance to slow down and enjoy one another's company against a beautiful natural backdrop should not be underestimated. *Photo courtesy of Kari Ahern.*

Girls show off their skills at Camp Wa Wa Segowea. *Photo courtesy of Camp Wa Wa Segowea.*

Another recent trend is that of posting photos online daily for parents to see all the fun their children are having. In his blog, Rabbi Jason Miller explains his and his wife's reaction to the sighting of their son on the camp's website. "On the slim chance that she caught a glimpse of our son in one of the photos, the analysis would begin. Was he wearing the same t-shirt that he was wearing in the photo two days ago? Did he misplace his glasses since he wasn't wearing them? Did he look sunburned? Did he make new friends since he was posing in the photo with the same friend from last time? Was he showering? Was he brushing his teeth? Was he having fun?"[417] *Time* ran an article in August 2012 about the widespread use of such online photo galleries. Psychologist Michael Thompson tells *Time,* "The camps are putting up pictures in an attempt to allay your anxiety and appease your need to know. You can look at them but know this: seeing pictures of your child online adds absolutely no value to your child's camp experience. It's 100% for the parents. One camp director told me about a boy whose mother said, 'When you see a photographer taking pictures of kids, jump in the picture and hold up two fingers if you're alright and three if you're not.'"[418] Twenty-first century parents, it seems, just can't leave well enough alone. Camp, Thompson argues, is as important for parents as it is for children. "If you are a parent who is constantly supervising and monitoring, when you send your child to camp, it throws you up against your own philosophy and habits of constant supervision and control. When you send your child to camp, you have to give that up."[419]

Additionally, whereas parents typically said goodbye on the first day of camp and then didn't see their children until the summer was over with, perhaps, the exception of visiting day, it has become more and more common for parents to pull their children out of camp for extended periods of time for any number of reasons: a grandparent's ninetieth birthday cruise, soccer camp, playing in the school band overseas and so on. Time at camp seems to be a casualty of twentiy-first century demands but luckily, many families are able to make competing schedules work so that children don't have to miss out on the camp experience.

The Christian Science Monitor laments that "spending the summer at camp is a fast disappearing tradition. It's being elbowed out by the viral pace of childhood, where the school year starts earlier and earlier, where high school sports—and their very specific skill sets—now dangle the promise of a free ride to college. Where the opportunities for travel are unprecedented. Where many kids need to make visitation time for a noncustodial parent."[420] The article continues to explain that "today's advocates consider [the traditional camp model] the ideal antidote to the too-fast, too-stressed, too-wired world of clinics and skill-building—a world many say is threatening childhood. They see camp as an incubator of personal resources that prove far more useful than a 50-point bump on someone's SAT score."[421] So as is the case with much else in today's fast-paced world, families are faced with difficult choices when it comes to summer activities.

"Rally" Ballentine behind the wheel of camp Kehonka's first automobile.

Photo courtesy of Roy Ballentine.

What Is the Future of Summer Camps?

It all used to be so simple. You shipped the kids off, dropped by on parents' day and welcomed them home in August. Now camp directors field phone calls and e-mails from helicopter parents. There is medication to manage and food allergies to accommodate.[422]

Carol Sudduth of Wyonegonic says that the most significant challenges to twenty-first century camps are adjusting to school calendars and offering a quality program while controlling costs.[423] Jeff Cheley, director of Cheley Colorado Camps, calls this the "school calendar creep." He explains that "the school calendar seems to be getting longer which limits our summer programming schedule. The fewer weeks available to offer summer camp, the harder it is to create the revenue to operate the business."[424] Another challenge for camps includes facility maintenance. Cheley explains that "we are fortunate that we are a 92-year institution in Colorado. With that comes a facility that has been around for 87 years (we were on a different location for the first 5 years). Our buildings are quality structures, but everything needs upgrading after many years. Whether it is replacing roofs, buildings, or water systems, it is one of our main responsibilities. The maintenance of the facility is paramount to the success of the program and must be an annual focus."[425]

And, as with any institution, government regulations often prove more of a hindrance than a help. Cheley comments on the situation: "it seems that the government wants to manage more aspects of our business. There are many different regulators that we meet with every year to make sure we are running a quality business. I feel that the number of people requesting visits, paperwork, and licenses has increased."[426] The passage of new legislation intended to make camps safer for children might mean camps must spend tens of thousands of dollars on new equipment or training that is likely to be out-of-date in just a year or two. While safety is the paramount concern of every camp, there is some legislation that is simply excessive.

Summer camp, like sports cars and fancy vacations, is a luxury item for most. So when the economy took a downward turn, many families had to reevaluate their priorities. Some families whose children had attended the same summer camp where their parents met suddenly found themselves unable to foot the bill for eight weeks of fun in the sun. The need for "camperships" increased. Camps, too, have felt the pinch of hard times. Enrollment has not been as robust for some, and the cost of food and gas has reduced overall profits.

In addition, many parents "want something more for their money. They want their children to come home with a better tennis serve, say, or a stronger backstroke, or perhaps a better technique for making chocolate soufflé." One camp director reports, "It is not enough anymore to just go to camp to have fun and make friends and improve independence and self-esteem...Some parents want actual takeaways. They want to see skills, achievements, patches, and certificates."[427]

Overall, however, while the twenty-first century poses its own set of unique challenges for summer camps, they are really no more or less significant than those overcome by camp directors of the past. In fact, as parents seek out opportunities for their children to be happy, well-rounded individuals with a healthy respect for the world around them, summer camps provide safe, creative opportunities for children to grow and mature. Corey Dockswell, director of Camp Wicosuta, believes, "the future of summer camps is bright, especially as the world is focused on twenty-first century Skills. Those skills—leadership, resilience, teamwork, etc.—are built at camp perhaps better than they are at school. Camps can and should be viewed as invaluable to the education of each child and the creation of a stronger world community."[428]

Coleman Country Day Camp emphasizes "the power of fun" while encouraging campers to discover themselves in a number of different ways. *Photo courtesy of Coleman Country Day Camp.*

9 The Lifelong Impact of Summer Camp

Green and white eventually unite after the fun of Color War. *Photo courtesy of Camp Wekeela.*

There are those who went to camp and those who didn't. Anyone who has ever tried to explain camp and what goes on there to someone who has never been to camp has, undoubtedly, experienced an utter loss of words to express themselves. Perhaps this is the result of the emotions that are tied up in one's camp experience or simply not knowing where and how to start. How do you explain certain camp rituals which, if performed outside of camp, might garner strange looks and concern?

In a 1998 edition of *This American Life,* Ira Glass explains how campers and staff feel when trying to relate their camp experiences to non-camp friends. "No one back home understands it. None of their friends, nobody. There is just a gap between camp people and non-camp people."[429] Glass sought to "understand what is the cult-like, mystical connection some people feel with their summer camps."[430]

What many non-campers have a hard time understanding is how—and why—twenty-first century kids willingly participate in camp where they are disconnected from their peers at home and willingly engage in silly behavior that they would never consider doing at home. "Camp is this unusually safe bubble, where kids can let themselves go, crying and screaming and singing. They all buy into this. None of them stands back. Nobody thinks they're too cool for it. Back at school, the rules are completely different. Everywhere the rules are completely different."[431]

The same struggle is likely to be experienced by friends from home who attend different camps. Everyone is usually convinced that their camp is the best for a variety of reasons—and this is why so many different types of camps are successful—but at least having a similar overall camp experience allows the two to relate to one another. In a recent blog post, writer Dan Duett explains, "there's a shared experience at the core, the result of common elements that are often deliberately, painstakingly cultivated."[432] Duett identifies the core elements of the summer camp experience as follows:

- Fun as a way of being
- An emphasis on growth and skill building
- Safety to take risks and be who you want to be
- Being part of something larger than yourself[433]

What Duett finds most salient is that "these common elements aren't simply product characteristics; they're deliberate community values of profound reach and importance. If I were asked to summarize the magic of summer camp in ten words or less, I'd describe it as *joyful, inspired, active immersion in something bigger than oneself,* which doubles as a pretty decent summation for the good life, in general."[434]

The most common recurring dream I have is being back at summer camp. It's at least once a month. I think it's because my eight years there are so deeply imprinted on my brain that my subconscious continues telling me to go back, even though I'm now 34 years old. As a kid, sometimes you don't really realize just how much you're enjoying something until you're older and then you remember just amazing it all was and how lucky you were.

—Chris Parsons [435]

It is astonishing how many people return to camps summer after summer. This is even more surprising in today's world where there are so many choices for summer activities and experiences. Sherri Maxman believes "it's a way to reinvent yourself. I was no one special at school, but somehow managed to be somewhat of a star at camp. I was allowed to try different things and find out that I was good at some of them, like swimming and acting. Also, the people I met at camp were so different from the people at home (Long Island, NY) and I really appreciated that difference."[436]

There are many values learned at camp regardless of the type of camp or its location. Chief among them, however, is tolerance and respect. Renee Tucknott explains the importance of respect in a camp setting.

> One of the most important values I brought away from camp is respect in all its forms... You meet so many people of different religions, race and social classes at camp... You often find that in life you surround yourself with people who are similar to you and share the same values and opinions. At camp you don't have this choice and you come across so many unique and different people. You learn to get to know people on a whole new level and respect them for their differences. And often you learn that you can be friends with people you never thought you would.[437]

A similar idea is echoed by Corinne Loder, a longtime camper turned counselor at Gold Arrow Camp, who hails from Los Angeles. When asked to reflect on the lessons she learned at camp, she said, "camp teaches you all about becoming who you want to be and it teaches you skills far beyond rock climbing and horseback riding. It teaches you how to work with other people, and how to solve problems—two of the most important skills I believe you can have in life."[438]

Alison McCarlie notes that explaining camp to her friends and family back home in Scotland is exceedingly difficult.

> My family and friends definitely do not get camp, despite my boring them to death talking about it. We don't have camps really here so it is a very foreign concept. My parents came to visit one year and said all that I had described started to make sense and they could see why I returned so many times. I think American camps are viewed by other countries as a babysitting service for American families who get less time off work than other countries. A lot of parents I speak to are shocked a parent could send their child away from home that long. Again I think they see camp as a set up for the parents (babysitting) rather than a chance for their child to develop social skills and gain independence.[439]

The difficulty in explaining such an emotional, all-encompassing experience seems to transcend age, gender, and nationality. Perhaps that is why reunions among camp friends are so sweet.

Making dream catchers is a favorite craft project among campers everywhere. *Photo courtesy of Camp Wa Wa Segowea.*

Friendships made at camp often last a lifetime. *Photo courtesy of Kari Ahern.*

Staff, some of whom have never sailed before, enjoy an evening sail during orientation at Cape Cod Sea Camps. *Photo courtesy of Justine Darmanian.*

Sunfish are a popular type of boat used by camps. They are relatively inexpensive and easy to master. *Photo courtesy of Kari Ahern.*

Campers listen intently to a story told by one of their counselors during an evening activity. *Photo courtesy of Kari Ahern.*

It has always been difficult for me to explain to people just how important camp was to me. At the end of each summer, my parents would pick me up and I would silently get in the car, wishing on everything I held dear that we would not actually have to drive down the long driveway, turn onto Route 6A and drive back to the world I had escaped 8 weeks prior. I would remain silent for pretty much the entire five-hour drive back to New York reliving every memory in my mind and trying to hold onto what one camp director would refer to each summer as the "afterglow." As time would pass, I would come around and start being myself again, but I would never talk about camp or tell camp stories. I had told my friends and family enough in my letters and postcards home (this was before email). I didn't want to have to put into words experiences that I did not think anyone would fully appreciate or understand. And I struggle now to capture the spirit of my experiences on paper.

We refer to it as the bubble. This alternate world that is summer camp where everything but your trunk full of clothes with your name tags sewn into them gets left behind. The day to day of this world consisted initially of meals in a dining hall, cleaning cabins, morning assemblies, moving from one activity to another (swimming, archery, art, field hockey, biking, etc.), gathering in evenings for evening activities under the stars. Each summer takes on a flavor of its own, with its own catch phrases, big personalities, and inside jokes.

As the years went by, the days were largely the same, but soon I was not taking activities, but teaching them, not being counseled, but counseling. But camp is so much more. Within this daily routine over the course of fourteen summers, I managed to accomplish some of my biggest achievements and suffer my biggest failures; I had bright shining moments and made some of my worst mistakes; I suffered through summers filled with unrequited summer love and had one perfect summer romance that I will always reflect on with a smile despite it's not so happy ending; I had summers during which I begged my parents to come pick me up due to seemingly incurable homesickness and summers when I barely remembered to write home; summers in which my intense shyness and anxiety prevented me from making friends and truly joining in the fun and then the summers in which I overcame those issues and felt truly at peace.

No matter the tenor of the particular summer though, or the particular mix of people, I was always deeply connected to the physical place. Even now, at any moment, I can conjure up the smell of camp in my head. When I see pictures of camp now, particularly of the perfect bay beach that borders CCSC, I have a visceral physical reaction to it. I feel the longing in my body. I truly believe, whether your particular camp is by the ocean, the lake, in the woods, or in the mountains, it is good for the soul to spend a dedicated period of time in a natural place without the distractions of the outside world. I imagine this is even truer today, with electronic devices dominating every moment of everyday life. This place, this camp, centered me in a way no other place could. Every summer, upon arriving at camp, I would walk the path down to the beach and I could quite literally feel the weight of my world lifting off my shoulders. As long as I could be a part of this beauty, breathe this air, feel this sand, everything would be ok. Divorce, moves, school pressures, and so much more did not stand a chance against this place. Camp was the calm in any storm that might have been raging in my life at the time. What did I learn from my time at camp? I think the better question is what didn't I learn at camp. I learned everything from the very basic (think tie dye and the backstroke) to the very profound (think how to be independent, how to appreciate life, how to learn from your mistakes, how to be myself, how to reflect on each day in a meaningful way).

I have not been the best at keeping in touch with the people who helped make my camp years so special, but that does not mean that I do not think about them and does not make their impact on my life any less important.

I am greatly looking forward to the day that I can send my own children to camp and they can form their own connections to this place I love so dearly.[440]

—Dianna Lamb Walsh

Camp leaders give instruction to a group prior to an activity.
Photo courtesy of Camp Towanda.

Values Learned at Camp

There is something unrelentingly analog about summer camp. To older generations of campers, it brought an immediate saturation of the senses. It was a dense, green world, scented with natural pine, pond water and aluminum canoe. To even young campers, camp carries a shock of digital deprivation. It will take a few days before the natural setting impinges upon them, before it feels natural to have no text messages or cellphone games to attend to—but instead, fireflies and slugs.

What goes on at camp is something of a mystery, just as it has always been. No one really knows besides the kids and the counselors. Perhaps it's the same thing that has always gone on—the cultivation of little habits and traditions that bring a fraternal and sororal order to the chaos of pubescence. But is there still woodcraft? Beading and leatherwork? Campfires and anthems? Does one still learn to walk like an Indian, straight-footed and silent? All we know is that we could use some summer camp ourselves, a chance to paddle out and listen to the loons.[441]

Parents send their children to camp in order for them to develop a sense of identity and new skills, to engage in positive social relationships and, perhaps most importantly, to develop independence and self-confidence. A safe, structured, and supportive environment, camp is the perfect place for children and teens to do these things. According to the American Camp Association, "in today's pressure-oriented society, camp provides a non-threatening environment for America's youth to be active, to develop competence in life skills, to learn about and enhance their own abilities and to benefit from meaningful participation in a community designed just for them."[442] Further, camp helps foster "a sense of industry and competency, a feeling of connectedness to others and to society, a belief in their ability to make decisions and a stable identity."[443] In short and as alluded to above, a camp experience provides all the things that school cannot: a willingness to take risks in a safe environment where people are not judged, healthy competition driven

Camp counselors play an important role in a camper's summer in terms of skill development. The impact a counselor can have on the life of a young camper is not to be underestimated. *Photo courtesy of Coleman Country Day Camp.*

not by the end result but by the camaraderie developed on teams, and the opportunity to develop life-long interests in things and friendships with people that would otherwise not be possible at home. While the so-called "experts" may beg to differ, summer camps are more equipped to prepare children and teens for real life than schools are. Just ask anyone who has ever been a camper.

Young adult authors Joanne and Karen Rock cite summer camp as a place where they learned important lessons as children that have continued to serve them well as adults. Joanne offers the following advice she learned from her camp experience: "Listen with your heart and not your eyes. It doesn't make you weak to trust in someone else's strength. That silly, goofy fun will lighten your heart and a shared smile is the fastest way to make a new friend. Life is happier with fewer barriers, and camp is full of outstretched hands to help you along tricky paths. I try to bring that lightness of heart into the rest of my life."[444] Karen suggests that camp taught her, "100% to be yourself. The world is better because people are different. Trying to be like everyone else would be so boring! The campers in our series are as varied in their personalities and interests. It's the way my real bunkmates were. I loved each one for who they were—especially the ways that each of us was different. In fact, it was the differences we liked best. So my lesson was not to try to fit in and not to try so hard to stand out."[445]

> *Maturity and responsibility. There we were, at age 16, put in shared charge of a cabin (sometimes with kids only three years younger than us). Our directors gave us a lot of freedom, but had indoctrinated in us just how important our jobs were. In addition to being vigilant about safety, we knew how important it was to quash any bullying or ganging up. For many of us, this camp was a respite from the peer pressure and social tension of school, and from growing up as campers we knew how important it was that nobody have to spend four or eight weeks being picked on. The summer was all about not just encouraging the kids to try new things, but get them to challenge themselves so they would leave with a feeling of accomplishment and pumped-up self-esteem. This was the place to reinforce what might have been beaten down in the school year. I've always kept that attitude in my career; as an editor and manager, I believe it's all about encouraging people and building them up, not intimidating them. Works on the archery range, works at a website.*[446]
>
> —Josh Wolk

Author Joanne Rock explains how the lessons she learned at camp serve her as an adult:

> I remember these lessons when I'm dealing with challenging people. I look for a shared laugh to connect with them and hope that we can be friends. I also reach out for new friendships all the time because I don't want to miss wonderful people! I have terrific friends, but that doesn't mean I can't always make more. Connecting with new people is a continual joy that all started at camp. I went into camp with a friend or two. I came home with dozens. I try to recreate this experience whenever possible![447]

Her sister-in-law and writing partner, Karen, explains how her former camp counselors inspire her work as a teacher:

> In addition to being an author, I'm also a teacher. So I get what it's like for the middle school students I work with. They've been in a small elementary school for six years and suddenly it's like WOW—one huge school with lots of new rules and new people. It can make kids feel lost and lonely so I reach out to them and make them feel included the way the counselors did for me. In fact, my hat is off to all counselors because it is just like being a teacher, and a babysitter, and a therapist all rolled into one. What amazing people! I learned how to work with kids from my amazing counselors and I will forever owe them for teaching me how to relate to young teenagers.[448]

Longtime Tripp Lake Camp camper Holly Zax Shuter explains how significant lessons learned at camp can be. "I learned a lot about feelings at camp—how easily they can be bruised… and how important unconditional friendship love can be in my life. I aspired to the attention of the older girls when I was young, and when I was an older camper, I learned how to pay attention to and care for other younger kids. I'm a youngest child, so I lived for being the big sister to younger girls. I think some of those qualities that I first learned at camp are actually quite maternal and tender and I think about them as a parent."[449]

Hence, campers who internalize the values espoused by their camps are likely to be more mature than many of their peers who spent their summers at home by the pool or playing video games in the air conditioning. What parent wouldn't want their child to have the opportunity to grow and develop while learning critical life lessons in a nurturing and safe environment?

Universality of the Camp Experience

Regardless of the location of one's camp, the unique traditions enmeshed in the culture, or the type of camp, there are certain sentiments and rites of passage that are universal. Such transcendence is what separates the campers from the non-campers. Simply put, this universality of experience is how you know whether you're talking to someone who "gets camp" or not. Again, author and journalist Josh Wolk eloquently explains this phenomenon.

> There are lots of different kinds of camp that leave kids with lots of different memories: My camp was all-boys, and wasn't a sports camp—it stressed more non-competitive activities (hiking, sailing, rock climbing, archery, etc). So when friends talk about their camp experiences related to Color War or making out in the woods, I can only shrug. And they can't imagine what the point was of going to a camp that didn't have those things. And yet I can't fathom going to their camps, either. The fact is, you always love your camp for what it was, and ultimately, once you get past those differences, there are still overarching commonalities that link all "camp people": the great friendship, the thrill of freedom, the traditions.[451]

> *It is not an exaggeration to say that I think daily about the lessons I learned at camp…chief among these is that attitude is literally everything.*[450]
>
> —Lindsey Mead Russell

Flutists rehearse for a performance at Camp Wa Wa Segowea. *Photo courtesy of Camp Wa Wa Segowea.*

A group of happy campers and staff at Camp Wa Wa Segowea. *Photo courtesy of Camp Wa Wa Segowea.*

I was never a camper growing up and, having started my summer camp experience as a young adult, I was definitely able to grasp one of the most important opportunities a person of any age should have. Summer camp teaches and reinforces so many of life's values: teamwork, diligence, and environmental awareness, to name just a few. I am so grateful to have found a place that has given me so much joy and rewarded me with incredible memories.[452]

—Michael Gomez

There are camps in the woods, camps near lakes, camps atop mountains, and camps by the ocean. Regardless of their location, their program, the people who run them, the children who attend them or their mission, all camps share a few things in common: making learning fun and fostering friendships and meaningful relationships. Camps, wherever they are, almost instantly become microcosms of society where a single day is the equivalent of an entire week in the real world because so much happens. Something inexplicable happens to the time-space continuum at camp; summers seem to fly by while simultaneously lasting forever. If only the summer *would* last forever…

And the irony is that even when something seems bad or unpleasant at camp, it is mitigated by the larger experience as a whole. "Despite the banality of institutional food, the tortures of blackflies and mosquitos, and the slippery black mud of Adirondack trails, thousands upon thousands of girls and boys and young women and men who attended or worked at Adirondack camps came back for more. As campers and counselors, they spent nights in damp sleeping bags and endured the cruelties that children and teenagers inevitably visit upon one another. Yet as adults, many say that the camp experience was one of the most positive of their lives."[453]

Now at 30 years old, I'm a Senior Director at a fashion company, and not someone anyone would refer to as incredibly nostalgic or emotional....except when it comes to camp. It's become the running joke amongst those who know me well. My first kiss, my first dance, first tennis match, first and only times I shot a bow and arrow—all happened at CCSC. I think it means as much as it does because I always felt very loved and protected at camp. Dances in the pavilion, sleeping out under the stars in front of the big house, counselors switching cabins with the boys in the middle of the night, the songs, the plays, Reveille and Taps, and Sundays at the beach. Camp helped me become independent, gave me a sense of time management, got a glimpse of real responsibilities … it shaped a lot of who I am.[454]

—Kim Ward Burt

Campers strike at pose at Camp Wekeela. *Photo courtesy of Camp Wekeela.*

At the ninetieth anniversary celebration of the Cape Cod Sea Camps, two former campers and counselors, Lucy Jane Lang and Seth Soulstein, delivered a speech similar to the one they had delivered at the camp's seventy-fifth anniversary when they were campers. It is remarkable what stands out to them as having been significant events in their camp experiences. Whether or not the specifics resonate, it is clear that the emotions and overall sentiments do.

Lucy: When he started camp at 12, he had never spent a night away from home.

Seth: When she started at camp, at 11, every night she pretended she had nightmares so the counselors would sit with her until she fell asleep.

Lucy: That whole first summer, he never took a shower without also wearing his swimsuit.

Seth: By the end of the summer, her parents had to tear her away from cabin 2 and she sobbed the whole car ride home.

Lucy: The next summer, he carved his first girlfriend's initials in the wood shop.

Seth: Her second summer she stayed for both sessions because she couldn't bear not to be in the final camp show.

Lucy: He had his first funnel cake, at the Barnstable County Fair.

Seth: She had her first kiss.

Lucy: As a Monomoy Senior, he played Kenicky in "Grease."

Seth: As a Wono Senior, she played Rizzo in "Grease."

Lucy: He fell in love with archery, and participated in tournaments all around the Cape.

Seth: She joined the race team and spent long afternoons learning how to roll tack on the bay.

Lucy: He loved getting up early on Sundays, to help the kitchen staff make fresh doughnuts.

Seth: She loved those doughnuts.

Lucy: He had an accident and broke his four front teeth in half, but he refused to go home until camp ended.

Seth: She actually preferred to have a little bit of sand in her bed when she went to sleep.

Lucy: He went to his first Red Sox game.

Seth: When she called the day after camp ended to register for the next year, Cheryl told her she was the first registration of the season.

Lucy: When, as an AC, he spent a week working at the day camp, he met people who became lifelong friends.

Seth: When, as captain of the green team during the Emma Del Cup, she and her fellow ACs couldn't agree on the outcome of the lip sync contest, they declared the first tie in Color Wars history.

Lucy: He tried, and failed, to windsurf.

Seth: She learned every single word of every verse of "American Pie."

Lucy: He learned how to use a darkroom.

Seth: She had her heart broken.

Lucy: As an AC, he read 12-year-old campers *The Old Man and the Sea* at night ... after they came back from the showers with their swimsuits on.

Seth: As a counselor, she held little girls' hands while they pretended to have nightmares just so that she would stay with them while they fell asleep.

Lucy: He went on to teach at arts camps around New England, using leadership skills he developed as a camper.

Seth: She came back to run Long Pond sailing while she studied for the bar exam.

Lucy: Years later, his wife doesn't quite understand how he managed to go to a "sea camp," but avoided doing basically every single water-based activity.

Seth: At camp, I had my first kiss.

Lucy: At camp, I made my best friends.

Seth: At camp, I learned to love the outdoors.

Lucy: At camp, I learned to throw a change of clothes in bag, go to the beach, and just see where the day takes me.

Seth: At camp, I fell in love

Lucy: At camp, I learned compassion.

Seth: I used to say that I learned more about life during my summers at camp than I ever did during the other three seasons at school ... I still believe it.

Lucy: I hope that if I have a son, someone at camp will read him *The Old Man and the Sea.*

Seth: If I have a daughter, I hope she will learn to love at camp.[455]

Friendships

The fact that camp seems to be unaffected by time is both stunning and disconcerting. While each day seems to be extremely long, the weeks somehow seem to fly by, and the entire summer passes in a heartbeat. Anyone who has a few years on the average camp counselor (who tends to be about nineteen or twenty) will tell you that camp is something of a fountain of youth. It is not unusual for forty-year-olds to consider twenty-year-olds among their closest friends nor is it uncommon for twelve-year-old campers to consider their eighteen-year-old counselors among their closest confidants. It is impossible to describe the friendships made at summer camp. They transcend time, age, and gender. They are often the most important relationships in one's life until college or even adulthood, which is not to say that they necessarily end once those milestones are reached.

The intensity of the friendships forged at summer camp is unlike any other. Perhaps what is most remarkable about them is that campers who gravitate towards one another are often markedly dissimilar, whereas in school and at home, children generally spend time with peers who share their interests and hobbies. Camp friends are often from different states and even different countries, have different backgrounds and talents, but are staunchly loyal in a way that friends from home aren't. Corrinne Loder discusses the differences between her camp friends and her friends from home.

> My friends at home have always been the ones who don't quite understand my obsession for camp. My good friends will listen to all my stories, but never having been to/worked at an overnight camp themselves, they don't understand the connection that I have not only to the people but to the place itself. My camp friends were/are always more open to new experiences, almost by default. You can't sign up to spend weeks at a time up in the mountains if you're not at least a little adventurous! With that openness to experiences comes a general open-mindedness that I don't tend to see as much in my friends back home, who are surrounded by the same things, opinions and experiences all the time.[456]

Author Joanne Rock explains, "Camp friends form strong bonds quickly because of the shared new experiences. We are sleeping in close quarters with strangers and sharing our strengths. I might help my new cabin mate hit the target in archery, while she helps me think my way through a tricky maze. Right away, we have a lot of shared, meaningful experiences together and

A group of assistant counselors prepares to welcome campers on opening day. *Photo courtesy of Kari Ahern.*

Campers greet each other after a long winter. *Photo courtesy of Camp Kupugani.*

Staff members enjoying their final night of camp. *Photo courtesy of Kari Ahern.*

Campers aren't the only ones who make friends for life while at camp. Here, a group of Cape Cod Sea Camps alumni gather at the wedding of Jim and Emily Fay who met at Cape Cod Sea Camps. *Photo courtesy of Emily Fay.*

that's like super-glue for a friendship."[457] Her sister-in-law and writing partner reflects on her own camp friends: "Camp friends are family. They become your sisters—which is probably why I joined a sorority in college. The bond is so strong because you eat, sleep, and play together for weeks on end. Secrets are exchanged, mistakes are forgiven, boys, hopes, and aspirations are discussed way past lights out... sometimes until the sun comes up. Friends at home have their own houses and their own families. But at camp, you make your home and family with your friends and there is no tighter bond."[458]

Rock continues, "I found an easy acceptance at camp that felt difficult to come by in school. I think it's because our guards are down a bit more at camp. There is less need to impress anyone. And in fact, you can't be terribly impressive when you're shivering your way through a swim test or wrestling with a tipped canoe. There is a natural camaraderie built into the challenges of camp activities that makes it easy to form fast, wonderful friendships. I still keep in touch with girls from camp."[459]

And it's not just the campers who are making great life-long friendships. Anyone who says that your college friends are your friends for life has obviously never been to camp. Coming to camp for the first time as a counselor is as nerve-wracking (if not more so) as coming to camp for the first time as a camper. Some staff members are nervous about fitting in with their peers, others worry whether the campers will like them. It is up to the veteran staff to show them the ropes and welcome them into the fold. And usually by the end of orientation week, friendships that will last a lifetime are made.

Relationships developed at camp are somehow stronger than those made at home or school for a number of reasons. First, staff is together around the clock in an intense environment. Camp friendships are built on genuine emotions and shared experiences. People are seeing each other at their best: helping others and having fun. They are participating in activities that they genuinely enjoy with others who feel the same; teaching how to throw a pot on a wheel or how to play soccer with someone who is equally passionate about the activity lays the groundwork for friendship.

It's hard to put into words the magic that is camp. There's just something about it that defies reason, that transcends geography and bends time. Camp isn't really a place at all—it's a feeling, a spirit. No matter where you went to summer camp or when, you know what I'm talking about. You feel it in your heart.[460]

And then there is simply the intensity of the camp experience. Being away from home in a somewhat idyllic environment for two months where everyone is wearing swim suits, sporting tans and smiles, while having the time of their lives is conducive to an atmosphere of romance. While this is often to the dismay of camp directors, many a summer romance has morphed into something greater and more permanent.

Camp Marriages

Overnight camp—where time stands still and yet everything happens all at once. Where you spend all summer long living with a bunk full of best friends you may have just met. Where days are spent hiking, swimming, making ceramics, or playing softball. Nights take place huddled around the campfire, or sneaking off to … whatever?

No homework, no commitments, no parents. What could be better than overnight camp?

How about camp with romance? Some might find simply a summer love, a crush, something to be packed away with the mementos in September. But others find the love of a lifetime.[461]

One of the greatest testimonies to the lifelong value of summer camp is the number of marriages that stem from summer romances. Many couples who meet at camp outlast the final campfire of the season. What is it about the collective experience and environment at summer camp that makes relationships formed there so successful? Likely, it is the values shared by all members of the community. Friendship is a critical element of both a marriage and a summer camp. Most families choose to send their children to camp not only to give them a chance to develop self-confidence, independence, and a unique set of skills, but also to provide the opportunity to make lasting friendships. When campers are asked what the best part of their summer was, they usually reference the friends they've made. Most adults would say that their spouse is their best friend. After all, a spouse, like a bunkmate, is the person you can wake up late at night if you can't sleep and the person with whom you share your successes, hopes, and fears. Honesty, too, is a cornerstone of both marriage and of friendships when living as part of a community. Bunkmates, like spouses, must understand the importance of honesty even when the truth may be difficult.

Camp marriages seem to be especially prevalent among Jewish camps. In fact, one Ramah camp in the Poconos has a "couples gazebo" that is filled with plaques honoring the couples who have met at the camp.[462] So many couples have met at Ramah camps that the National Ramah Commission maintains a searchable online database of over 300 couples, though many more camp

Jim Fay wed Emily Woodfill in September 2003. The couple met at Cape Cod Sea Camps where they continue to work. Their son, Crosby, attends camp and is sure to be followed by his sisters, Madeline and McKinley. Emily's sister, Angie, also met her husband, Elliott McDermed, at CCSC in the 1990s.

marriages are believed to be unregistered. According to the Commission, there are sixty-seven couples in which both husband and wife spent over a decade at Ramah and 187 couples met when both were staff members at their camp. Many of these couples report that the affirmation of their Jewish identity through their experiences at Ramah had a significant impact on their relationship. Simply by choosing to have a Jewish camp experience, campers share an important foundation in their friendships and relationships.[463]

Noam Neusner attended Ramah as did his parents. Like them, Neusner met his wife there. He explains that campers who attend Ramah are together for eight or nine years in a row as campers, finishing around tenth or eleventh grade. Many return as staff while they are in college or after they have graduated, a time when many begin looking for a mate. Neusner says that it is at this point that Ramah becomes "kind of like a marriage factory."[464] When asked why he thinks Ramah boasts such a high marriage rate among its population, he explained that Jews "are a small people and within our small people, those who are actively Jewish are smaller. With Ramah, you're dealing with a self-selective group of kids. They have a similar background, similar life values, professions, et cetera. From a sociologist's point of view, most people choose a mate who they have a lot in common with. [At camp there is] so much comfort and relationships are deep. You really know about somebody."[465]

A number of camps boast a "camp couples" page on their web site. Pine Forest Camp in Greeley, Pennsylvania, currently highlights thirty-one couples who met their spouses as campers or counselors. Beber Camp features eight couples' stories. In the past decade, Cape Cod Sea Camps has witnessed at least seven weddings of longtime camp couples, some of whom were campers and others of whom were counselors when they met. "Sure, many marrieds started their relationship as childhood sweethearts. But for those who met at overnight camp, the bond, many say, can be much more profound. Not only has each member of the partnership witnessed the other's growth (literally and figuratively), but they also understand the crazy adventures and secret codes that are part of camp. Most important, the lessons learned at their home away from home are also the ones cited as necessary for a good marriage."[466]

Critical to the success of camp and marriage is the notion of acceptance. Camp provides children and teens a safe environment devoid of the pressures of school in which they can simply be themselves and be appreciated and accepted for who they are and for the talents they have. Because of camp, countless happy couples have found one another as the result of a set of shared values and experiences that cannot be found elsewhere. These couples will have children who will continue to understand and embrace the importance of spending a summer by the bay, in the mountains, on a lake, or in the woods with friends who share the same passion for bug juice, s'mores, mosquito bites, care packages, and camp traditions.

Garran Peterson (a member of the fourth generation of owners of Cape Cod Sea Camps) met and married his wife, Christie, at Cape Cod Sea Camps. The two are now year-round staff at the camp.

Hollis von Summer wed Mike Kennedy on October 14, 2006. Hollis and Mike, both longtime campers and counselors, met at Cape Cod Sea Camps. Their son, Dean, now attends CCSC's Monomoy Day Camp.

Christina Quirk married Chris Peterson, a fourth generation member of the Delahanty family that continues to run Cape Cod Sea Camps. The couple now works year-round at the CCSC's Monomoy Day Camp.

Reunions and Returning to Camp

At some point during the long winter months, the distance becomes too much for campers and counselors to bear. Of course, today's technology makes it possible for campers to text before they have even reached the end of the camp's driveway and to Skype on their way home. However, prior to these innovations, letters were written and the occasional phone call placed in an effort to reminisce about the summer past and look forward to the one ahead. Today, campers often organize their own impromptu reunions, meeting up over long weekends or school vacations. Friends who are unable to make it in person join via Skype, while everyone marvels at how different people look in sweaters and pants as opposed to t-shirt and shorts and how pale everyone is, their tans having faded long ago.

Many camps hold reunions during the year in locations that boast heavy concentrations of campers. Boston, New York City, and Washington, D.C., are popular locations for such events, which also (not accidentally) often coincide with camp fairs in the area. Generally, reunions organized by the camps themselves are held at JCC facilities, hotels, or similar facilities.

Other camps hold reunions on the camp grounds in significant anniversary years; Cheley Colorado Camps, for example, held its first reunion in 1970 as the camp celebrated its fiftieth anniversary. Cheley reunions were also held in 1990, 1995, 2000, and 2010 over Labor Day weekends. Cape Cod Sea Camps hosted its ninetieth anniversary celebration in 2012, complete with fireworks enjoyed by over 250 alumni.

But even more popular is the concept of camp for adults. Today, former campers and those who weren't fortunate enough to attend camp as a child are able to go as an adult. Campers-at-heart can choose from sports camps, fantasy camps, adventure camps, special interest camps, volunteer vacations, and performing arts camps. A recent *Wall Street Journal* article reports that there are over 800 adult camps in the United States. "What defines an adult camp can be somewhat different from marshmallow roasts and singalongs. Most let campers explore a hobby or live out a childhood fantasy. Accommodations range from rustic to luxurious."[467]

Camp Grounded in Anderson Valley, California is marketed as "summer camp for adults." "Campers" are encouraged to "trade in your computer, cell phone, Instagrams, clocks, schedules, and work-jargon for an off-the-grid weekend of pure unadulterated fun. Together we'll create a community where money is worth little... and individuality, self-expression, friendship, freedom, and memories are valued most."[468] Campers can stargaze, make friendship bracelets, swim in the river, visit the canteen, play a game of kickball, and roast marshmallows. The Camp Grounded Web site bears an important disclaimer: "This is not a conference. This is summer camp. Let's be clear. This is not a conference, a networking event or meet-up opportunity to make contacts that further your career. There will be no cocktail hour or welcoming reception for anyone to explain what they do, play the 'we know the same people' game, or try and figure out how they can connect again after they return to the workplace. Instead, we create an atmosphere for personal freedom, creative thinking, liberation from technology, and a space from the working world where we can all once again be... human. Friendships at camp are based on real-life connections, and the most important status we'll update is our happiness."[469]

Adult Color Wars is yet another example of grown-ups' desire to reconnect with not only the friends they had at camp but also with the entire camp experience. A 2013 *Los Angeles Times* article explains:

> It looks a little like a frat house basement dragged into the light of day, but this competition is much more innocent. It's part of Adult Color Wars, a weekend designed to give adults a chance to relive their days at camp. It's a chance to recapture, says founder Jennifer Rheuban, a fleeting childhood moment of no responsibilities, no school walls and the freedom to explore the person you were and the person you hoped to become.[470]

Regardless of where one attended camp or how many years ago, nearly everyone describes visceral memories of cabins, dining halls, and other camp venues. Writer Don Steinberg describes his "informal hunt for evocative smells" as he returned to Camp Kweebec in 2012. Upon returning to camp to write an article of *Philadelphia Magazine,* he explained, "One thing I was determined to investigate upon my arrival was whether camp still smelled the same."[471] Finally, after a week spent at camp, Steinberg wrote, "There's probably something about the rite of fire, the burning, the breaking of the rope, that symbolizes a departure from childhood. Anyway, it was intense. The heat of the flames was warming the crowd. The fires crackled audibly and threw off orange embers that twinkled against the dark sky and disappeared. The smoke blew in my face. Now it smelled like camp."[472]

Moving On

At some point, the vast majority of people fortunate enough to have attended camp as either a camper or counselor or both come to the realization that it is time to move on. Internships and "real jobs" beckon and, short of becoming a teacher with summers off, there will be a final summer spent at camp. This decision is not made lightly and many hours are spent trying to figure out how returning to camp might be possible. Once the realization sets in that returning to camp is not a possibility, an immense sense of loss overcomes the individual. It is similar to the agony of hearing "Taps" played for the last time on one's last night at summer camp; it is symbolic not just of the end of a summer, but also of the end of an important part of childhood and way of life. And although friendships are easily maintained beyond camp, things are never quite the same in the outside world. However, the lessons learned at summer camp are the kind that stay with someone forever.

Josh Wolk, author of *Cabin Pressure*, reflects on his final summer at camp:

> I did my last year as a counselor after my freshman year of college, and knew deep down that the next summer I would try something different and slowly graduate to internships and higher paying jobs. But that age is not known for its ability to look that far in the future. I had had perhaps my greatest summer ever that year, so it was easy to convince myself that I would someday be back, perhaps in a summer before grad school, who knew? But as college is kind of like camp with homework, I was eager to get there and it didn't feel like I was leaving a place of innocence for a black-and-white adult world at the time. Plus, I knew I would be back to visit.
>
> When I left in 2003 at 34 years old, however, I knew I would not be back. However, the summer had convinced me that while I still adored camp and all of its memories, it was no longer the right place for me. It would only be the same if everyone my age came back with me. My nostalgia was so intertwined with my friends from that era that just working there was only half the experience. However, my camp holds Family Camp for two weeks after all the kids go home at the end of the summer, where alumni return with their clans and stay in the cabins, swim, sail, and do the other activities. Last summer I returned with my family for the first time and captured exactly what had been missing in 2003: Not only was it fantastic to see the camp through my kids' eyes (both girls, and as it's an all-boys camp, sadly this is as much of the experience as I'll be able to pass on), but I was surrounded by fond familiar faces. And so the kids would go to bed and a bunch of us would make a campfire and start out with some very adult musings on life, but gradually, after a couple of beers, regress to reminiscing about ridiculous stories and all was as it should be: a bunch of guys acting really immature by the side of the lake. That made me feel far younger at 43 years old than working at the camp at age 34 did.[473]

I'm glad I went in an era without digital cameras or I would constantly find myself procrastinating by rifling through hundreds of old online photos. At best, I have a few envelopes of old photos buried somewhere in my basement. But I still remember it vividly; every time I smell Ivory soap I get lost in a reverie since that was the default soap there. Same with Dr. Bonner's biodegradable shampoo: we used it in the lake and if it ever gets anywhere near my nose I picture myself taking a late-night dip. Luckily I am now able to go for Family Camp to get a taste; I could just walk in circles around the grounds all day long listening to echoes of the kids yelling in the water or the thwack of tennis balls and it feels like nothing has changed. Of course, then my back hurts when I try to get a kayak down from the boat rack and I am snapped back to reality. But as I said in my book [Cabin Pressure], the great thing about camp is that it defies modernization: tennis courts and canoes will never get a high-tech makeover, so you always know it will just like you left it.[474]

—Josh Wolk

The lifelong impact of summer camp should never be underestimated. Independence, self-confidence, compassion, empathy, and respect are among the most important qualities one needs in virtually all aspects of life: college, the work force, teams, relationships, and so on. A willingness to work with others, an open mind, and flexibility are also traits of successful individuals who often become leaders in their chosen fields, and, while these traits can be honed elsewhere, summer camps provide a safe, fun, and positive atmosphere in which to develop them. In short, the skills and experiences gained as a result of the summer camp experience add immeasurably to the quality of one's life and generally help children and teens to grow into exemplary adults and community members.

And while the "real world" doesn't include rest hour, care packages, or Color Wars, perhaps it should; if it were a bit more like summer camp we might all be the best possible versions of ourselves and enjoy life that much more. Professor Daniel Dustin writes:

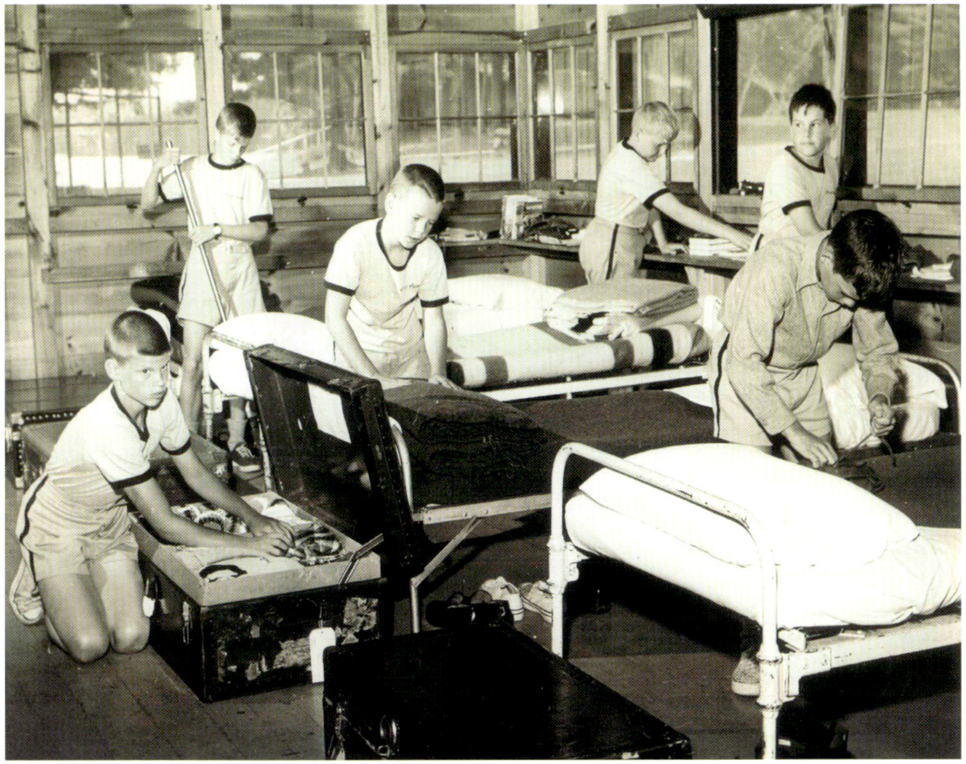

Boys prepare their beds, trunks, and bunk for morning inspection at Camp Agawam in the 1950s. *Photo courtesy of Camp Agawam archives.*

If only the world were more like a camp, occupying a few acres nestled in the woods somewhere, people would come from everywhere to marvel at it. They would marvel at the community spirit, the cooperation and the caring. They would marvel at the intensity of giving, the extension of self and the dedication to the common good. The people would marvel at the atmosphere of hope enveloping the world, and at the good deeds accomplished there. The people would regard it as magical because of its powers, and they would protect it so that it would not be hurt. Such a world would be the greatest wonder known, and people would come to pray to it, to be healed, to gain knowledge, to know beauty and to wonder how it could be. People would love it and defend it with their lives because they would know that their lives, their own roundness, could be nothing without it. If only the world were more like a camp.[475]

Frances Horn and Crosby Fay are "chips" at Cape Cod Sea Camps. Franny's parents, Chris and Rachel Horn met at camp as did Crosby's parents, Jim and Emily Fay. Both now attend CCSC's Monomoy Day Camp and are sure to be friends for life. *Photo courtesy of Kari Ahern.*

Afterword

On the last night of the summer at Camp Echo every child and staff member launches a candle into the lake. Wishes are made and hugs and tears are shared. *Photo courtesy of Camp Echo.*

> *You know, I grew into my skin as I browned it on sailboats on Lake of the Woods, and I got used to the way it fit. I became me at camp. All my confidence, my attitude and my aptitude were found and figured out because of all of those summers and all of those people and all of those friends.*[476]
>
> —David Himmel

I was at a Starbucks in New York City in March 2012 and was on my way to meet up with camp friends. While I waited for my latte, I picked up a copy of *USA Today* that had been left behind by another patron. Lo and behold, there was an editorial entitled "Why the World Needs Summer Camp." Though the article had originally run in *Camping Magazine* a few months earlier, I thought that it was fateful that I encountered it while visiting friends who I never would have met had it not been for camp. The editorial's author, Jeff Merhige, wrote that, "summer camp is an opportunity for children to be exposed to the best of human character."[477] Though the entire editorial is absolutely perfect and spot-on, this is what really resonated with me. I always felt that at camp I was the best version of myself and that those around me were the best versions of themselves as well. Each June, I feel as though I literally shed my old skin and my winter persona and bring my best self out of winter storage. It is such a pleasure and such a relief to welcome her back after a long "off season." The arrival of the camp season means that my very best friends will be with me for two glorious months, that my biggest decision of the day is which pair of flip flops to wear, and that I get to have a hand in helping campers make new friends, try new activities, and, most importantly, be their best selves too.

I treasure the opportunity to meet new people and make new friends each summer. I relish the day when the new staff arrives and I try to explain what they're in for and realize that words cannot adequately describe the experience that they are going to have. I love how at the end of the summer they say that they finally understand what I was talking about when they arrived. I seize the opportunities that each day brings, I cherish each and every memory that I make and I lament the speed with which each summer passes. I sometimes cannot believe my good fortune and how fate has bestowed upon me so many incredible experiences and people with whom to share them. I cannot imagine my life or my world without camp.

Antoine de Saint-Exupéry wrote, "It is in the time you have wasted for your rose that makes your rose so important."[478] Aside from the incredible people in my life, each of whom is most definitely a rose, there are two other roses. The first is rowing and, not coincidentally, that is what my first book is about. *A History of Collegiate Rowing in America* required an incredible amount of research and many interviews with people who know much more about the sport than I do, despite my fanatical involvement in it during college. It was often difficult to get people on the phone or to get responses to emails and photo requests were a huge challenge. This book, however, was different in many ways, mainly because it is about the biggest and most significant rose in my life: camp. When I started a Facebook page for the book and put out a call for those interested to email me, I got countless messages from people I didn't even know wanting to share their camp memories and experiences with me. Everyone, it seemed, was convinced that their camp was the best and that they had the most interesting stories. I found it interesting that I heard more from people who hadn't attended camp in many years who were excited to relive their camp days.

I suspect that the reason this book was more challenging for me is that the emotions tied up in my own camp experience sometimes precluded me from seeing the subject matter objectively and with clarity; hence, the writing process took longer than usual for me. My time at camp has been nothing short of transformative and miraculous. I am the person I am today entirely because of my years at camp. I would never have become a teacher had it not been for camp. I would never have met my husband had it not been for camp. And I would never have made the world's best friends were it not for my many years at camp. After all, camp was where I learned about hair products (not inconsequential to a teenage girl), boys, and sailing, among other things! However, in all seriousness, when something has had such a profound of an impact on you, it can be difficult to see it clearly. Furthermore, so many people had entrusted me with their precious camp memories that I agonized over how to do them all justice. I knew that their camp memories were just as sacred to them as mine are to me. Over and over people told me how their summers at camp were the best times of their lives. To be charged with writing a book about something that is so special to so many people in so many places is a big—and sometimes paralyzing—responsibility.

So I owe a great debt of gratitude to the strangers who shared their stories with me; they no longer feel like strangers and I hope I adequately relayed their love for camp. However, I owe an even greater debt to my friends and camp family which have changed my life forever in ways I never thought possible. When my aforementioned best friend, Kathie, picked up her daughter, Sophie, from her second summer at CCSC, Kathie's husband, Jon, snapped a photo of us and posted it to Facebook. I liked the photo and commented, "With my BFF!" Under that, Kathie commented, "What would your life be like had I not done such a good CCSC sales pitch at age 11?!" This possibility is something I cannot even begin to wrap my head around. I cannot imagine not having had this experience and not knowing the incredible people with whom I have been lucky enough to cross paths.

Standing on the beach of Cape Cod Sea Camps with my best friend, Kathie, who introduced me to the place that changed my life.

A singing telegram shark was delivered to me at camp on my fortieth birthday by camp friends Hollis von Summer and Mike Kennedy.

About a month after turning forty in August 2012, I was having a heart-to-heart with my friend Hollis (another camp friend, another camp marriage, another happy camper child) while our husbands were out on some adventure in a plane or a boat. She is the most direct person I know and, true to form, she told me that she was worried that my refusal to give up camp was not allowing me to move forward. She told me how she always dreaded "the lasts" of every season—the last dance, the last sail, the last council ring—but how she knew that meant there would always be a new bunch of "firsts" the following season. She explained that she never thought she'd get over camp but that she somehow did. Eventually she stopped coming to camp and I just don't think I can do that. While there may be a lot that I have sacrificed in my determination to return to camp each summer, I believe that what I have gained far outweighs anything I could possibly have missed out on. I have determined that there are some things I cannot live without and camp is one of those things. After all, I'm pretty convinced that camp is the elusive fountain of youth.

I wish to close with a poem that used to be read at camp often and that always made me cry (perhaps because its reading signaled that there were just a few days left of camp) when very few things in this world do. There are no other words to do justice to the feelings I have about the people I've met at camp. And, perhaps a bit selfishly, I will also conclude with a photographic tribute to some of the amazing people I have met and befriended at camp. Without them, my camp experience would not have been nearly as meaningful and joyous as it has been and will continue to be. There is simply not enough gratitude in the world to express what these people mean to me. But the best part about this is that I know that everyone out there who has been to camp for any amount of time has camp friends who are just as meaningful to them as mine are to me. There is simply no substitute for the relationships built at camp.

And finally, a million thanks to everyone who has been and will continue to be a part of camps everywhere. Summer camps are, without question, among America's finest traditions.

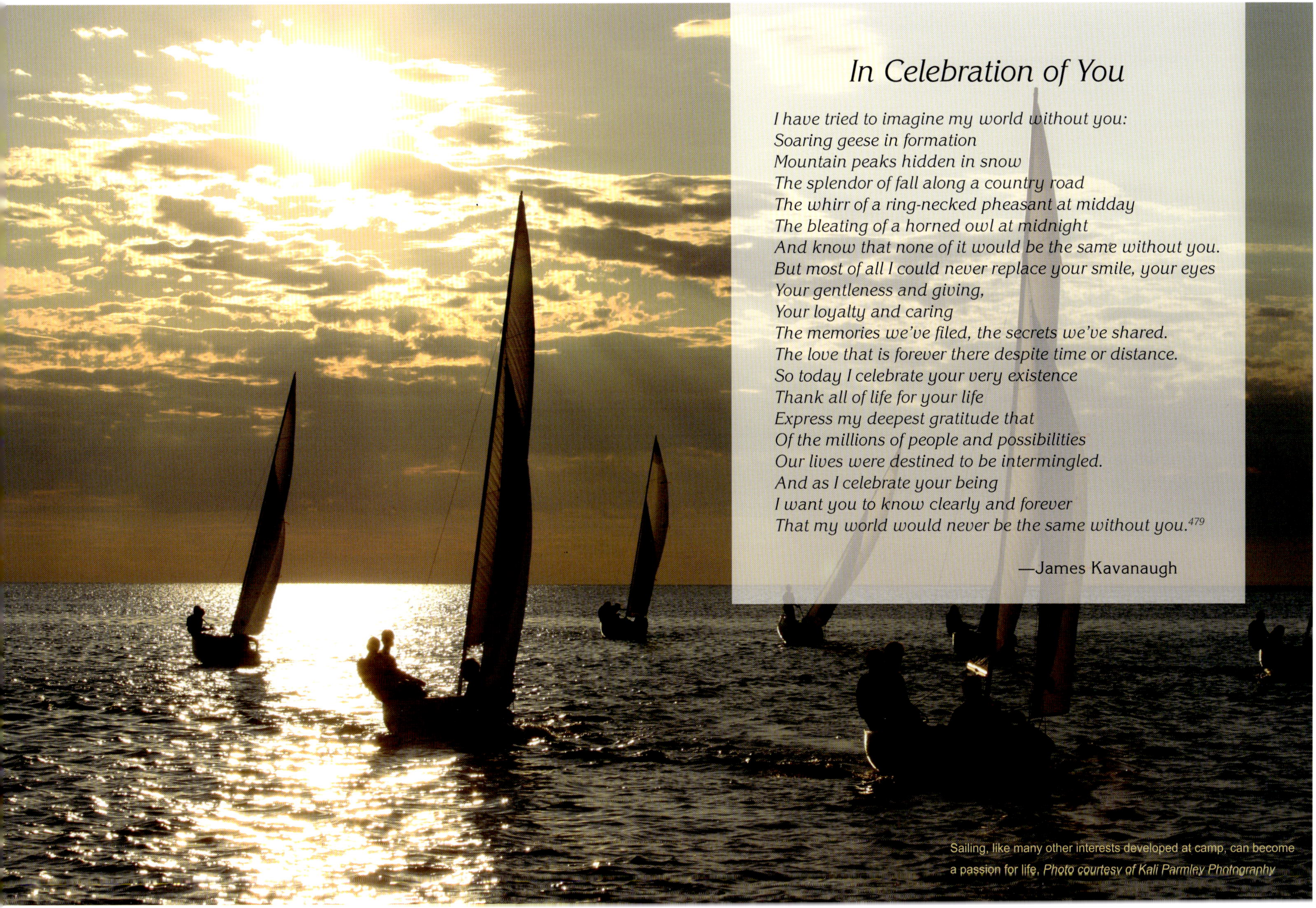

In Celebration of You

I have tried to imagine my world without you:
Soaring geese in formation
Mountain peaks hidden in snow
The splendor of fall along a country road
The whirr of a ring-necked pheasant at midday
The bleating of a horned owl at midnight
And know that none of it would be the same without you.
But most of all I could never replace your smile, your eyes
Your gentleness and giving,
Your loyalty and caring
The memories we've filed, the secrets we've shared.
The love that is forever there despite time or distance.
So today I celebrate your very existence
Thank all of life for your life
Express my deepest gratitude that
Of the millions of people and possibilities
Our lives were destined to be intermingled.
And as I celebrate your being
I want you to know clearly and forever
That my world would never be the same without you.[479]

—James Kavanaugh

Sailing, like many other interests developed at camp, can become a passion for life. *Photo courtesy of Kali Parmley Photography*

The author (left) with colleagues Christie Peterson, Sherry Mernick, and Michael Halperson enjoying Sunday "bay play." *Photo courtesy of Kari Ahern.*

Three of the author's very best friends from camp.

Joanna Flanagan and her oldest daughter, Kelly, have spent many summers at Cape Cod Sea Camps where Joanna is an assistant director of the Monomoy Day Camp and Kelly served as a head counselor. *Photo courtesy of Kari Ahern.*

The author's husband, Jeff, and two close camp friends, Jim Fay and Rob Percarpio, at the wedding of another camp friend.

Camp friends are friends for life! Emily Fay andthe author celebrate the wedding of Katie Percarpio to Colin Carpenter who also met at camp.

Camp friends reunite at the wedding of Jim and Emily Fay who met at camp.

New Year's camp reunion! The author and her husband celebrate the arrival of 2007 with their camp friends Rob Percarpio, his sister, Katie, and her husband, Colin Carpenter.

Just another day at work.

A huge group of friends from camp celebrate the wedding of Ed and Ellen Waller in 2012.

Siblings Kelly and Max Flanagan attended camp as campers and then worked together as staff members.

Prior to sending their children to Cape Cod Sea Camps where they spent our summers as children, Kathie Guben Wachs and her sister, Alison Guben Waldman, brought their husbands and children for a tour.

A few of the author's "summer spouses" whom she regularly sees more of than her actual husband in the summer.

The author, flanked by fellow staff members Bridget Roche, Philipp Luerzer, Will Brodt, and Katie Kass, celebrates the completion of another successful camp season on Cup Night in 2010.

The author's dear friends Julie and Joanna who have made camp such a special place to be.

Philip Luerzer supervising bay sail on a beautiful summer day.

Friends Hollis von Summer and Caitlin Doggart, together with Caitlin's daughter, Belen, who now attends CCSC.

Working with Jim Flanagan and Christie Peterson each summer is an honor.

The author's husband, Jeff, who despite being insanely jealous that she is still able to work at camp every summer, indulges her desire never to grow up or leave camp.

Peace Love
Happiness

Appendices

The sun sets on another summer.
Photo courtesy of Kari Ahern.

Glossary of Terms

Archery—Activity in which campers shoot at targets using bows and arrows.
Buddy check—A system used by lifeguards to be sure that all swimmers are accounted for
Bug juice—A drink that is often either too sugary or too watery and is served at camp meals
Bunk—Cot-sized beds which are stacked so that there is a top bunk and a bottom bunk. Sometimes used to refer to one's cabin as well
Cabin—Also referred to as a bunk, the building in which campers and counselors live while at camp
Camp feet—A perpetual state of one's feet being positively filthy after spending a prolonged period of time in flip-flops or barefoot at camp walking in sand, dirt and grass
Canteen—Also known as the camp store, this is where candy is sold along with camp t-shirts, sweatshirts, etc.
Capture the Flag—A game in which each team tries to steal the other's flag without being tagged
Care package—A box full of magazines, whoopee cushions, water guns, extra bug spray and toothpaste, comic books, Frisbees, Mad Libs, glo sticks, and (most importantly) edible treats including cookies, candy, gum and other potential contraband
C.I.T.—Counselor in Training; a teenager who is part camper, part counselor and who is given just enough responsibility but is still supervised (see J.C.)
Color war—Event in which the camp is divided up into teams to compete in a series of athletic events
Colors—the formal ceremony in which the American flag is lowered.
Council Ring—A group of benches (usually around a campfire) where a group of campers sit to hear the day's announcements.
Dining Hall—Building in which all meals are served
Dry lesson—Method used by archery instructors to teach campers who have never shot before
Duty chart—List of jobs to be done during cabin clean up
Freeze—A game played at meals to see who will clean the table
Friendship bracelet—Bracelets made of embroidery floss and given from one camper to another as a symbol of friendship
Gimp—A synthetic material used to make lanyards and bracelets most often employing the barrel stitch
Gold Rush—An activity in which campers are divided into teams (alternately, the activity can be done so that it's every camper for him or herself) and run around camp searching for gold-painted rocks. These rocks are then brought to the camp store and exchanged for points or some form of camp currency
Homesickness—Feelings of missing one's family, pet and home, generally accompanied by tears, a headache and a stomach ache
Ice breakers—Get-to-know-you games played on the first day of camp
Infirmary—Building housing the camp nurse(s) where health care is provided
J.C.—Junior Counselor (see C.I.T.)
Landsports—Generally any team sport such as soccer, baseball, lacrosse, field hockey and football
L.I.T—Leader-in-Training (see C.I.T. and J.C.)
Macrame—Craft using embroidery floss, string, or rope to make jewelry, wall hangings or other decorative arts
PFD—Personal Floatation Device, also known as a lifejacket
Plaque—Generally made in the woodshop, cabins or other groups design a plaque to depict a theme or item that was significant that summer that also lists campers' names for posterity
Resident camp—Synonym for "sleepaway" or "overnight" camp
Rest hour—The time after lunch when campers and counselors "rest" in their cabins before the afternoon activities.
Reveille—The tune played on a bugle to wake up the camp.
Riflery—An activity in which campers shoot .22s at paper targets
Shabbat-o-grams—A nice note sent from one camper to another on Shabbat at Jewish camps
S'more—A tasty treat made in the evening by a campfire. Traditionally, the graham cracker "sandwich" is made using a roasted marshmallow and half of a chocolate bar but more recently other ingredients have been added like peanut butter or other types of candy
Senior staff—Directors, program specialists, and others who are responsible for running a camp
Spirit award—Given to campers who demonstrate sportsmanship and otherwise excel in activities and cabin life
Taps—The tune played on the bugle signaling the end of the day
Tattoo—The bugle call played 15 minutes before "Taps"
Tetherball—A game where two players try to hit a ball attached to the top of a pole by a rope all the way around the pole. Often results in injuries
Visiting Day—A day on which parents and family members visit campers
Watersports—Activities including canoeing, kayaking, sailing, waterskiing, windsurfing, tubing, and the like

Cheley Colorado Camps are situated amongst the Rocky Mountains, providing rugged and beautiful terrain for campers. *Photo courtesy of Cheley Colorado Camps.*

Fried Ham

Fried Ham
Fried Ham
Cheese and Bologna
After the macaroni
They'll be pickles
Ketchup and onions
After the ham
Fried Ham
Fried Ham

Linger

Mmm, I want to linger
Mmm, a little longer
Mmm, a little longer here with you
Mmm, its such a perfect night
Mmm, it doesn't seem quite right
Mmm, that this should be my last with you
Mmm, and as the years go by
Mmm, I'll think of you and sigh
Mmm, This is good night and not good bye
Mmm, I want to linger
Mmm, a little longer
Mmm, a little longer here with you
Mmm, and come September
Mmm, I will remember
Mmm, our camping days and friendships true
Mmm, I want to linger
Mmm, a lttle longer
Mmm, a little longer here with you

Little Bunny Foo Foo

Chorus:
Little bunny Foo Foo
Hopping through the forest
Scooping up the field mice
And bopping 'em on the head

And down came the Good Fairy
And she said
"Little bunny Foo Foo
I don't like you're attitude
Scooping up the field mice
And bopping 'em on the head"

I'll give you 3 chances.
Then I'll turn you into a goon!
The next day…

(Chorus)
Repeat two more verses with 2 and 1 chances

"I gave you three chances.
Now I'll turn you into a goon!"
(POOF!)
And the moral of the story is:
Hare today, goon tomorrow!

House at Pooh Corner

Christopher Robin and I walked along
under branches lit up by the moon.
Posing our questions to owl and Eeyore
as our days disappeared all too soon.
But I've wandered much further today than I should
and I can't seem to find my way back to the wood.

So, help me if you can I've got to get
back to the house at Pooh corner by one.
You'd be surprised there's so much to be done,
count all the bees in the hive,
chase all the clouds from the sky.
Back to the days of Christopher Robin and Pooh.

Winnie the Pooh doesn't know what to do,
got a honey jar stuck on his nose.
He came to me asking help and advice
and from here no one knows where he goes.
So I sent him to ask of the Owl if he's there,
how to loosen a jar from the nose of a bear

So, help me if you can I've got to get
back to the house at Pooh corner by one
You'd be surprised there's so much to be done,
count all the bees in the hive,
chase all the clouds from the sky .
Back to the days of Christopher Robin and Pooh,
back to the days of Christopher Robin,
back to the ways of Pooh

Cottage In A Wood

In a cottage in a wood
Little old man at the window stood,
Saw a rabbit running by
Frightened as could be.
"Help me, help me, sir," she said,
"Before the huntsman shoots me dead."
"Come, little rabbit, come with me,
Happy we will be."

Actions:
Cottage—draw shape of cottage in air
Little old man at the window stood—hold hands up to eyes like binoculars looking out window
rabbit running by—hold hand in "peace" sign with two fingers extended to look like rabbit ears, and move hand from one side to the other in "hopping" motion
frightened as could be—cross arms across chest and twist from side to side
help me, help me—throw arms up in air
shoots me dead—clap one hand against the other
come little rabbit—"come here" gesture with finger
happy we will be—stroke one hand with the other

Keep repeating and with each repeat replace a line of the song with the appropriate action until no words are sung.

Photo courtesy of Philip Luerzer

Counselors entertain the girls at Camp Kehonka. *Photo courtesy of Roy Ballentine.*

Song that Never Ends

This is the song that never ends
It just goes on and on, my friend
Some people started singing it
Forever just because... *(Repeat)*

Baby Bumble Bee

I'm bring home my baby bumble bee
Won't my mommy be so proud of me
I'm bring home my baby bumble bee
Ouch! It stung me!

I'm smashing up my baby bumble bee
Won't my mommy be so proud of me
I'm smashing up my baby bumble bee
Ugh! What a mess!

I'm licking up my baby bumble bee
Won't my mommy be so proud of me
I'm licking up my baby bumble bee
Eww! I feel sick!

I'm puking up my baby bumble bee
Won't my mommy be so proud of me
I'm puking up my baby bumble bee
Yuck! What a mess!

I'm sweeping up my baby bumble bee
Won't my mommy be so proud of me
I'm sweeping up my baby bumble bee
Well, I won't do that again!

Tall Girls, Short Girls

Tall girls, short girls, fat or thin
Whatcha gonna do when the heat rolls in?
Nothing to do, nothing to say
That's the time to pack your bags and go away.

Come to (*name of camp)* where the breezes blow
Come to (*name of camp)* where we swim and row
Answer the ever-luring call;
Come to (*name of camp)* it's the best of all!

Girls at Camp Kehonka enjoy a beautiful sunset.

Photo courtesy of Roy Ballentine.

Day is Done

Day is done, Gone the sun,
From the lake, from the hills,
From the sky;
All is well,
Safely rest, God is nigh.

Fading light dims the sight,
And a star gems the sky
Gleaming bright, from a far,
Drawing nigh, Falls the night.

A Timeline of Summer Camp

1851— YMCA founded by Thomas Sullivan in Boston
1860— First Boys' Club begun in Hartford
1861— The Gunnery Camp (Connecticut) is the first summer camp in the country
1864— First Girls' Club established in Waterbury, Connecticut
1866— YWCA begun in Boston
1874— YWCA camps develop, the first of which is Sea Rest in Asbury Park, New Jersey
1876— North Mountain School of Physical Culture, the first private camp (PA), opened by Dr. Joseph Rothrock
1877— The Fresh Air Movement gains popularity in New York, Pennsylvania
1880— West Hartford, Connecticut Reverend George W. Hinckley founds the first church-sponsored boys' camp, The Good Will Farm
1881— Dartmouth College student Ernest Balch builds a small cabin on Squam Lake in New Hampshire where he establishes Camp Chocorua; Reverend Willard Parsons appeals to the New York Tribune for financial assistance for the Fresh Air Fund
1882— Camp Harvard opened by Harvard Theological student William Ford Nichols
1884— Winthrop Talbot takes over Camp Harvard on Asquam Lake
1885— Sumner Dudley offers a camping trip through the YMCA; Camp Harvard in Rindge, New Hampshire opened
1886— Camp Algonquin, a science camp, opened on Lake Squam and directed by Edwin DeMerritte; C. Hanford Henderson opens Camp Marienfeld in New Hampshire; New York's Church of Incarnation opens Incarnation Camp, the nation's oldest coed summer camp (now called Camps Pequot & Sherwood and Pioneer Village)
1887— Camp Harvard moved to Squam Lake and renamed Camp Asquam; Trail Blazer Camps opened in New Jersey by John Ames Mitchell, the publisher of *Life* magazine
1888— The Tribune Fresh Air Fund Aid Society is incorporated
1889— Typhoid fever sweeps through Camp Chocura; Camp Farwell, the first overnight girls' camp in the country, is founded in Vermont
1891— Camp Chocorua closes; Camp Dudley moves to Westport, NY
1892— Camp Arey is the first camp to admit girls (New York) by allowing them to camp for a month; St. Ann's, the first private Catholic camp for boys, established on Lake Champlain
1893— Groton School Camp opened; Camp Lehman opened by the Jewish Working Girls Vacation Society of New York City
1894— Keewaydin Camp founded in Canada; longest-running canoe trip camp in the world; Dr. Winthrop Talbot moves Camp Harvard and renames it Camp Asquam
1895— Camp Pasquaney founded on Newfound Lake, New Hampshire
1896— Camp Marienfield founded on the Upper Delaware River by C. Hanford Henderson; Ronald Mulford opens Camp Choconut, a camp for boys in Friendsville, Pennsylvania
1897— Sumner Dudley dies unexpectedly and "camper #1" George Peck assumes his responsibilities as director
1898— Camp Greenbrier for Boys is established in Alderson, West Virginia
1899— A meeting of camp directors takes place at Camp Asquam
1900— First Boys' Club camp founded by the Salem Fraternity (Massachusetts); Camp Awosting (currently in Lakeville, Connecticut) begins in Ellenville, New York; Camp Redcroft, the first girls' camp, is founded in Hebron, New Hampshire
1902— Camp Kehonka, a girls' camp, is started on Lake Wentworth in New Hampshire by Laura Mattoon; Camp Pinelands for girls opened in Maine; Wyonegonic Camps founded in New Hampshire by the Cobbs; Surprise Lake Camp founded in Cold Spring, New York to provide an escape for boys from Manhattan's Lower East Side tenements; Camp Cobbossee founded in Winthrop, Maine for Jewish boys; the Marsans family arrives in Monmouth, Maine and opens Camp Cobbossee for boys
1903— Sherwood Forest camp opened; Camp Barnard founded in Vermont; first meeting of camp directors takes place in Boston; Camp Becket founded in the Berkshire Mountains of Massachusetts; Tecumseh is founded by three Olympic athletes in Center Harbor, New Hampshire; Camp Belknap opens in Tuftonboro, New Hampshire with the motto, "God first, the other fellow second, and myself last;" Camp Wyonegonic charges $125 for eight weeks; Elizabeth Ford Holt purchases the Barnard Farm on Newfound Lake where she opens Camp Mowglis for boys; Camp Wachusett opened as one of New England's first boys' camps
1904— Pasquaney Nature Club (also known as Mrs. Hassan's Camp) founded in New Hampshire; Kareless Club also founded in New Hampshire; Camp Quanset opened in Orleans, Massachusetts; Hayo-Went-Ha founded at Torch Lake, MI; Adirondack Camp founded by Dr. Elias Brown; George Peck is succeeded by Raymond Kaighn at Camp Dudley

1905— Camp Cloyne opened on Squam Lake; Camp Aloha founded in Vermont; Sons of Daniel Boone established by Daniel Cater Beard; *World's Work Magazine* lists 700 private camps in the United States; Forest Service established; Quanset Sailing Camp opened by Mary Hammatt in Orleans, MA; Camp Pok-O-Moonshine for boys opened by Dr. Charles Alexander Robinson; George Carlton "King" Shafer opens Susquehannock Camp

1906— Schroon Lake Camp, one of the earliest Jewish camps, opened; The Children's Outing Association is begun by a group of women in Almond, Wisconsin in order to provide a fresh air experience for needy local children; Boy's Club is renamed Boys' Club Organization; Rev. Ernest Dennen founds Camp O-AT-KA in East Sebago, Maine; Reverend William Parsons, founder of the Fresh Air Fund, dies; Life's Fresh Air Fund is incorporated in New York City

1907— Camp Asquam shut down because of debt; Walter Wood, superintendent of the Chicago YMCA, lists recreation as one of the ten objectives of camp; Dr. George Meylan establishes the White Mountain Camp for Boys; Alfred Lake Camp opened in South Hope, Maine by Dr. Susan Kingsbury and Florence Marshall; Camp Algonquin started by Chicago's United Charities; Camp Kohut founded by Dr. George Alexander Kohut in Oxford, Maine; Camp Runoia opened in Belgrade Lakes, Maine

1908— Hanoum Camps founded; "Chief" Becky Beckman takes over Camp Dudley, beginning a forty-year tenure; Camp Cedar founded in Pottersville, New York

1909— Owissa (later renamed Tonset) opened for girls 10-16 on Cape Cod by Norma White; Camp St. Croix, a YMCA camp, opens in Hudson, Wisconsin; William Blake establishes Blake Camp to reward good students at the Blake School

1910— The American Camping Association (ACA) is founded as Camp Directors Association of America (CDAA); Boy Scouts of America and Camp Fire USA are also founded; Camp WoHeLo started in New London, Connecticut; Porter Sargent begins to list camps in *A Handbook of American Private Schools*; Charles Scott becomes president of the American Camp Association; the Boy Scouts of America is incorporated and their first camp is held at Silver Bay in New York; Black Elephant Camp begun on Lake George

1911— Camp Fire Girls organized; *Camping for Boys* written by Henry Gibson; Dr. Elias Brown becomes president of the American Camp Association; Camp Greystone, a girls' camp, is opened (NC); Camp Michigamee opened (MI); Tripp Lake Camp opened in Poland, Maine, by Cyd Bettelheim and Eva Rosenheim who directed the camp until 1949

1912— Girl Scouts of America founded; First Girl Scout Camp (Georgia); first Girl Guide troops founded; Camp Gulick (soon renamed Camp Wohelo) founded by Camp Fire Girls; the Boy Scouts begin publishing *Boys' Life*; J. Clark Reed becomes president of the American Camp Association; Camp Sandstone and Minnewawa opened in Wisconsin; Camp Wyonegonic boasts two seven-passenger cars

1913— The National Playground Association's magazine, *Playground*, begins reporting camps in its annual publication; the city of Los Angeles establishes camps; Highland Nature Camps opened in South Naples, Maine; Camp Dudley erects the Avery Boathouse; William Lawrence Camp in New Hampshire begins as a non-profit organization affiliated with the Episcopal Church; Admiral Robert Peary speaks at Camp Kohut in Maine

1914— First Camp Fire Girls camp founded; Dr. George Meylan becomes president of the American Camp Association; Holiday camps open in Iowa; Rocky Mountain Dancing Camp (Colorado) opened by Portia Mansfield and Charlotte Perry; Camp Seely opened in San Bernadino National Forest; Camp Cayuga opened for Jewish boys on Schroon Lake; Camp Dixie founded in Georgia's Blue Ridge Mountains; Camp Dixie begun by "Pop J" Jameson in Clayton, Georgia; Dr. John B. May opens Winnetaska Canoeing Camps

1915— Camp Chinqueka founded in Bantam Lake, Connecticut; Camp Dixie founded in Georgia to serve southern Christian families; Camp Dudley's dining hall is destroyed in a fire; Echo Hill Camp opened in Worton, Maryland; Camp Kawaga opened in Minocqua, Wisconsin by Doc Ehrenreich; School of the Woods is opened by Charles Eastman and his wife

1916— National Association of Directors of Girls' Camps is formed (New York); Edward Healy becomes president of the American Camp Association; National Park Service established; Boulder Point camp founded on Rainbow Lake; Camp Lochearn, a private girls' camp, opened in Post Mills, Vermont; Florence Ellis and Fannie Holt begin Keystone Camp in western North Carolina; Camp Walden opened in Denmark, Maine

1917— Camp Wabanaki opened by Emily Welch; Brant Lake Camp founded by Robert Gerstenzang; Camp Cunningham started on Cape Cod as a sailing camp for underprivileged girls from Milton, Massachusetts; New York State developed a camping department; Camp Timanous for boys started in Maine

1918— Pierce Country Day Camp, the first day camp in the nation, opens; Ellen Farnsworth becomes president of the American Camp Association; Camp Willapa opened in Washington state by Dorothy Elliott

1919— Camp Boiberik, affiliated with the Sholem Aleichem Folk Institute founded; Eugene Lehman becomes president of the American Camp Association; Camp Radford established by the city of Los Angeles; Balfour Lake Camp for boys opens; Helen Van Buren founds Camp Kiniya for girls; Camp Cejwin founded for Jewish children; YMCA Camp Mohawk for Girls opened in Litchfield, Connecticut; Frederick "Chief" Guggenheimer opens Camp Winnebago in Fayette, Maine; Dammie Day founds Camp Merrie-Woode; Samuel and Lila Vanderbilt Webb open an all-girls' YWCA camp in Vermont; the first permanent Girl Scout camp opened in Springfield, Massachusetts

1920— Frank Bryant becomes president of the American Camp Association; Camp Mayflower opened on Crystal Lake on Cape Cod by Norman White and Katherine McLoon Bryan; Camp Wicosuta founded by Anna Rothman in Hebron, New Hampshire; Camp Winaukee opened by three teachers on Lake Winnipesaukee; Camp Greystone for Girls opened by Dr. Joseph Sevier in Tuxedo, North Carolina; Colonel L.L. Rice founded Nakanawa Camps for Girls in Tennessee

1921— Mid-West Camp Directors Association formed (Illinois); Camp Atwood, the first camp founded by an African-American church, founded; Philip Fagans becomes president of the American Camp Association; the Des Moines Playground Association opens the nation's second day camp; Camp Andree Clark opened to older Girl Scouts in Westchester County; Camp Juliette Low opens to Girl Scouts hailing from southern states; Frank Cheley opens Bear Lake Trail School; Camp Waukeela opened in Eaton, New Hampshire; Rockbrook Summer Camp opened for girls in North Carolina; Joe Tinsley opens Camp Illahee on land he purchased two years earlier; Camp Riva-Lake opened by Mrs. William Rutland on the Elk River in Tennessee; the YWCA files Articles of Association for Camp Hochelaga Corporation; the Girl Scouts of America open their first nationally owned and operated camp facility as Camp Andree Clark for older Girl Scouts

1922— The Girl Scouts Camp Department is established; Camp Becket hosts its first Dads' Weekend; Harvey Went becomes president of the American Camp Association; Harvard University President Charles W. Eliot states, 'the organized summer camp is the most important step in education that America has given the world.'; Camp Greylock opened on Raquette Lake; Camp Modin founded in Maine for Jewish children; Catalina Island Camps founded; Camp Monomoy founded in Harwich, Massachusetts by Robert and Emma Delahanty; Emma Graumann opens a camp for girls on Little Bear Pond in Maine called We-You-Wega; Camp Sangamon for boys started in Rutland, Vermont; Camp Louise opened by Lillie and Aaron Straus in Cascade, Maryland; Camp Sangamon opened near Rutland, Vermont; Ruth McIntyre opens Camp Jeanne d'Arc in Merrill, New York; Camp Mondamin opened by Frank "Chief" Bell, Sr. in Tuxedo, North Carolina

1923— Camp Mary Day founded as a Girl Scout camp; *Red Book* associate director Henry Wack publishes *Summer Camps—Boys and Girls*; Louise Price, secretary of the Girl Scout National Camp Committee, tours a number of Girl Scout camps to assess the militaristic nature of the camps; Walter Keyes becomes president of the American Camp Association; Star Lake Music Camp founded in New Jersey; Camp Chaparral opened in California and is the first to have no shelters for campers; Camp WeHaKee is started by the Dominicans of Sinsinawa near Marinette, Wisconsin; Elizabeth S. Johnston, a public health nurse in Cedar Rapids, began a week-long outing for sickly children at Camp Wapsie Y; Camp Carysbrook opened in Riner, Virginia; Brownie Cote buys Blake Camp and renames it Camp Lincoln; Camp Carysbrook opened in the New River Valley of Virginia; Leibush Lehrer purchases Stratford Lake Camp for $29,000 and opens Camp Boiberik, one of the earliest Jewish camps; Life's Camp at Branchville becomes all-girls

1924— Porter Sargent begins publishing the *Handbook of Summer Camps* annually; Pioneer Youth Camp is founded and serves mostly Jewish campers; *Red Book* magazine begins to publish information about camps; the Swimming, Canoe and Campcraft Conference is held at Camp Quinibeck on Lake Fairlee in Vermont; Dr. George Meylan becomes president of the American Camp Association; the Camp Fire Girls hire Barbara Ellen Joy as director of camping services; CDAA and NADGC merge to become the Camp Directors Association (CDA); 4-H for Youth for America started by the U.S. Department of Agriculture; Camp Hilltop established in Hancock, New York; Camp Airy started by Aaron and Lillie Straus in Maryland's Catoctin Mountains; ; Camp Hilltop opened in Hancock, New York; Camp Carolina begun by Professor David Meade Bernard in Brevard, North Carolina

1925— Camp Kinderland, a Jewish summer camp, is founded; Henry Wack publishes *The Camping Ideal: The New Human Race* in which he estimates that there are 1200 private camps serving 150,000 children; the YWCA alone reports 90,000 girls attending 200 camps in 1925 alone; William Gould Vinal becomes president of the American Camp Association; Griffith Park camps opened in Los Angeles; Adirondack Woodcraft Camp opens; Camp Chéri founded on Arey's Pond in Orleans, MA; Camp Namequoit opens as a boys' sailing camp on Pleasant Bay on Cape Cod; Owissa closes; Camp Towanga, one of the nation's first Jewish camps, opens in Groveland, California; Governor and former U.S. Senator Bert Fernald opens the July fourth festivities at Camp Kohut; Camp Foley opened in Minnesota by Father John P. Foley; Tanager Lodge opened as a wilderness camp in Merrill, New York; Kickapoo Camp for Girls started by Charles "Chief" Ford and his wife, Budgie, in Monteney, Arkansas; Lloyd Burgess Sharp becomes the Executive Director of Life's Camps

1926— Camp Edith Macy is established by the Girl Scouts in Briarcliff Manor, New York; Henry Wack publishes *More About Summer Camps, Training for Leisure;* H.W. Gibson becomes president of the American Camp Association; John Cittadino founds Seashore Day Camp, New Jersey's first day camp; Tom Sawyer Camps begin in Laguna Beach, California; *Camping* is published for the first time by the CDA; Cloudmont Camp for Boys founded in Mentone, Alabama; Camp Grizzly Lodge Summer Camp founded in Portola, California by "Mom and Pop" Walton; Elizabeth Johnston expands her one-week program to eight weeks at Camp Wapsie which is eventually renamed Camp Tanager; Birch Rock Camp opened on Lake McWain under the guiding principle that "home and school aren't enough for boys to build self-reliance and character."; Camp Cody opened on Lake Ossipee in New Hampshire; Camp Green Lane opened in Green Lane, Pennsylvania; Forest Lake Camp for boys opened by Harold Confer after purchasing 200 acres around Forest Lake; Camp Swannanoa for girls opens for its first of only two summers in Ridgecrest, North Carolina; Chief and Budgie Ford move Kickapoo Camp to Branson, Missouri; Ora Johnson established Camp Waldemar in Hunt, Texas; Camp Anokijig founded in Wisconsin; Camp Hochelaga moves to Vermont's Lake Champlain

1927— Camp Kinder Ring founded; the Boy Scouts establish their own Department of Camping which subsequently issues *Camp Site Development Plans*; twentys-four Girl Scouts sent on an exchange to a camp in Switzerland; Camp Lake Hubert for Girls is opened and led by Grace Rogers; Camp Kinder Ring opened by the Workmen's Circle/ Arbeter Ring, a Jewish organization designed to help immigrants; H.R. Dobson brings his football team to Wolf Lake in North Carolina to train and discovers a perfect site for Camp Pinnacle which opened the following summer; Camp Killooleet opened in Vermont's Green Mountain National Forest; first national 4-H Camp held on the grounds of the Department of Agriculture

1928— Camp Guilford Bower founded by St. Philip's Church of New York City; Charlotte Gulick dies after a lengthy illness; the National High School Orchestra Camp opens in Interlochen, Michigan; Camp La Junta started by Dr. Ralph Walsh of Corpus Christi, Texas; Winnetaska Canoeing Camps closed

1929— Charles Hendry pens *Camping and Character*; Bernard Mason writes *Camping and Education;* Dr. John Perley Sprague becomes president of the American Camp Association; Morris Libman founds Camp Hillard in Westchester, New York; Camp Viking, a boys sailing camp, opened by Katherine McLoon Bryan and Norman White, Jr. on Cape Cod; Charles and Harriet Cobb hand over the operation of Camp Wyonegonic to their son, Roland, and daughter-in-law, Catherine; YMCA Camp Ihduhapi (a Lakota word meaning "independence") opens in Loretto, Minnesota; Camp Ridgecrest for Boys opened as a Christian camp in Ridgecrest, North Carolina

1930— Lloyd Sharp writes *Education and the Summer Camp;* Camp Mohawk opened by Glen Loucks in White Plains, New York; Margery Plimpton opens Lake Farm Camp on Cape Cod with eight of her students from New York City; Chief Ford purchased land to start Kuggaho, a brother camp to Kickapoo

1930s—The National Park Service develops Recreation Demonstration Areas for camp groups lacking their own grounds and facilities; between 5000 and 7000 camps exist in the United States; Ben Solomon delivers a speech at Teachers' College at Columbia University emphasizing the importance of camping in the education of children; Camp Sealore for boys and Camp Seamaid for girls open on Cape Cod

1931— *Creative Camping* written by Joshua Lieberman; Dr. Frank Hackett becomes president of the American Camp Association; Heart of the Hawkeye Camp Fire Council opens a day camp in Newton, Iowa; E. Carlos Ward writes *Organized Camping and Progressive Education;* Camp Augusta donated to "the girls of Piedmont [California]" by Freda Ehmann in memory of Augusta Collins; Hughie and Selma Black start Pine Forest Camp in Greeley, Pennsylvania; Camp Walden opened in Diamond Point, New York; Camp Pinnacle for Girls opened by Laura Mae Dobson in North Carolina; Lois Goodrich hired by Lloyd Sharp as a "scouting counselor" for the Girls' Camp at Branchville

1932— Labor Zionist Habonim camps founded; Emily Welch becomes president of the American Camp Association; the first YMCA day camps open (White Plains YMCA and Camp Iriquois by the Syracuse and Onondaga County Association); Camp Chickagami opened for boys

1933— Col. Raymond Purcell becomes president of the American Camp Association; Gold Arrow Camp started by Manny Vezie in California's Sierra National Forest; Grace Haynes opens Camp Ton-A-Wandah in western North Carolina

1934— Camp Dudley celebrates its Golden Jubilee; Camp Chéri closes; Jameson Ranch Camp opened in Glennville, California; Jameson Ranch Camp opened; Lois Goodrich becomes director of the Girls' Camp at Branchville

1935— Camp Directors' Association is renamed American Camping Association (ACA) and a list of "Suggested Tentative Standards" was adopted; Camp Brosius founded to serve German-American campers from the midwest; Carlos Ward writes *Organized Camping and Progressive Education;* Herbert Twining becomes president of the American Camp Association; The ACA partners with the American Council on Education, the Progressive Education Association and the National Education Association; cabins replace tents completely at Camp Dudley; Camp Nor-wester founded in Edmonds, Washington; Lake of the Woods Camp for Girls and Greenwoods Camp for Boys started in Decatur, Michigan by Louis and Florence Greenberg; Otto "Cap" Endres and Helen "Mom" Endres open Camp Chippewa on Cass Lake in Minnesota; Mary Gwynn founds Gwynn Valley Camp for boys and girls in Brevard, North Carolina; Chief and Budgie Ford move Kickapoo Camp to New Mexico for the summer

1936— Camp Wo-Chi-Ca, the Workers' Children's Camp is founded and is affiliated with local Communist groups; Dr. Portia Mansfield becomes president of the American Camp Association; the Girl Scouts sponsor the first international camp; Camp Quinebargeopened by Tom Kenly on the shores of Lake Kanasatka

1937— Hazel Allen becomes president of the American Camp Association; Camp Wyonegonic initiates the Wyonegonic Abroad program through which older campers travel to Europe for seven weeks; Camp Arrowhead opened in North Carolina's Blue Ridge Mountains; Richard and Helen Wittenkamp open Red Pine Camp for Girls in Wisconsin; Louis and Florence Greenberg open Camp Greenwoods for Boys

1938— Pleasant Bay Camp founded by Mr. and Mrs. James Bartlett Melcher, Sr. on Cape Cod; Francis "Poppa" Hammatt assumes leadership of Quanset Sailing Camp

1939— Dr. Charles Wilson becomes president of the American Camp Association; Camp Wono founded in Brewster, Massachusetts by Robert and Emma Delahanty

1940— Maestro and Mrs. Arturo Toscanini visit Camp Kohut in Maine; Chief and Budgie Ford move Kickapoo Camp to Colorado for the summer (and for 1941 as well)

1941— Esther Waldo becomes president of the American Camp Association; Frank Cheley opens the Boys' and Girls' Trail's End camps; Friendly Pines Camp opened in Prescott, Arizona by Bud and Isabelle Brown

1942— Dr. Taylor Statten, Sr. becomes president of the American Camp Association; Camp Chickagami closes; Camp Sealore for boys and Camp Seamaid for girls close due to the threat of attack on the Atlantic Coast by Axis forces; Buck's Rock Camp founded in Connecticut by Ernst and Ilse Bulova in the Montessori tradition; Chief and Budgie Ford move Kickapoo Camp to Texas when it becomes impossible to get train cars to bring in campers

1943— West Klusmann becomes president of the American Camp Association

1944— Barbara Ellen Joy becomes president of the American Camp Association; Adirondack Swim Camp opened; Ann and Wendall Schrader open Camp Nicolet for Girls in Eagle River, Wisconsin; Camp Catawba opened by German émigré Vera Lachmann

1945— Camp Echo Lake opened; Girls' Club is renamed Girls, Inc.; Skylake Yosemite Camp founded in Wishon, California; Alice McBride and Doris Tucker begin Camp Bridewood

1946— Camp Fire Girls issue *When You Plan Your Camp;* YMCA publishes *Layout, Building Designs, and Equipment for Y.M.C.A. Camps;* the New York City Department of Education establishes a camp committee to determine the value of the summer camp experience and how it can relate to schooling; Girl Scouts open the first intercultural camp for Native American and non-Native America girls ; Camp Chateaugay founded on Upper Chateaugay Lake by Lil and Aaron Rose; Max and Rose Caldwell begin Kennolyn Camps in Soquel, California; Camp Pinehurst begun by George Hartley Curtis and his wife in Raymond, Maine; Honey and Speedy Altman open Camp Thunderbird for Boys in Minnesota

1947— Carol Gulick Hulbert becomes president of the American Camp Association; Eloise Hart Temple founds Camp Skyline in Mentone, Alabama; Trail's End Camp opened on Chestnut Lake in Pennsylvania by Joe Laub

1948— ACA adopts a set of standards that serve as the foundation for camp accreditation; Girl Scouts issue *Camp Site Development;* Camp Fire USA reports 95 day camp programs; Aldersgate Camp opens; Camp Birchwood opened on Lake Placid; Bob Marshall succeeds "Chief" Beckwith as director at Camp Dudley; Sanborn Western Camps opened in Florissant, Colorado; Lee Horowitz and Herb Blumenfeld open Camp Skylemar in Maine; Camp Walt Whitman opened in New Hampshire's White Mountains; Hal and Dean Tiffany open Hidden Valley Camp as a farm camp in Montville, Maine

1949— Dr. Reynold Carlson becomes president of the American Camp Association; Camp Askenonta founded on Lake Placid by Eugene Schwabach; the Camp Dudley Association (CDA) is established in an effort to stay connected during the off season; Camp Tonset founded on Cape Cod by Roderick and Mary Hagenbuckle as a sailing camp for boys; Camp Laurel opened on Echo Lake in Maine; Caroline Lavenson assumes the directorship at Tripp Lake Camp

1950— 431 different YMCA associations report a total of 67,999 campers attending various day camp programs; state parks report 296 camping facilities with facilities to accommodate 32,457 campers; Camp Danbee for girls started in Hinsdale, Massachusetts; Camp Bridewood is renamed Merri-Mac

1951— Elmer Ott becomes president of the American Camp Association; Jack and Marilyn Williams buy Camp Kiniya; Barbara Morgan publishes *Summer's Children: A Photographic Cycle of Life at Camp*, chronicling life at Camp Treetops; White Eagle Camp (later renamed Camp Kupugani) is opened in Leaf River, Illinois by the 4-H; Camp Voyager opened in Ely, Minnesota by Mim and Charlie Erdmann; White Eagle Camp opened as a 4-H camp in northwestern Illinois; Doris Duke funds the season for Life Camps after *Life* magazine withdraws its corporate support

1952— Camp Fire USA reports 252 day camps; Herbert Sweet becomes president of the American Camp Association; Circle F Dude Ranch Camps founded in Lake Wales, Florida

1953— Catherine Hammett becomes president of the American Camp Association; Heart O' the Hills Camp opened along Texas' Guadalupe Hills; Art and Mollie Lustig open Weequahic in Wayne County, Pennsylvania

1954— Camp Arcady founded on Lake George by Louis and Bingo Brant; Camp Betsey Cox founded by Jean Smith Davies in Vermont; Spencer Boyd starts a small camp for boys to avoid the polio epidemic; Camp Kanata opened in Wake Forest, North Carolina

1955— Theodore Cavins becomes president of the American Camp Association; Camp Netop founded in Casco, Maine; Camp Crestridge for Girls opened as the sister camp of Camp Ridgecrest for Boys in North Carolina and was directed by Arvine Bell; Fred and Evelyn Greenberg start Timber Ridge Camp in West Virginia's Shenandoah Mountains

1956— The ACA adopts its first set of standards for day camps; Camp Rockmount founded as a Christian boys' camp in North Carolina; Nield Gordon, Everette Pigg and their wives purchase land in North Carolina to open Camp Chatuga; the twenty-sixth and final national 4-H camp is held

1957— T.R. Alexander becomes president of the American Camp Association; Elizabeth Nale and Marion Currier purchase Lake Farm Camp on Cape Cod; Mr. and Mrs. James Bartlett, Jr. take over Pleasant Bay Camp; Camp Cayuga opened in Pennsylvania's Pocono Mountains; Ruth and Doc Spahn become directors of Tripp Lake Camp; the Buynak family opens Camp Lohikan in the Pocono Mountains; Ben and Polly Wax purchased Camp Parrydice, a girls' camp in Highlands, North Carolina and founded Camp Highlander

1958—Camp High Rocks opened on Cedar Mountain, North Carolina

1959— Fred Rogers becomes president of the American Camp Association; Mike and Arline Buynak purchase Lake Greeley Camp in Greeley, Pennsylvania; Falcon Camp opened in Ohio

1960— 811 different associations report a total of 171,989 campers attending various YMCA day camps; Camp Fire celebrates its Golden Jubilee with a project entitled "The World Around Us;" the ACA celebrates its fiftieth anniversary; Camp Judaea opened in Hendersonville, North Carolina

1961— Stanley Michaels becomes president of the American Camp Association; Camp Askenonta closed; Camp Dudley begins its German Exchange Program in which campers traveled to Camp Abbensen in Hannover, Germany; Hughie and Selma Black and their children start Lake Owego for boys; Camp Piankatank bought by the Virginia Baptist Mission Board as a Royal Ambassador camp

1963— Camp Birchwood's property purchased by New York state; Camp Timber Tops opened by the Black and Halpern families as a sister camp to Lake Owego for boys

1964— John Dreasen becomes president of the American Camp Association; Adirondack Wilderness Camp opens

1965— Earl Adams ("Daddy Earl") opens Camp Huawni in Texas; Camp Highlander reopened as a coed camp

1966— Howard Gibbs becomes president of the American Camp Association; Camp Mayflower closes; Bruce Hammatt buys Quanset Sailing Camp and serves as owner and director until the camp closes in 1976

1967— Jack Swan expands Camp Pok-O-Moonshine by opening a sister camp called Camp MacCready

1968— Frank Washburn becomes president of the American Camp Association; University of Texas football players Chris Gilbert and Corby Robertson, Jr., establish Camp Olympia in Trinity, Texas

1969— Colvig Sulver camps founded by Craig and Mary Colvig outside Durango, Colorado; Jay Stager purchases Hidden Valley Camp; Long Lake Adventure Camp opens in New York; Falling Creek Camp opened by Jim Miller as a Christian boys' camp in Tuxedo, North Carolina

1970s— Camp MacCready and Camp Pok-O-Moonshine merge into Pok-O-MacCready Camps

1970— John Kirk becomes president of the American Camp Association; Camp Arcady closed; Camp Cayuga closed; Claire and Dusty Drew open Camp Wekeela in Maine; Honey and Speedy Altman open Camp Thunderbird for Girls in Minnesota; Camp Tall Timbers founded by Jerry Smith in High View, West Virginia; Camp Catawba closes

1971— Adirondack Wilderness Camp closes; Camp Greylock closes

1972— Nelson Waters becomes president of the American Camp Association; Camp Tonset closes after its final season

1974— Armin Luehrs becomes president of the American Camp Association; Balfour Lake Camp for boys closes; Camp Highlander purchases Camp Blue Ridge in Mills River, North Carolina after outgrowing its facility;

1975— Camps Monomoy and Wono merge into the Cape Cod Sea Camps in Brewster, Massachusetts

1976— Thomas Curtain becomes president of the American Camp Association; Quanset Sailing Camp closes; Camp Wyonegonic celebrates its seventy-fifth season

1977— First computer camp (National Computer Camps) established

1978— John Howe becomes president of the American Camp Association

1979— Pleasant Bay Camp closes; Camp Chatuga in North Carolina goes coed

1980— Betty van der Smissen becomes president of the American Camp Association; Camp Woodbrooke opened by a Quaker couple near Richland Center, Wisconsin

1981— Camp Woodmont founded on Lookout Mountain in Georgia by Jane and Jim Bennett; Bev and Jon Myers become Tripp Lake Camp's directors

1982— Charles Kujawa becomes president of the American Camp Association; Camp Sierra Vista for Girls opened in Ingram, Texas

1983— International Camping Congress is held and the International Camping Fellowship is formed; Riverview becomes a private camp for girls in Mentone, Alabama; Merri-Mac (formerly Camp Bridewood) becomes Camp Timberlake

1984— Jean McMullan becomes president of the American Camp Association; Adirondack Swim Camp closes; Camp Viking closes; Pat and Joyce Caughlan open Kingsley Pines Camp in Raymond, Maine

1985— Camp Kehona closes after 84 years of operation

1986— Richard Chamberlain becomes president of the American Camp Association; Island Lake opened by Bev and Mike Stoltz in Starrucca, Pennsylvania

1987— Camp Netop in Casco, Maine closes

1988— Edie Klein becomes president of the American Camp Association; Camp Namequoit, one of the oldest camps on Cape Cod, closes

1990— Charles Ackenbom becomes president of the American Camp Association; the National Music Camp changes its name to Interlochen Arts Camp; Forest Lake Camp for Girls opened as a sister camp to Forest Lake Camp for Boys

1993— Connie Coutellier becomes president of the American Camp Association; Rich Morell opens Camp Birch Hill
1994— Nancy Gilbert Brenner is named director of Tripp Lake Camp
1995— Suzanne Welch becomes president of the American Camp Association; former Gwynn Valley Camp owners Howie and Betty Boyd create a conservation easement to protect the camp's 320 acres; Camp Merrie-Woode is named to the National Register of Historic Places
1996— Don Cheley becomes president of the American Camp Association
1998— Foundation for Jewish Camping started by Elisa and Robert Bildner
1999— Rodger Popkin becomes president of the American Camp Association; Leslie Konigsberg Levy becomes director of Tripp Lake Camp
2001— Camp Micah, a traditional Jewish camp, is opened on Peabody Pond in Maine
2002— Marla Coleman becomes president of the American Camp Association; Sandra Schmitt and her staff open Camp Honey Creek for Girls in Hunt, Texas
2003— Camp Piankatank becomes coeducational
2004— Camp Dudley at Kiniya is "reinvented" as a non-profit camp for girls
2005— Ann Sheets becomes president of the American Camp Association; Netop Summer Camp reopened with new facilities in Casco, Maine, by alumnus Steve Hallowell and family
2006— Camp Dudley at Kiniya opens on Lake Champlain in Vermont; the Board of Camp Susquehannock decides to merge its holdings and share the same facility for its boys' and girls' camps; Meg and Clayton Clark open Camp Lonehollow in Texas
2008— Peter Surgenor becomes president of the American Camp Association; following a meeting of the "Board of Campers" at Dylan's Candy Bar in Manhattan, Trail's End Camp rebranded as Chestnut Lake Camp led by Marc Honigfeld
2009— ACA launches "Because of Camp..." campaign nationwide; Camp Lincoln and Camp Lake Hubert celebrate one hundred years of camping
2010— Camp Walden celebrates its ninety-fifth anniversary
2011— Grand reopening of Camp Pinnacle in Flat Rock, North Carolina; Tripp Lake Camp celebrates its centennial summer
2012— Cape Cod Sea Camps celebrates its ninetieth anniversary
2013— Camp Ridgecrest celebrates its eighty-fifth summer; Camp Carysbrook celebrates its ninetieth summer

Sea Camps Colors is an artist's rendering of a Sunday colors ceremony.
Painting by Deborah Fowler Greenwood.

Endnotes

[1] Edward M. Hallowell. *The Childhood Roots of Adult Happiness: Five Steps to Help Kids Create and Sustain Lifelong Joy*. New York: Ballantine, 2002.

[2] Chiam Potok. "Chaim Potok Writes about Going to Summer Camp." 26 Jan. 2013. http://potok.lasierra.edu/Teachers.camp.html.

[3] Leslie Paris. *Children's Nature: The Rise of the American Summer Camp*. New York: New York University Press, 2008, 2.

[4] Mary S. Edgar. "To An Old Camper." *Camp Marlyn*. 21 May 2013. http://campmarlyn.com/old_camper.htm.

[5] Jon Malinowski and Christopher Thurber. "Summer Camp Handbook." *: 16.1 A History of Summer Camp*. 2009. Accessed: 17 Mar. 2012. http://www.summercamphandbook.com/161-a-history-of-summer-camp.html.

[6] Paris, 2.

[7] "Urban Dictionary: Summer Camp." *Urban Dictionary*. 02 Oct. 2012. http://www.urbandictionary.com/define.php?term=summer camp.

[8]"Urban Dictionary: Sleepaway Camp." *Urban Dictionary*. 02 Oct. 2012. http://www.urbandictionary.com/define.php?term=sleepaway camp.

[9] Eleanor Eells. *Eleanor Eells' History of Organized Camping: The First 100 Years*. Martinsville: American Camping Association, 1986, 4.

[10] Jeff Merhige. "Why the World Needs Summer Camp: An Essay to Parents." Editorial. *Camping Magazine* Nov.-Dec. 2011. *American Camp Association*. Nov.-Dec. 2011. 17 Mar. 2012. http://www.acacamps.org/campmag/1111/why-world-needs-summer-camp.

[11] ibid.

[12] "ACA Logos: Eligibility Requirements." *American Camp Association*. 23 Sept. 2012. http://www.acacamps.org/logos/rights.

[13] Abigail Ayres Van Slyck. *A Manufactured Wilderness: Summer Camps and the Shaping of American Youth, 1890-1960*. Minneapolis: University of Minnesota, 2006, xxiv.

[14] Eells, 3.

[15] ibid., 3.

[16] Van Slyck, xix.

[17] Lance Ozier. "Camp: At the Crossroads of America's Past and Future." *American Camp Association*. American Camp Association, June-July 2012. 09 Sept. 2012. http://www.acacamps.org/campmag/1207/camp-crossroads-americas-past-future.

[18] ibid.

[19] Donald R. Hammerman and William M. Hammerman. *Outdoor Education; a Book of Readings*. Minneapolis: Burgess Pub., 1973, 66.

[20] ibid 65 quoting E.H. Lehman *Camps and Camping 1929*.

[21] Paula G. Krimsky. "ConnecticutHistory.org." *ConnecticutHistory.org Reading Writing and the Great Outdoors Frederick Gunns School Transforms Victorianera Education Comments*. 18 May 2013. http://connecticuthistory.org/reading-writing-and-the-great-outdoors-frederick-gunns-school-transforms-victorian-era-education/.

[22] Hammerman 65 quoting Davis Keiser *Camper and Hiker*.

[23] Carlos E. Ward. "Organized Camping and Progressive Education." *Archive.org*. 29 Dec. 2012.

[24] Malinowski and Thurber.

[25] Eells, 8.

[26] ibid., 8.

[27] "WayBack . Summer Vacation . Summer Camp | PBS KIDS GO!" *WayBack*. PBS Kids. 09 Sept. 2012. http://pbskids.org/wayback/summer/features_summer.html.

[28] Eells, 9.

[29] ibid., 26.

[30] Paris., 36.

[31] "CAMP MARIENFELD CHESHAM NEW HAMPSHIRE." *CAMP MARIENFELD CHESHAM NEW HAMPSHIRE*. 02 Mar. 2013.

[32] Van Slyck, xxi.

[33] ibid., xxi.

[34] ibid., xxiii.

[35] ibid., xxiii.

[36] ibid., 171.

[37] Christiaan P. Vorkink "Ernest Thompson Seton and the Woodcraft Indians." *YMCA Camp Belknap*. YMCA Camp Belknap. 29 Aug. 2012. http://www.campbelknap.org/pages/woodcraft_history.htm.

[38] "History of the Woodcraft Movement | The Ernest Thompson Seton Pages." *The Ernest Thompson Seton Pages*. 22 Feb. 2013.

[39] Vorkink.

[40] ibid.

[41] "History of the Woodcraft Movement | The Ernest Thompson Seton Pages." *The Ernest Thompson Seton Pages*. 22 Feb. 2013.

[42] "History of the Woodcraft Movement | The Ernest Thompson Seton Pages." *The Ernest Thompson Seton Pages*. 22 Feb. 2013.

[43] "History of the Woodcraft Movement | The Ernest Thompson Seton Pages." *The Ernest Thompson Seton Pages*. 22 Feb. 2013.

[44] "American President: A Reference Resource." *The Miller Center*. University of Virginia. 29 Aug. 2012. http://millercenter.org/president/roosevelt/essays/biography/1.

[45]Eells, vi.

[46] Malinowski and Thurber.

[47] Paris, 208.

[48] Bonnie Dunn and Denise Frebertshauser. "Native Americans—The First Campers." *American Camp Association*. Sept.-Oct. 2002. Accessed: 02 Mar. 2013.

[49] Richard Gutman and Kellie O. Gutman. *The Summer Camp Memory Book: A Pictorial Treasury of Everything, from Campfires to Color Wars, You Loved about Camp*. New York: Crown, 1983, 22.

[50] George Eastman. "Indian Scout Talks," www.gutenberg.org. 2 Mar. 2013.

[51] Marta Gutman and Ning De Coninck-Smith, eds. *Designing Modern Childhoods: History, Space and the Material Culture of Children*. Rutgers UP, 2008. 25-26.

[52] Van Slyck, 19.

[53] Caille Millner. "America's Summer Camps Have a Surprisingly Political History." *The Daily*. 11 May 2012. Accessed: 24 Dec. 2012.

[54] Anna W. Coale. "Life in a Girls' Camp." *The Outlook* 25 July 1914: 710+. *The Outlook*. 2 Sept. 2012. http://www.unz.org/Pub/Outlook-1914jul25-00687.

[55] ibid.

[56] ibid.

[57] ibid.

[58] Anna Worthington Coale. *Summer in the Girls' Camp,*. New York: Century, 1919.

[59] ibid.

[60] Eells, 14.

[61] "Girls in Tents." *National Women's History Museum*. 23 Sept. 2012. http://www.nwhm.org/blog/girls-in-tents/.

[62] "Camp Kehonka (1902-1985)." *Camp Kehonka (1902-1985)*. 23 Sept. 2012. http://kehonka.wordpress.com/about/.

[63] Gulick, 3.

[64] ibid., 3.

[65] ibid., 7.

[66] ibid., 8-9.

[67] ibid., 9.

[68] ibid., 21-23.

[69] Anna W. Coale. "Life in a Girls' Camp." *The Outlook* 25 July 1914: 710+. *The Outlook*. 2 Sept. 2012. http://www.unz.org/Pub/Outlook-1914jul25-00687.

[70] Coale., 65.

[71] Coale., 45.

[72] Coale., 98.

[73] Van Slyck, xxiv.

[74] "Kehonka History and Lore." *Camp Kehonka (1902-1985)*. 23 Sept. 2012. http://kehonka.wordpress.com/history-and-lore/.

[75] Nancy Ferguson and Jennifer Burch. "Religious Camps: Common Roots and New Sprouts." *American Camp Association*. Nov.-Dec. 2011. 21 May 2013. http://www.acacamps.org/campmag/1111/religious-camps.

[76] "History | Campdudley.org." *www.campdudley.org*. 23 Sept. 2012. http://campdudley.org/alumni/history-2/.

[77] "Mission & Motto." *Mission & Motto*. 2011. 23 Sept. 2012. http://campdudley.org/camp-information/mission-motto/.

[78] "Fast Facts." *www.campdudley.org*. 03 Mar. 2013.

[79] "History." *Becket-Chimney Corners YMCA*. 03 Mar. 2013.

[80] Abigail A. Van Slyck. "Connecting with the Landscape." *Designing Modern Childhoods: History, Space and the Material Culture of Children*. Rutgers University Press, 2008, 25.

[81] "Yesterday, Today, Tomorrow...For Good." *The Y: History*. 09 Mar. 2013. http://www.ymca.net/history/1870-1890s.html.

[82] "Anniversary Timeline." *American Camp Association*. 22 May 2013. http://www.acacamp.org/anniversary/timeline/.

[83] "The Seaside Boarding House for Working Women. NYTimes.com." *The New York Times*. 04 Aug. 1874. Accessed: 03 Mar. 2013.

[84] Abbie Graham. "The Girls' Camp." *Hathi Trust Digital Library*. 03 Mar. 2013, 137.

[85] Peter Marks. "Bunk Beds, Bug Juice and Cultural Identity; Jewish Museum Exhibit Celebrates Summer Camp as a Crucible of Ethnic Tradition." *The New York Times*, 27 May 1994. Accessed: 26 Jan. 2013.

[86] Ramie Arian, Elisa S. Bildner, Dr. Gary A. Tobin, Amy L. Sales, Leonard Saxe, Abraham Wahrhaftig, Jeffrey Eisenstat, Anita Diamant, Emilia Diamant, and Jordan Dale. "Jewish Summer Camps: Our Precious Resource." *www.jewishlife.org*. Ed. Eli Valley. Summer 2002. Accessed: 26 Jan. 2013.

[87] Jeri Zeder. "Summer Camps." *My Jewish Learning*. 03 Feb. 2013.

[88] Sales & Saxe, 17.

[89] ibid., 24-25.

[90] ibid., 25-26.

[91] ibid., 26.

[92] ibid., 26.

[93] Nancy Mykoff. "Summer Camping in the United States | Jewish Women's Archive." *Summer Camping in the United States | Jewish Women's Archive*. N.p., 2005. Accessed: 04 Nov. 2012. http://jwa.org/encyclopedia/article/summer-camping-in-united-states.

[94] Sales & Saxe, 26-27.

[95] ibid., 29.

[96] Zeder, 2013.

[97] "Camp Boiberik." *Omega*. N.p., n.d. Accessed: 20 Feb. 2013. http://www.eomega.org/about-omega/camp-boiberik.

[98] Marla Sokolsky. "Article from The Forward." *Http://boiberik.media.mit.edu*. 29 May 1998. Accessed: 20 Feb. 2013.

[99] Noam Neusner. 5 April 2013. Telephone interview.

[100] Sales & Saxe, 55.

[101] Jason Miller. "The Magic of Jewish Summer Camp." *The Huffington Post*. TheHuffingtonPost.com, 30 Mar. 2012. Accessed: 03 Feb. 2013.

[102] Arian, et al., 2013.

[103] Neusner, 5 April 2013.

[104] Sales and Leonard Saxe, 40.

[105] "The Fresh Air Fund / History & Mission." *The Fresh Air Fund*. N.p., n.d. Accessed: 03 Mar. 2013.http://www.freshair.org/history-and-mission.

[106] "A Place With Real Stars." *The New York Times*. N.p., 02 Apr. 2006. Accessed: 03 Mar. 2013. http://www.nytimes.com/2006/04/02/opinion/nyregionopinions/LIfreshair.html?ref=freshairfund.

[107]"The Fresh Air Fund." *The New York Times*. N.p., 2009. Accessed: 3 Mar. 2013. http://www.nytimes.com/2006/04/02/opinion/nyregionopinions/LIfreshair.html?ref=freshairfund.

[108] ibid.

[109] ibid.

[110] "The Fresh Air Fund / Media Room." *The Fresh Air Fund*. N.p., n.d. Accessed: 29 Dec. 2012.

[111] "A Quick Look at Trail Blazer Camps." *www.trailblazers.org*. N.p., Mar. 2011. Accessed: 3 Mar. 2013.

[112] "Facts and Figures." *Trail Blazers RSS*. N.p., 2012. Accessed: 03 Mar. 2013.http://www.trailblazers.org/about/facts/.

[113] DeGraff, 45.

[114] ibid., 45.

[115] ibid., 48-9.

[116] Ozier.

[117] Chicago Council of Social Agencies. *Character Education in the Summer Camp*. New York: Association, 1935, 3.

[118] "The Annual Trek to Summer Camps; A Million Boys and Girls From the Cities Are Expected to Go This Year to the Woods-- An Organized Camp Movement." *The New York Times*. 03 June 1928. Accessed: 19 Jan. 2013.

[119] Eunice F. Barnard. "Young america Is Off to Summer Camp." *The New York Times*. 29 June 1930. Accessed: 19 Jan. 2013.

[120] Ozier.

[121]Dawn Ewing. *Continuing a Tradition of Education: 2009 Annual Report*. Rep. www.projectmorry.org, 2009. Accessed: 20 Feb. 2013.

[249] Emily Bernstein. "A Summer at Camp: Arriving; Short Sheets, and a Long Way From Home." *The New York Times,* 9 July 1995.

[250] Elissa Gootman. "Red vs. White." *The New York Times,* 13 Aug. 2010. Accessed: 1 Apr. 2012. http://www.nytimes.com/2010/08/15/nyregion/15ritual.html?pagewanted=all.

[251] Tucknott.

[252] Werlin.

[253] Emily Bernstein. "A Summer at Camp: Arriving; Short Sheets, and a Long Way From Home." *The New York Times* 9 July 1995.

[254] Paris, 136.

[255] Paris, Leslie. "Please Let Me Come Home." *The American Child: A Cultural Studies Reader.* Ed. Caroline Levander and Carol Singley. N.p.: n.p., n.d. 246-61.

[256] ibid., 250.

[257] Paris, *Children's Nature,* 141.

[258] ibid., 136.

[259] Diane Falanga. "Celebrating Summer Camp." Message to the author. 21 March 2012. E-mail.

[260] Timothy Noah. "What Your Enjoyment of Sleep-away Camp, or Lack of Same, Says about Your Character." *Slate Magazine.* N.p., 23 July 2010. Accessed: 24 Dec. 2012.

[261] Michael Rosenzweig. "Summer Camp Got in the Way of Blogging." *Boulder Jewish News.* N.p., 9 Sept. 2012. Accessed: 07 Apr. 2013. http://boulderjewishnews.org/2012/summer-camp-got-in-the-way-of-blogging/.

[262] Ira Glass. "Notes on Camp | This American Life." *This American Life.* WBEZ, Chicago, Illinois, 28 Aug. 1998. *This American Life.* Accessed: 30 Mar. 2013. http://www.thisamericanlife.org/radio-archives/episode/109/notes-on-camp.

[263] Bussel, Bette. "How to Prepare for Summer Camp." *Seacoast Online.* N.p., 15 Feb. 2013. Accessed: 22 Feb. 2013.

[264] "5,000 Children Speed to Camps Amid Bedlam in Grand Central." *The New York Times.* N.p., 01 July 1935. Accessed: 19 Jan. 2013.

[265] ibid.

[266] ibid.

[267] Christine Haughney. "To Reach Simple Life of Summer Camp, Lining Up for Private Jets." *The New York Times,* 25 July 2011. Accessed: 22 Dec. 2012.

[268] Sandy Lederman. "Bonding on the Camp Bus." Editorial. *The New York Times* 25 July 2011: n. pag. Accessed: 22 Dec. 2012.

[269] Minsberg, Talya. "What Parents Don't Get About Camp." Web log post. *Motherlode Blog. The New York Times,* 17 Aug. 2012. Accessed: 28 Oct. 2012. http://parenting.blogs.nytimes.com/2012/08/17/what-parents-dont-get-about-camp/.

[270] Elizabeth Donnan Kintz. "Celebrating Summer Camp." Message to the author. 21 May 2012. E-mail.

[271] Potok.

[272] Van Slyck, *A Manufactured Wilderness,* 51.

[273] Van Slyck, *A Manufactured Wilderness,* 58.

[274] Paris, *Children's Nature,* 117.

[275] "Camps of Orleans." *Orleans Historical Society.* N.p., n.d. Accessed: 28 Oct. 2012. http://www.orleanshistoricalsociety.org/collections-camps.html.

[276] Kevin Nicolai. "Sailing." Message to the author. 13 Oct. 2012. E-mail.

[277] Jim Fay. "Sailing." Message to the author. 15 Oct. 2012. E-mail.

[278] Andy Stern. "Sailing." Message to the author. 26 Nov. 2012. E-mail.

[279] Anna W. Coale. "Life in a Girls' Camp." *The Outlook* 25 July 1914: 710+. *The Outlook.* Accessed: 2 Sept. 2012. http://www.unz.org/Pub/Outlook-1914jul25-00687.

[280] Van Slyck, 88.

[281] ibid., 88.

[282] Christie Peterson. Personal communication. 30 August 2012.

[283] ibid.

[284] Paris, *Children's Nature,* 114.

[285] ibid.,115.

[286] Wack, 71.

[287] ibid., 60.

[288] ibid., 63.

[289] ibid., 63.

[290] ibid., 67.

[291] Loder email 5/16/12.

[292] Kali Parmley. Personal communication. 29 October 2012.

[293] Kelly Flanagan. Personal communication. 22 February 2013.

[294] Jim Flanagan. "Landsports." Message to the author. 30 August 2012. E-mail.

[295] Coale, Anna W. "Life in a Girls' Camp." *The Outlook* 25 July 1914: 710+. *The Outlook.* Accessed: 2 Sept. 2012. http://www.unz.org/Pub/Outlook-1914jul25-00687.

[296] Paris, 116.

[297] Van Slyck, 63.

[298] Lucy J. Norvell. "Play at Summer Camp." *Seacoast Online.* N.p., 15 Feb. 2013. Accessed: 23 Feb. 2013.

[299] Karen Alexander. "Jewish Camps Spawn a U.S. Playground Hit." *The New York Times.* N.p., 18 July 2012. Accessed: 4 Nov. 2012. http://www.nytimes.com/2012/07/19/us/gaga-playground-game-is-popular-at-camps.html.

[300] Douglas Mann. "Going Gaga Over Gaga Ball." *Camp Business.* Northstar Publishing, 5 July 2008. Accessed: 16 June 2013. http://www.northstarpubs.com/articles/cb/going-gaga-over-gaga-ball.

[301] Eden Foster. "Art Matters: The Creative Side of the Summer Camp Experience." *American Camp Association.* N.p., Nov.-Dec. 2003. Accessed: 28 Oct. 2012. http://www.acacamps.org/campmag/cm0311art.

[302] ibid.

[303] Richard Frost. Personal communication. 1 November 2012.

[304] Deborah Fowler Greenwood. "Arts at Summer Camp." Message to the author. 24 February 2013. E-mail.

[305] "Summer Camps." *Discover Archery.* N.p., n.d. Accessed: 02 Nov. 2012. http://www.discoverarchery.org/from-the-basics-to-the-podium/summer-camps/.

[306] Doug Engh. "Camps and Archery." Message to the author. 20 Feb. 2013. E-mail.

[307] "CMP—Camp Riflery Program." *CMP—Camp Riflery Program.* N.p., 2012. Accessed: 03 Nov. 2012. http://www.odcmp.com/Training/CRProgram.htm.

[308] Ben Bertolino. Personal communication, 28 October 2012.

[309] Tommy Cusano. Personal communication. 2 March 2013.

[310] Olivia Barker. "Can Summer Camps Revive the Lost Art of Letter Writing?" *USA Today* 28 July 2010: n. pag. *www.usatoday.com.* 28 July 2010. Accessed: 23 Dec. 2012. http://usatoday30.usatoday.com/life/lifestyle/2010-07-28-lettersfromcamp28_CV_N.htm.

[311] Lisa Belkin. "Letters From Camp." *The New York Times* 29 July 2010. *www.newyorktimes.com.* 29 July 2010. Accessed: 23 Dec. 2012. http://parenting.blogs.nytimes.com/2010/07/29/letters-from-camp/

[312] Diane Falanga. "Celebrating Summer Camp." Message to the author. 21 March 2012. E-mail.

[313] Halliday, Ayun. "How Not to Write to Your Child at Camp." *The New York Times*. N.p., 9 Aug. 2012. Accessed: 23 Dec. 2012.

[314] ibid.

[315] ibid.

[316] Kate Kelly. "Summer Care Packages Have Honorable Heritage." *The Huffington Post*. TheHuffingtonPost.com, 21 July 2009. Accessed: 17 Mar. 2013. http://www.huffingtonpost.com/kate-kelly/summer-care-packages-have_b_242199.html.

[317] ibid.

[318] "Sealed With A Kiss." *Camp Care Packages by Sealed With A Kiss (SWAK)*. N.p., n.d. Accessed: 31 Aug. 2012. https://www.eswak.com/pages/home.

[319] ibid.

[320] Susan Domius. "A Place and an Era in Which Time Could Stand Still." *The New York Times*. N.p., 14 Aug. 2008. Accessed: 16 June 2013. http://www.nytimes.com/2008/08/15/nyregion/15bigcity.html?_r=2.

[321] Kathy Thurber. "Riding Programs at Camp: Enrichment of a Different Kind." *American Camp Association*. N.p., Mar.-Apr. 2004. Accessed: 04 Nov. 2012. http://www.acacamps.org/members/knowledge/program/cm/043riding.

[322] ibid.

[323] Sue Ballentine. "Celebrating Summer Camp." Message to the author. 16 Mar. 2013. E-mail.

[324] Richard Gutman and Kellie O. Gutman. *The Summer Camp Memory Book: A Pictorial Treasury of Everything, from Campfires to Color Wars, You Loved about Camp*. New York: Crown, 1983.

[325] Thomas Adler. *Campingly Yours*. Chandler: Five Star Publications, Inc., 2008, 71-72.

[326] Tomas Ayala. "Reflections on Camp." Message to the author. 22 Mar. 2013. E-mail.

[327] Kelly Flanagan. Personal communication. 22 February 2013.

[328] Personal interview with anonymous source, July 20, 2012.

[329] Jari A. Villanueva. "24 Notes That Tap Deep Emotions." N.p., n.d. Accessed: 29 Dec. 2012.

[330] ibid.

[331] Albion G. Hart. "Thoughts at Bedtime."

[332] Van Slyck 52.

[333] Allan Peterson. Personal communication. 24 March 2013.

[334] Katy Jack Goerke. Personal communication. 24 March 2013.

[335] Frank Rich. "Camp Visiting Day." *The New York Times*, 24 July 1994. Accessed: 27 Apr. 2013. http://www.nytimes.com/1994/07/24/opinion/journal-camp-visiting-day.html.

[336] Susan J. Gordon. "Parenmts' Guide to Visiting Day at Camp." *The New York Times*. N.p., 26 July 1981. Accessed: 19 Jan. 2013.

[337] "Summer Camp." *Rookie*. N.p., 10 June 2013. Accessed: 15 June 2013. http://rookiemag.com/2013/06/summer-camp/.

[338] Tom Schweinhart. "The Camp Community and the World Community." *American Camp Association*. N.p., Mar.-Apr. 2002. Accessed: 25 Mar. 2013. http://www.acacamps.org/members/knowledge/participant/cm/023camp.

[339] Jeff Cheley. "Celebrating Summer Camp." Message to the author. E-mail 14 March 2012.

[340] Barbie Cobb. "Celebrating Summer Camp." Message to the author. 29 April 2012. E-mail.

[341] Timothy Noah. "You Are How You Camped: What Your Enjoyment of Sleep-away Camp, or Lack of Same, Says about Your Character." *Slate Magazine*. N.p., 23 July 2010. Accessed: 24 Dec. 2012.

[342] Gutman and Gutman, 139.

[343] Hallie E.Bond, Joan Jacobs Brumberg, and Leslie Paris. *"A Paradise for Boys and Girls": Children's Camps in the Adirondacks*. [Syracuse, N.Y.]: Adirondack Museum/Syracuse UP, 2006. Print, 2.

[344] Maxman, 14 March 2012. E-mail.

[345] Cheley, E-mail 14 March 2012.

[346] Dawn Swindle. "Camp Traditions: Memories in the Making." *American Camp Association*. American Camp Association, May-June 2010. Accessed: 09 Sept. 2012. http://www.acacamps.org/campmag/1005/camp-traditions.

[347] ibid.

[348] Shelby Bruselof. "Celebrating Summer Camp." Message to the author. 10 May 2012. E-mail.

[349] Carol Sudduth. "Camp traditions." Message to the author. 25 March 2013. E-mail.

[350] Glass. "Notes on Camp | This American Life," 28 Aug. 1998.

[351] Paris, 99.

[352] Mary Beth McCauley. "Summer Camp: Sunset for an American Tradition?" *The Christian Science Monitor*. The Christian Science Monitor, 16 June 2010. Accessed: 22 Mar. 2013. http://www.csmonitor.com/USA/Society/2010/0616/Summer-camp-Sunset-for-an-American-tradition.

[353] Paris, 103.

[354] Audrey Monke. "Celebrating Summer Camp." Message to the author. 12 May 2012. E-mail.

[355] Adler, 14.

[356] ibid., 35.

[357] Paris 121.

[358] ibid., 121.

[359] ibid., 121.

[360] Gutman and Gutman, 133.

[361] ibid., 134.

[362] "About Adult Color Wars." *Adult Color Wars*. N.p., n.d. Accessed: 23 Mar. 2013. http://www.adultcolorwars.com/about/.

[363] ibid.

[364] Jack Pearse. "Camp Songs—History and Traditions." *American Camp Association*. American Camp Association, July-Aug. 2010. Accessed: 09 Sept. 2012. http://www.acacamps.org/campmag/1007/camp-songs-history-and-traditions.

[365] ibid.

[366] ibid.

[367] Maxman, 14 March 2012. E-mail.

[368] Michael Eisner. "What I Did During Summer Vacation." Tri-State Camping Conference. New York. 8 Mar. 2001. Speech.

[369] "Building Creativity Through Campfire." *Camp Laurel Maine Summer Camp Blog*. N.p., 15 Mar. 2011. Accessed: 28 Apr. 2013. http://www.camplaurel.com/blog/uncategorized/building-creativity-through-campfire/.

[370] Gutman and Gutman, 123.

[371] Adler, 72.

[372] Talya Minsberg. "What Parents Don't Get About Camp." Web log post. *Motherlode Blog. The New York Times*, 17 Aug. 2012. Accessed: 28 Oct. 2012. http://parenting.blogs.

nytimes.com/2012/08/17/what-parents-dont-get-about-camp/.

[373] Maxman, 14 March 2012. E-mail.

[374] Personal interview with anonymous source, July 20, 2012.

[375] Personal interview with anonymous source, July 20, 2012.

[376] Paris, 258.

[377] Gutman and Gutman, 146.

[378] Paris, 258.

[379] Malinowski, Jon, and Chris Thurber. "Closing Day." *'Summer Camp Handbook'* N.p., 2009. Accessed: 29 June 2013. http://www.summercamphandbook.com/141-closing-day.html.

[380] Paris, 258.

[381] Marjorie Ingall. "Home Again." *Tablet Magazine.* N.p., 26 July 2010. Accessed: 30 Mar. 2013. http://www.tabletmag.com/jewish-life-and-religion/40375/home-again.

[382] ibid.

[383] ibid.

[384] April Smith. "Off to Summer Camp." *The New York Times*, 26 Apr. 1981. Accessed: 27 Mar. 2012.

[385] Jon Malinowski. "Summer Camps in Popular Culture." *American Camp Association.* American Camp Association, May-June 2011. Accessed: 09 Sept. 2012. http://www.acacamps.org/campmag/1105/summer-camps-popular-culture.

[386] Scott Tobias. "The New Cult Canon: Wet Hot American Summer." *AV Club Live.* N.p., 11 June 2008. Accessed: 27 Jan. 2013.

[387] JK Rock. "Celebrating Summer Camp." Message to the author. 20 Mar. 2013. E-mail.

[388] ibid.

[389] Laurie Susan Kahn. *Sleepaway: The Girls of Summer and the Camps They Love.* New York: Workman Publishing, 2003, p.242.

[390] "Camp Inspirations: Look Who Went to Camp!" *American Camp Association.* N.p., n.d. Accessed: 16 Jan. 2013.

[391] "Hello Muddah Hello Fadduh Lyrics." *MetroLyrics.* N.p., n.d. Accessed: 04 July 2013. http://www.metrolyrics.com/hello-muddah-hello-fadduh-lyrics-sherman-allan.htmldah-lyrics-allan-sherman.html.

[392] "Summer Camp: Board Game (2003)." *Board Game Geek.* N.p., n.d. Accessed: 04 May 2013. http://boardgamegeek.com/boardgame/7069/summer-camp.

[393] "CampAntics." *CampAntics.* Accessed: 04 July 2013. http://campantics.com/index.php.

[394] Elliot E. Cohen. "A Teen-Age Bill Of Rights." *The New York Times.* 07 Jan. 1945. Accessed: 09 Mar. 2013.

[395] Nancy Mykoff. "Summer Camping in the United States | Jewish Women's Archive." *Summer Camping in the United States | Jewish Women's Archive.* N.p., 2005. Accessed: 04 Nov. 2012. http://jwa.org/encyclopedia/article/summer-camping-in-united-states.

[396] Fielden, 92.

[397] Camp Trends Fact Sheet." *American Camp Association.* American Camp Association, n.d. Accessed: 09 Sept. 2012. http://www.acacamps.org/media-center/camp-trends/fact.

[398] Bond, Jacobs, Brumberg, and Paris, 2

[399] Cheley, E-mail 14 March 2012.

[400] Coleman, Marla. "Camp Is the Antidote..." *American Camp Association.* 19 Mar. 2013. Accessed: 02 June 2013. http://www.acacamps.org/blog/word-peg/camp-antidote.

[401] ibid.

[402] ibid.

[403] ibid.

[404] Jess Michaels. "Camp Revamped." *The Right Camp.* Accessed: 21 Jan. 2013.

[405] Fielden, 103.

[406] Peg L.Smith. "The Great Education Debate: Camp Has A Place In Childhood Development." *Parents & Families.* N.p., n.d. Accessed: 31 Mar. 2013. http://www.campparents.org/case-for-camp/great-education-debate.

[407] ibid.

[408] Don Steinberg. "Rites of Passage: A Summer at Camp Kweebec | Philadelphia Magazine—Page 2." *Philadelphia Magazine Articles.* July 2012. Accessed: 29 Mar. 2013. http://www.phillymag.com/articles/rites-passage-summer-camp-kweebec/2/.

[409] Tina Kelley. "Dear Parents: Please Relax, It's Just Camp." *The New York Times.* N.p., 26 July 2008. Accessed: 27 Dec. 2012.

[410] ibid.

[411] Coutellier, 44.

[412] William Hageman. "Camp 21st Century." *Chicago Tribune.* Chicago Tribune, 22 Feb. 2011. Accessed: 09 Sept. 2012. http://articles.chicagotribune.com/2011-02-22/features/sc-fam-0222-specialty-camp-20110222_1_academic-camps-summer-camp-three-camp-sessions.

[413] Fielden, 102.

[414] Natasha Singer. "Summer Camps Are Facing New Economics." *The New York Times* 10 July 2011: n. pag. *The New York Times*, 10 July 2011. Accessed: 23 Dec. 2012.

[415] Fielden, 103.

[416] Don Steinberg. "Rites of Passage: A Summer at Camp Kweebec | Philadelphia Magazine—Page 2." *Philadelphia Magazine Articles.* N.p., July 2012. Accessed: 29 Mar. 2013. http://www.phillymag.com/articles/rites-passage-summer-camp-kweebec/2/.

[417] Jason Miller. "Summer Camp Online Photos: The Good, the Bad and the Oy Vey. Online Photos: The Good, the Bad and the Oy Vey." *Rabbi Jason Miller—Blog: Summer Camp Online Photos: The Good, the Bad and the Oy Vey.* N.p., 29 Aug. 2012. Accessed: 21 Sept. 2012. http://blog.rabbijason.com/2012/08/summer-camp-online-photos-good-bad-and.html.

[418] Alexandra Sifferlin, Alice Park, and Maia Szalavitz. "Summer Camp: Great for Kids, Maybe Even Better for Parents." *Time.* Time, 3 Aug. 2012. Accessed: 22 Sept. 2012. http://healthland.time.com/2012/08/03/summer-camp-great-for-kids-maybe-even-better-for-parents/.

[419] ibid.

[420] Mary Beth McCauley. "Summer Camp: Sunset for an American Tradition?" *The Christian Science Monitor.* The Christian Science Monitor, 16 June 2010. Accessed: 22 Mar. 2013. http://www.csmonitor.com/USA/Society/2010/0616/Summer-camp-Sunset-for-an-American-tradition.

[421] ibid.

[422] Natasha Singer. "Summer Camps Are Facing New Economics." *The New York Times* 10 July 2011: n.p. *The New York Times*, 10 July 2011. Accessed: 23 Dec. 2012.

[423] Sudduth, 25 March 2013. E-mail.

[424] Cheley, 14 March 2012. E-mail.
[425] ibid.
[426] ibid.
[427]Singer.
[428] Corey Dockswell. "Celebrating Summer Camp." 12 Oct. 2012. E-mail.
[429] Ira Glass. "Notes on Camp | This American Life." *This American Life*. WBEZ, Chicago, Illinois, 28 Aug. 1998. *This American Life*. Accessed: 30 Mar. 2013. http://www.thisamericanlife.org/radio-archives/episode/109/notes-on-camp.
[430] ibid.
[431] ibid.
[432] Dan Duett. "Thoughts on Summer Camp." *Dan Duett*. N.p., n.d. Accessed: 30 Mar. 2013. http://danduett.com/thoughts-on-summer-camp.html.
[433] ibid.
[434] ibid.
[435] Chris Parsons. Personal communication. 4 February 2013.
[436] Sherry Maxman. "Celebrating Summer Camp." Message to the author. 14 March 2012. E-mail.
[437] Tucknott, 1 May 2012. E-mail.
[438] Loder, 15 May 2012. E-mail.
[439] McCarlie. Personal communication. 16 October 2012.
[440] Dianna Lamb Walsh. Personal communication. 5 September 2012.
[441] "Into the Woods and Onto the Water." Editorial. *The New York Times*. *The New York Times*, 02 July 2012. Accessed: 24 Dec. 2012.
[442] "Benefits of Camp: Skill Development." *American Camp Association*. Accessed: 30 Dec. 2012. http://www.acacamps.org/media-center/benefits-of-camp/skill.
[443]ibid.
[444] JK Rock. "Celebrating Summer Camp." Message to the author. 30 Mar. 2013. E-mail.
[445] ibid.
[446] Josh Wolk. Personal communication. 21 March 2013.
[447] JK Rock, 30 Mar. 2013. E-mail.
[448] ibid.
[449] Holly Zax Shuter. Personal communication. 14 July 2012.
[450] Russell, 30 April 2012. E-mail.
[451] Wolk, 21 March 2013.
[452] Mike Gomez. Personal communication. 20 March. 2013.
[453] Bond, Brumberg, and Paris, vii.
[454]Kim Ward Burt. Personal communication. 22 December 2012.
[455] Lucy J. Lang, and Seth Soulstein. "The Speech: 15 Years Later." Cape Cod Sea Camps 90th Anniversary. Cape Cod Sea Camps, Brewster. 11 Aug. 2012.
[456] Corrinne Loder. "Celebrating Summer Camp." 15 May 2012. E-mail.
[457] JK Rock. 20 Mar. 2013. E-mail.
[458] ibid.
[459] ibid.
[460] "Summer Camp." *Rookie*. 10 June 2013. Accessed: 15 June 2013. http://rookiemag.com/2013/06/summer-camp/.
[461] Amy Oscar. "A Fine Romance: Couples Find Love of a Lifetime at Jewish Summer Camp." *A Fine Romance: Couples Find Love of a Lifetime at Jewish Summer Camp*. N.p., July-Aug. 2009. Accessed: 30 Mar. 2013. http://www.jewishrockland.org/page.aspx?id=202324.
[462] Sarah Singer. "Some Enchanted Summer..." *Washington Jewish Week* 28 Aug. 2008: B14-15.
[463] Nancy B. Scheff. "Romance at Ramah." *Ramah Marriages*. Accessed: 30 Mar. 2013. http://www.campramah.org/content/ramahmarriages.php.
[464] Neusner, Noam. 5 April 2013. Telephone interview.
[465] ibid.
[466] Steinberg.
[467] Anne Tergesen. "The Best Summer Camps for Grown-Ups." *The Wall Street Journal*. 18 Mar. 2013. Accessed: 23 Mar. 2013. http://online.wsj.com/article/SB100014241278873246105045782757441436570 34.html.
[468] "Camp Grounded." *Camp Grounded*. N.p., n.d. Accessed: 23 Mar. 2013. http://campgrounded.org/.
[469] ibid.
[470] ,Jessica P. Ogilvie. "Welcome to Camp Wannabe a Kidagin." *Los Angeles Times*. Los Angeles Times, 18 May 2013. Accessed: 18 May 2013. http://www.latimes.com/health/la-he-color-wars-20130518,0,2269399.story.
[471] Steinberg.
[472] ibid.
[473] Wolk.
[474] ibid.
[475] "Why Camping Is Important." *Why Camping Is Important*. Accessed: 12 May 2013. http://www.friendsofcrowellhilaka.org/camping_reasons.htm.
[476] David Himmel. *A Camp Story: The History of Lake of the Woods and Greenwoods Camps*. Charleston, SC: History, 2012. Print, 152.
[477] Jeff Merhige. "Why the World Needs Summer Camp: An Essay to Parents." Editorial. *Camping Magazine* Nov.-Dec. 2011. *American Camp Association*. Nov.-Dec. 2011. Accessed: 17 Mar. 2012. http://www.acacamps.org/campmag/1111/why-world-needs-summer-camp.
[478] De Saint-Exupery, Antione. "The Little Prince by Antione De Saint-Exupery." *The Little Prince by Antione De Saint-Exupery*. Accessed: 20 July 2013. http://www.poetryfountain.com/littleprince/chapter21.html.
[479] "James Kavanaugh (1928—2009)." *James Kavanaugh (1928—2009)*. N.p., n.d. Accessed: 20 July 2013. http://james-kavanaugh.memory-of.com/About.aspx

Bibliography

"About 4-H Camp Farley." Camp Farley Outdoor Education Center. N.p., n.d. Accessed: 17 Mar. 2013. http://www.campfarley.com/about4-H.htm.

"About Adult Color Wars." N.p., n.d. Accessed: 23 Mar. 2013. http://www.adultcolorwars.com/about/.

"About FJC." Homepage. N.p., n.d. Accessed: 26 Jan. 2013.

"ACA Logos: Eligibility Requirements." *American Camp Association*. N.p., n.d. Accessed: 23 Sept. 2012. http://www.acacamps.org/logos/rights.

Adler, Thomas. *Campingly Yours*. Chandler: Five Star Publications, Inc., 2008.

Alexander, Karen. "Jewish Camps Spawn a U.S. Playground Hit." *The New York Times*. N.p., 18 July 2012. Accessed: 4 Nov. 2012. http://www.nytimes.com/2012/07/19/us/gaga-playground-game-is-popular-at-camps.html.

"The American Child: A Cultural Studies Reader." Google Books. Ed. Caroline Levander and Carol Singley. N.p., n.d. Accessed: 15 June 2013. http://books.google.com/books/about/The_American_child.html?id=MMI-sS1J6ekC.

"American President: A Reference Resource." The Miller Center. University of Virginia, n.d. Accessed: 29 Aug. 2012. http://millercenter.org/president/roosevelt/essays/biography/1.

"Anniversary Timeline." *American Camp Association*. 22 May 2013. http://www.acacamp.org/anniversary/timeline/.

"The Annual Trek to Summer Camps; A Million Boys and Girls From the Cities Are Expected to Go This Year to the Woods—An Organized Camp Movement." *The New York Times*. N.p., 03 June 1928. Accessed: 19 Jan. 2013.

Arian, Ramie, Elisa S. Bildner, Dr. Gary A. Tobin, Amy L. Sales, Leonard Saxe, Abraham Wahrhaftig, Jeffrey Eisenstat, Anita Diamant, Emilia Diamant, and Jordan Dale. "Jewish Summer Camps: Our Precious Resource." www.jewishlife.org. Ed. Eli Valley. N.p., Summer 2002. Accessed: 26 Jan. 2013.

Ayala, Tomas. "Reflections on Camp." Message to the author. 22 Mar. 2013. E-mail.

Ballentine, Sue. "Celebrating Summer Camp." Message to the author. 16 Mar. 2013. E-mail.

Barker, Olivia. "Can Summer Camps Revive the Lost Art of Letter Writing?" *USA Today*, 28 July 2010: n. pag. www.USATODAY.com. 28 July 2010. Accessed: 23 Dec. 2012. http://usatoday30.usatoday.com/life/lifestyle/2010-07-28-lettersfromcamp28_CV_N.htm

Barnard, Eunice F. "Young America Is Off to Summer Camp." *The New York Times*. N.p., 29 June 1930. Accessed: 19 Jan. 2013.

Barstead, Matthew. "The Human Need to Belong: An Evolution in How We Think about Camps." *American Camp Association*. N.p., July-Aug. 2012. Accessed: 09 Sept. 2012. http://www.acacamps.org/campmag/1207/human-need-belong.

Belkin, Lisa. "Letters From Camp." *The New York Times* 29 July 2010: n. pag. www.newyorktimes.com. 29 July 2010. Accessed: 23 Dec. 2012. http://parenting.blogs.nytimes.com/2010/07/29/letters-from-camp/

Belkin, Lisa. "Sleep-Away Separation Pains." *The New York Times*. N.p., 22 June 2010. Accessed: 01 Feb. 2013.

"Benefits of Camp: Skill Development." *American Camp Association*. N.p., n.d. Accessed: 30 Dec. 2012. http://www.acacamps.org/media-center/benefits-of-camp/skill

Benjamin, Grace. "Celebrating Summer Camp." Message to the author. 13 May 2012. E-mail.

Bergmann, Jenna. "Camp Personal Essay." 19 August 2012. E-mail.

Bermel, Joyce. "Speaking Personally: Ah, Summer Camp." *The New York Times*. N.p., 29 July 1979. Accessed: 19 Jan. 2013.

Bernstein, Emily. "A Summer at Camp: Arriving; Short Sheets, and a Long Way From Home." *The New York Times*, 9 July 1995.

Bertolino, Ben. Personal communication, 28 October 2012.

Black, Kathryn. *In the Shadow of Polio: A Personal and Social History*. N.p.: De Capo, 1997. Google Books. Accessed: 20 Feb. 2013.

"Boiberik Home Page." Boiberik Home Page. N.p., n.d. Accessed: 19 Feb. 2013.

Bond, Hallie E., Joan Jacobs. Brumberg, and Leslie Paris. "A Paradise for Boys and Girls": Children's Camps in the Adirondacks. [Syracuse, N.Y.]: Adirondack Museum/Syracuse UP, 2006. Print.

Bouchier, David. "Out of Order; The Rise and Fall of Summer Camp." *The New York Times*. N.p., 21 July 1996. Accessed: 19 Jan. 2013.

Bruselof, Shelby. "Celebrating Summer Camp." Message to the author. 10 May 2012. E-mail.

"Building Creativity Through Campfire." Camp Laurel Maine Summer Camp Blog. N.p., 15 Mar. 2011. Accessed: 28 Apr. 2013. http://www.camplaurel.com/blog/uncategorized/building-creativity-through-campfire/.

Burgess, Colin. "Celebrating Summer Camp." Message to the author. 23 August 2012. E-mail.

Burt, Kim Ward. Personal communication. 22 December 2012.

Bussel, Bette. "How to Prepare for Summer Camp." Seacoast Online. N.p., 15 Feb. 2013. Accessed: 22 Feb. 2013.

Bussel, Bette. "Shopping for Summer Camp." Seacoast Online. N.p., 15 Feb. 2013. Accessed: 22 Feb. 2013.

"Camp and 21st Century Skills: Oxymoron or Ideal?" *American Camp Association*. N.p., 23 Feb. 2012. Accessed: 11 June 2013. http://www.acacamps.org/blog/parents-place/oxymoron-or-ideal.

"The Camp around the Corner: Day Camp." *American Camp Association*. N.p., n.d. Accessed: 16 Mar. 2013.

"Camp Boiberik." Omega. N.p., n.d. Accessed: 20 Feb. 2013. http://www.eomega.org/about-omega/camp-boiberik

"Camp Dudley 1885–1907: The Pioneering Years." www.campdudley.org. N.p., n.d. Accessed: 23 Sept. 2012. http://campdudley.org/wp-content/uploads/2011/08/1885-1907-History.pdf.

"Camp Dudley 1908 to 1930: Chief Beckman...the Early Years." www.campdudley.org. N.p., n.d. Accessed: 23 Sept. 2012. http://campdudley.org/wp-content/uploads/2011/08/1908-1930-History.pdf.

"Camp Dudley 1930–1947: The Thirties and Forties." www.campdudley.org. N.p., n.d. Accessed: 23 Sept. 2012. http://campdudley.org/wp-content/uploads/2011/08/1930-1947-History.pdf.

"Camp Dudley 1948 to 1970: "The Marshall Years"" www.campdudley.org. N.p., n.d. Accessed: 23 Sept. 2012. http://campdudley.org/wp-content/uploads/2011/08/1948-1970-History.pdf.

Camp Fire Girls "hiking" N.d. Photograph. Bain Collection, Washington, D.C. Accessed: 19 Feb. 2013.

Camp Fire Girls at Lake Sebago. N.d. Photograph. Bain Collection, Washington, D.C. Accessed: 19 Feb. 2013.

"A Camp for Every Child—Girls Only, Boys Only, or Coed?" *American Camp Association.* N.p., n.d. Accessed: 17 Mar. 2013.

"Camp Grounded." http://campgrounded.org/.N.p., n.d. Accessed: 23 Mar. 2013.

"Camp Inspirations: Look Who Went to Camp!" *American Camp Association.* N.p., n.d. Accessed: 16 Jan. 2013.

"Camp Kehonka (1902-1985)." Camp Kehonka (1902–1985). N.p., n.d. Accessed: 23 Sept. 2012. http://kehonka.wordpress.com/about/.

"Camp Knowledge Center." *American Camp Association.* Accessed: 22 Nov. 2012. http://www.acacamps.org/knowledge.

"Camp Marienfeld Chesham New Hampshire." N.p., n.d. Accessed: 02 Mar. 2013.

"Camp Trends Fact Sheet." *American Camp Association.* American Camp Association, n.d. Accessed: 09 Sept. 2012. http://www.acacamps.org/media-center/camp-trends/fact.

"CampAntics." N.p., n.d. Accessed: 04 July 2013. http://campantics.com/index.php.

"Camps of Orleans." Orleans Historical Society. N.p., n.d. Accessed: 28 Oct. 2012. http://www.orleanshistoricalsociety.org/collections-camps.html.

Cheley, Jeff. "Celebrating Summer Camp." Message to the author. E-mail 14 March 2012.

Chicago Council of Social Agencies. Character Education in the Summer Camp. New York: Association, 1935. Print.

"CMP—Camp Riflery Program." N.p., 2012. Accessed: 03 Nov. 2012. http://www.odcmp.com/Training/CRProgram.htm.

Coale, Anna W. "Life in a Girls' Camp." *The Outlook,* 25 July 1914: 710+. The Outlook. Accessed: 2 Sept. 2012. http://www.unz.org/Pub/Outlook-1914jul25-00687.

Coale, Anna Worthington. *Summer in the Girls' Camp.* New York: Century, 1919. Print.

Cobb, Barbie. "Celebrating Summer Camp." Message to the author. 29 April 2012. E-mail.

Cohen, Elliot E. "A Teen-Age Bill Of Rights." *The New York Times.* N.p., 07 Jan. 1945. Accessed: 09 Mar. 2013.

Cohen, Helen H. "A Camp Director Remembers World War II." *American Camp Association.* N.p., July-Aug. 2003. Accessed: 31 Mar. 2013. http://www.acacamps.org/members/knowledge/strategic/cm/037wwii.

Coleman, Jessica. "The Power of Camp: Camp Changes Lives in Positive Ways." American Camp Association, May-June 2009. Accessed: 09 Sept. 2012. http://www.acacamps.org/campmag/issues/0905/power-of-camp.

Coleman, Marla. "Camp Is the Antidote..." *American Camp Association.* 19 Mar. 2013. 02 June 2013. http://www.acacamps.org/blog/word-peg/camp-antidote.

Coleman, Marla. "Campfire Stories for Parents." N.p., 28 Sept. 2010. Accessed: 10 Mar. 2013.

Coleman, Marla. "Why Day Camp?" *American Camp Association.* N.p., n.d. Accessed: 16 Mar. 2013.

Cook, Joan. "The Specialized Summer Camp." *The New York Times.* N.p., 26 Feb. 1966. Accessed: 19 Jan. 2013.

Coutellier, Connie. "Years of Adventures and Challenges: The History of Day Camp." *Camping Magazine,* Jan.-Feb. 2011: 40-45.

Cusano, Tommy. Personal communication. 2 March 2013.

Darmanian, Justine. Personal communication. 6 February 2013.

Davis, Warren. Personal communication. 24 May 2012.

DeGraaf, Donald G., Ronald D. Ramsing, Julianne Gassman, and Kathy H. DeGraaf. *Camp Leadership: A Staff Development Approach.* Peosta, IA: Eddie Bowers Pub., 2002. Print.

Dell'Antonia, KJ. "How to Pack a Camp Care Package." Web log post. Motherlode Blog. *The New York Times,* 10 July 2012. Accessed: 28 Oct. 2012. http://parenting.blogs.nytimes.com/2012/07/10/how-to-pack-a-camp-care-package/.

Dell'Antonia, KJ. "Is It Too Late to Send Myself to Camp?" Web log post. Motherlode Blog. *The New York Times,* 31 May 2012. Accessed: 28 Oct. 2012. http://parenting.blogs.nytimes.com/2012/05/31/is-it-too-late-to-send-myself-to-camp/.

De Saint-Exupery, Antione. *The Little Prince.* N.p., n.d. Accessed: 20 July 2013. http://www.poetryfountain.com/littleprince/chapter21.html.

Di Dio, Ombretta. "What Happens in Summer Camp Doesn't Necessarily Have to Stay There." *The Huffington Post.* TheHuffingtonPost.com, 19 July 2012. Accessed: 16 Mar. 2013. http://www.huffingtonpost.com/ombretta-di-dio/summer-camp_b_1688072.html

Dockswell, Corey. "Celebrating Summer Camp." 12 Oct. 2012. E-mail.

Domius, Susan. "A Place and an Era in Which Time Could Stand Still." *The New York Times.* N.p., 14 Aug. 2008. Accessed: 16 June 2013. http://www.nytimes.com/2008/08/15/nyregion/15bigcity.html?_r=2.

Duett, Dan. "Thoughts on Summer Camp." Dan Duett. N.p., n.d. Accessed: 30 Mar. 2013. http://danduett.com/thoughts-on-summer-camp.html.

Dunn, Bonnie, and Denise Frebertshauser. "Native Americans—The First Campers." *American Camp Association.* N.p., Sept.-Oct. 2002. Accessed: 02 Mar. 2013.

Eastman, George. "Indian Scout Talks." www.gutenberg.org. N.p., n.d. Accessed: 2 Mar. 2013.

Edgar, Mary S. "To An Old Camper." Camp Marlyn. N.p., n.d. Accessed: 21 May 2013. http://campmarlyn.com/old_camper.htm.

Eells, Eleanor. "Camps of a Different Sort." www.acacamp.org. N.p., n.d. Accessed: 3 Mar. 2013.

Eells, Eleanor. *Eleanor Eells' History of Organized Camping: The First 100 Years.* Martinsville: American Camping Association, 1986.

Egerman, Laura. Personal communication, 11 October 2012.

Eisner, Michael D. *Camp.* New York: Warner Books, 2005.

Eisner, Michael. "What I Did During Summer Vacation." Tri-State Camping Conference. New York. 8 Mar. 2001. Speech.

Elkind, David. "The Values of the Traditional Camp Experience: The Power of Play." *American Camp Association.* N.p., Jan.-Feb. 2007. Accessed: 29 Mar. 2013. http://www.acacamps.org/campmag/0701elkind.

Engh, Doug. "Camps and Archery." Message to the author. 20 Feb. 2013. E-mail.

Ernest Thompson Seton, on Bench. N.d. Photograph. Bain Collection, Washington, D.C. Accessed: 19 Feb. 2013.

Ewing, Dawn. *Continuing a Tradition of Education: 2009 Annual Report.* Rep. www.projectmorry.org, 2009. Accessed: 20 Feb. 2013.

"Facts and Figures." Trail Blazers RSS. N.p., 2012. Accessed: 03 Mar. 2013. http://www.trailblazers.org/about/facts/

Falanga, Diane. "Celebrating Summer Camp." Message to the author. 21 March 2012. E-mail.

Falanga, Diane. *P.S.: I Hate It Here! Kids' Letters from Camp.* New York: Abrams Image, 2010.

"Fast Facts." www.campdudley.org. N.p., n.d. Accessed: 03 Mar. 2013.

Fay, Jim. "Sailing." Message to the author. 15 Oct. 2012. E-mail.

Ferguson, Nancy, and Jennifer Burch. "Religious Camps: Common Roots and New Sprouts." *American Camp Association.* N.p., Nov.-Dec. 2011. Accessed: 21 May 2013. http://www.acacamps.org/campmag/1111/religious-camps.

Fielden, Jay. "Sleepaway Days." Editorial. *Town & Country,* June-July 2012: 14.

"Find a Camp." *American Camp Association.* N.p., n.d. Accessed: 1 June 2013. http://find.acacamps.org/search_results.php.

Fishback, Brian. "The Comedy News: Clique That Went to Jewish Summer Camp Together Still Won't Shut Up About Jewish Summer Camp." N.p., 16 Jan. 2013. Accessed: 16 Jan. 2013.

"5,000 Children Speed to Camps Amid Bedlam in Grand Central." *The New York Times.* N.p., 01 July 1935. Accessed: 19 Jan. 2013.

Flanagan, Joanna. "Celebrating Summer Camp." 27 April 2013. E-mail

Flanagan, Kelly. "Quotes." Message to the author. 22 Feb. 2013. E-mail.

Fleshler, Dan. "The Camp Counselor vs. the Intern." Web log post. Motherlode Blog. *The New York Times,* 29 May 2012. Accessed: 28 Oct. 2012. http://parenting.blogs.nytimes.com/2012/05/29/the-camp-counselor-vs-the-intern/.

Foster, Eden. "Art Matters: The Creative Side of the Summer Camp Experience." *American Camp Association.* N.p., Nov.-Dec. 2003. Accessed: 28 Oct. 2012. http://www.acacamps.org/campmag/cm0311art.

"4-H Motto, Creed and Pledge." National 4-H History Preservation Program. N.p., n.d. Accessed: 15 June 2013. http://4-hhistorypreservation.com/History/M-C-P/.

"Framework for 21st Century Learning—The Partnership for 21st Century Skills." N.p., n.d. Accessed: 10 June 2013. http://www.p21.org/overview/skills-framework.

"The Fresh Air Fund." *The New York Times.* N.p., 2009. Accessed: 3 Mar. 2013. http://www.nytimes.com/2006/04/02/opinion/nyregionopinions/LIfreshair.html?ref=freshairfund

"The Fresh Air Fund / History & Mission." The Fresh Air Fund. N.p., n.d. Accessed: 03 Mar. 2013. http://www.freshair.org/history-and-mission

"The Fresh Air Fund / Home." The Fresh Air Fund. N.p., n.d. Accessed: 29 Dec. 2012.

"The Fresh Air Fund / Media Room." The Fresh Air Fund. N.p., n.d. Accessed: 29 Dec. 2012.

Friedman, Sally. "Marriages Made in Camp." *Philadelphia Inquirer.* N.p., 24 June 2009. Accessed: 30 Mar. 2013. http://www.philly.com/philly/living/celebrations/weddings/20090624_Marriages_made_in_camp.html?mr=1.

Frost, Richard. Personal communication. 1 November 2012.

Gabordi, John. "Living with Campers." Message to the author. 19 Feb. 2013. E-mail.

Garran, Nancy. "Quote." Message to the author. 30 April. 2013. E-mail.

Geist, William E. "About New York: The Joys of Summer Camp for Parents." *The New York Times.* N.p., 13 July 1985. Accessed: 19 Jan. 2013.

Gillis, Charles. (2010) "1970-1979." *American Cultural History.* Lone Star College-Kingwood Library. Last modified August 2010. http://wwwappskc.lonestar.edu/popculture/decade70.html.

"Girls in Tents." National Women's History Museum. N.p., n.d. Accessed: 23 Sept. 2012. http://www.nwhm.org/blog/girls-in-tents/.

Glass, Ira. "Notes on Camp | This American Life." This American Life. WBEZ, Chicago, Illinois, 28 Aug. 1998. This American Life. Accessed: 30 Mar. 2013. http://www.thisamericanlife.org/radio-archives/episode/109/notes-on-camp.

Goerke, Katy Jack. Personal communication. 24 March 2013.

Goldstein, Meredith. "At Summer Camp, Love Is in the Air." www.boston.com. N.p., 22 July 2009. Accessed: 30 Mar. 2013. http://www.boston.com/lifestyle/relationships/articles/2009/07/22/at_summer_camp_love_is_in_the_air/.

Golub, Michael. "Station Two: Chapter III." N.p., n.d. Accessed: 20 Feb. 2013.

Gomez, Mike. Personal communication. 20 March. 2013.

Goodwin, Susan and Becky Bradley. "1960-1969." *American Cultural History.* Lone Star College-Kingwood Library. Last modified July 2010. http://wwwappskc.lonestar.edu/popculture/decade60.html.

Gootman, Elissa. "Red vs. White." *The New York Times.* 13 Aug. 2010. Accessed: 1 Apr. 2012. http://www.nytimes.com/2010/08/15/nyregion/15ritual.html?pagewanted=all.

Gordon, Susan J. "Parents' Guide to Visiting Day at Camp." *The New York Times.* N.p., 26 July 1981. Accessed: 19 Jan. 2013.

Gottesman, Itzik. "Boiberik History." Boiberik History. N.p., n.d. Accessed: 19 Feb. 2013.

Graham, Abbie. "The Girls' Camp." Hathi Trust Digital Library. N.p., n.d. Accessed: 03 Mar. 2013.

Greenwood, Deborah. "Arts at Summer Camp." Message to the author. 24 Feb. 2013. E-mail.

Greenwood, Deborah. "Summer Camp." Message to the author. 24 Feb. 2013. E-mail.

Greenwood, Deborah Fowler. "Arts at Summer Camp." Message to the author. 24 February 2013. E-mail.

Gulick, Luther Halsey. *Camp Fire Girls (of America).* Carlisle, MA: Applewood, 1912. Print.

Gulick, Luther H. *The Dynamic of Manhood.* New York: Association, 1918. Google Books. Accessed: 01 Apr. 2012. http://books.google.com/books?id=Ek8WAAAAYAAJ.

Gundersheim, Jillian. "Camp." Message to the author. 2 Mar. 2013. E-mail.

Gutman, Marta, and Ning De Coninck-Smith, eds. *Designing Modern Childhoods: History, Space and the Material Culture of Children.* N.p.: Rutgers UP, 2008. Print.

Gutman, Richard, and Kellie O. Gutman. *The Summer Camp Memory Book: A Pictorial Treasury of Everything, from Campfires to Color Wars, You Loved about Camp.* New York: Crown, 1983. Print.

Hackett, Frank S. "THE Summer Camp: An Outdoor School." *The New York Times.* N.p., 24 May 1931. Accessed: 19 Jan. 2013.

Hageman, William. "Camp 21st Century." *Chicago Tribune*, 22 Feb. 2011. Accessed: 09 Sept. 2012. http://articles.chicagotribune.com/2011-02-22/features/sc-fam-0222-specialty-camp-20110222_1_academic-camps-summer-camp-three-camp-sessions.

Hageman, William. "Specialized Pursuits in a New Breed of Summer Camp." www.ohio.com. N.p., 25 Feb. 2012. Accessed: 11 July 2013. http://www.ohio.com/lifestyle/specialized-pursuits-in-a-new-breed-of-summer-camp-1.266893?localLinksEnabled=false.

Halliday, Ayun. "How Not to Write to Your Child at Camp." *The New York Times.* N.p., 9 Aug. 2012. Accessed: 23 Dec. 2012.

Hallowell, Edward M. *The Childhood Roots of Adult Happiness: Five Steps to Help Kids Create and Sustain Lifelong Joy.* New York: Ballantine, 2002. Print.

Hallowell, Edward. "Sustaining Lifelong Joy: Camp Is a Key Connector." American Camp Association, Jan.-Feb. 2009. Accessed: 09 Sept. 2012. http://www.acacamps.org/campmag/issues/0901/lifelong-joy.

Hammerman, Donald R., and William M. Hammerman. *Outdoor Education; a Book of Readings.* Minneapolis: Burgess Pub., 1973. Print.

Hardin, Dayna G. "Embracing Change: Ensuring the Camp Experience Remains Relevant in 2020 and Beyond." American Camp Association, Mar.-Apr. 2010. Accessed: 09 Sept. 2012. http://www.acacamps.org/campmag/issues/1003/embracing-change-ensuring-camp-experience-remains-relevant-in-2020.

Hart, Albion G. "Thoughts at Bedtime."

Haughney, Christine. "To Reach Simple Life of Summer Camp, Lining Up for Private Jets." *The New York Times*, 25 July 2011. Accessed: 22 Dec. 2012.

"Heavy Weights." IMDb. IMDb.com, n.d. Accessed: 27 Jan. 2013.

"Hello Muddah Hello Fadduh Lyrics." MetroLyrics. N.p., n.d. Accessed: 04 July 2013. http://www.metrolyrics.com/hello-muddah-hello-fadduh-lyrics-sherman-allan.htmldah-lyrics-allan-sherman.html.

Hill, Thomas and Steve Slavkin. *Salute Your Shorts: Life at Summer Camp.* New York: Workman Publishing, 1986.

Himmel, David. *A Camp Story: The History of Lake of the Woods and Greenwoods Camps.* Charleston, SC: History, 2012. Print.

"History." Becket-Chimney Corners YMCA. N.p., n.d. Accessed: 03 Mar. 2013.

"History." Trail Blazers RSS. N.p., 2012. Accessed: 03 Mar. 2013.

"History | Campdudley.org." www.campdudley.org. N.p., n.d. Accessed: 23 Sept. 2012. http://campdudley.org/alumni/history-2/.

"History of the Woodcraft Movement." The Ernest Thompson Seton Pages. N.p., n.d. Accessed: 22 Feb. 2013.

"Camp Fuller History." *History.* N.p., n.d. Accessed: 06 Apr. 2013. http://www.ymcagreaterprovidence.org/Branches/CampFuller/AboutCampFuller/History/tabid/193/Default.aspx.

Hoffman, Jan. "At Camp, It's Not Grub, It's Cuisine." *The New York Times*, 11 July 2012. Accessed: 19 Jan. 2013.

Hyland, William G. "Books: Richard Rodgers." *The New York Times.* N.p., 1998. Accessed: 11 Feb. 2013.

"Into the Woods and Onto the Water." Editorial. *The New York Times. The New York Times*, 02 July 2012. Accessed: 24 Dec. 2012.

Ingall, Marjorie. "Home Again." *Tablet Magazine.* N.p., 26 July 2010. Accessed: 30 Mar. 2013. http://www.tabletmag.com/jewish-life-and-religion/40375/home-again.

"James Kavanaugh (1928–2009)." Accessed: 20 July 2013. http://james-kavanaugh.memory-of.com/About.aspx.

James, Penny. "Cyclic Trends in the History of Camping: Reflections on the Past/Implications for the Future." *American Camp Association.* N.p., 2009. Accessed: 4 Nov. 2012. http://www.acacamps.org/sites/default/files/images/research/connect/presentations/2009/Cyclic_Trends_in_the_History_of_Camping.pdf.

Kahn, Laurie Susan. *Sleepaway: The Girls of Summer and the Camps They Love.* New York: Workman Publishing, 2003.

"Kehona's Contribution to Camping (1902-1985)." Camp Kehonka (1902-1985). N.p., n.d. Accessed: 23 Sept. 2012. http://kehonka.wordpress.com/history-and-lore/kehonkas-contribution-to-camping/.

"Kehonka History and Lore." Camp Kehonka (1902-1985). N.p., n.d. Accessed: 23 Sept. 2012. http://kehonka.wordpress.com/history-and-lore/.

Keller, Jared. "In Praise of Summer Camp." *The Atlantic.* N.p., 28 June 2012. Accessed: 24 Dec. 2012.

Kelly, Kate. "Summer Care Packages Have Honorable Heritage." *The Huffington Post.* TheHuffingtonPost.com, 21 July 2009. Accessed: 17 Mar. 2013. http://www.huffingtonpost.com/kate-kelly/summer-care-packages-have_b_242199.html.

Kelley, Tina. "Dear Parents: Please Relax, It's Just Camp." *The New York Times.* N.p., 26 July 2008. Accessed: 27 Dec. 2012.

Kimmelman, Andy. "Why Day Camp Matters." American Camp Association, Nov.-Dec. 2011. Accessed: 09 Sept. 2012. http://www.acacamps.org/campmag/1111/why-day-camp-matters.

Kintz, Elizabeth Donnan. "Celebrating Summer Camp." Message to the author. 21 May 2012. E-mail.

Konarska, Amanda. "Celebrating Summer Camp." Message to the author. 24 April 2012. E-mail.

Kowalczyk, Kristin. "Celebrating Summer Camp." Message to the author. 30 April 2012. E-mail.

Krimsky, Paula G. "ConnecticutHistory.org." ConnecticutHistoryorg Reading Writing and the Great Outdoors Frederick Gunns School Transforms Victorianera Education Comments. N.p., n.d. Accessed: 18 May 2013. http://connecticuthistory.org/reading-writing-and-the-great-outdoors-frederick-gunns-school-transforms-victorian-era-education/.

Lang, Lucy J., and Seth Soulstein. "The Speech: 15 Years Later." Cape Cod Sea Camps 90th Anniversary. Cape Cod Sea Camps, Brewster. 11 Aug. 2012.

Lazarowitz, Elizabeth. "Kid Consultants Design Their Ultimate Camp." *New York Daily News*. N.p., 11 June 2007. Accessed: 20 Jan. 2013.

Lederman, Sandy. "Bonding on the Camp Bus." Editorial. *The New York Times*, 25 July 2011: n. p. Accessed: 22 Dec. 2012.

Lehrer, Leibush. *Camp Boiberik: The Growth of an Idea*. New York: n.p., 1959. Print.

Levinsky, Nancy S. "Summer Camps." Colby's Maine Jewish History Project. N.p., 9 July 2012. Accessed: 03 Feb. 2013.

"List of Job Description Titles." *American Camp Association*. Accessed: 22 Nov. 2012. http://www.acacamps.org/members/jobdesc/titles.

Loder, Corrinne. "Celebrating Summer Camp." 15 May 2012. E-mail

Madeyski, Tom. "What Do You Do the Rest of the Year? Camp Director Has Become a Year-Round Job." *American Camp Association*. N.p., May-June 2000. Accessed: 31 Mar. 2013. http://www.acacamps.org/members/knowledge/human/cm/005whtdoyr.

Malanga, Gina. Personal communication, 29 April 2012.

Malinowski, Jon, and Chris Thurber. "Closing Day." *Summer Camp Handbook*. N.p., 2009. Accessed: 29 June 2013. http://www.summercamphandbook.com/141-closing-day.html.

Malinowski, Jon, and Chris Thurber. "Coed or Single Sex?" *Summer Camp Handbook*. N.p., 2009. Accessed: 11 June 2013. http://www.summercamphandbook.com/54-coed-or-single-sex.html.

Malinowski, Jon, and Chris Thurber. "The Goals of Camping." *Summer Camp Handbook*. N.p., 2009. Accessed: 11 June 2013. http://www.summercamphandbook.com/22-the-goals-of-overnight-camping.html.

Malinowski, Jon, and Chris Thurber. "Selection Checklist." *Summer Camp Handbook*. N.p., 2009. Accessed: 11 June 2013. http://www.summercamphandbook.com/71-selection-checklist.html.

Malinowski, Jon. "Summer Camps in Popular Culture." *American Camp Association*. American Camp Association, May-June 2011. Accessed: 09 Sept. 2012. http://www.acacamps.org/campmag/1105/summer-camps-popular-culture.

Malinowski, Jon, and Christopher Thurber. *Summer Camp Handbook*: "16.1 A History of Summer Camp." 2009. Accessed: 17 Mar. 2012. http://www.summercamphandbook.com/161-a-history-of-summer-camp.html.

Mann, Douglas. "Going Gaga Over Gaga Ball." *Camp Business*. Northstar Publishing, 5 July 2008. Accessed: 16 June 2013. http://www.northstarpubs.com/articles/cb/going-gaga-over-gaga-ball.

Marcus, Jon. "How to Choose a Summer Camp." Boston.com. N.p., 26 Feb. 2012. Accessed: 16 Mar. 2013.

Marcus, Jon. "The More Camps Change..." Boston.com. N.p., 26 Feb. 2012. Accessed: 16 Mar. 2013.

Marks, Peter. "Bunk Beds, Bug Juice and Cultural Identity; Jewish Museum Exhibit Celebrates Summer Camp as a Crucible of Ethnic Tradition." *The New York Times*, 27 May 1994. Accessed: 26 Jan. 2013.

Martin, Bruce, Christine Cashel, Mark Wagstaff, and Mary Breuning. *Outdoor Leadership: Theory and Practice*. Google Books. N.p., 2006. Accessed: 23 Sept. 2012. http://books.google.com/books?id=D4ewmFjesOcC.

Maxman, Sherry. "Celebrating Summer Camp." Message to the author. 14 March 2012. E-mail.

McCarlie, Alison. Personal communication. 16 October 2012.

McCauley, Mary Beth. "Summer Camp: Sunset for an American Tradition?" *The Christian Science Monitor*, 16 June 2010. Accessed: 22 Mar. 2013. http://www.csmonitor.com/USA/Society/2010/0616/Summer-camp-Sunset-for-an-American-tradition.

McCurdy, Tom. Personal communication, 1 July 2012.

McCurdy, Tom and Carol Ann. "Camp Answers." 27 May 2012. E-mail.

McMullan, Jean G. "Camp Truths Are Forever." *American Camp Association*. N.p., 20 May 2013. Accessed: 02 June 2013. http://www.acacamps.org/blog/word-peg/camp-truths-are-forever.

"Meatballs." IMDb. IMDb.com, n.d. Accessed: 27 Jan. 2013.

Merhige, Jeff. "Why the World Needs Summer Camp: An Essay to Parents." Editorial. *Camping Magazine*, Nov.-Dec. 2011. *American Camp Association*. Nov.-Dec. 2011. Accessed: 17 Mar. 2012. http://www.acacamps.org/campmag/1111/why-world-needs-summer-camp.

Mernick, Sherry. "Daniella-camp Book." Message to the author. 5 Apr. 2013. E-mail.

Michaels, Jess. "Camp Revamped." The Right Camp. N.p., n.d. Accessed: 21 Jan. 2013.

Miller, Jason. "The Magic of Jewish Summer Camp." *The Huffington Post*. TheHuffingtonPost.com, 30 Mar. 2012. Accessed: 03 Feb. 2013.

Miller, Jason. "Summer Camp Online Photos: The Good, the Bad and the Oy Vey. Online Photos: The Good, the Bad and the Oy Vey." Rabbi Jason Miller—Blog. N.p., 29 Aug. 2012. Accessed: 21 Sept. 2012. http://blog.rabbijason.com/2012/08/summer-camp-online-photos-good-bad-and.html.

Millner, Caille. "America's Summer Camps Have a Surprisingly Political History." *The Daily*. N.p., 11 May 2012. Accessed: 24 Dec. 2012.

Minsberg, Talya. "What Parents Don't Get About Camp." Web log post. Motherlode Blog. *The New York Times*, 17 Aug. 2012. Accessed: 28 Oct. 2012. http://parenting.blogs.nytimes.com/2012/08/17/what-parents-dont-get-about-camp/.

"Mission & Motto." N.p., 2011. Accessed: 23 Sept. 2012. http://campdudley.org/camp-information/mission-motto/.

"Modern Methods Urged for Camps." *The New York Times*. N.p., 26 Jan. 1946. Accessed: 19 Jan. 2013.

Monke, Audrey. "GAC question." Message to the author. 2 May 2012. E-mail.

Monke, Audrey. "Why Kids Flourish at Camp." *American Camp Association*. 02 June 2013. http://www.campparents.org/newsletter/1305/why-kids-flourish-camp.

"Mrs. C Gulick Dies in Camp in Maine." *The New York Times*. N.p., 29 July 1928. Accessed: 19 Jan. 2013.

Mykoff, Nancy. "Summer Camping in the United States | Jewish Women's Archive." N.p., 2005. Accessed: 04 Nov. 2012. http://jwa.org/encyclopedia/article/summer-camping-in-united-states.

Neusner, Noam. "Carving Our Niches at Summer Camp." *The Jewish Daily Forward.* N.p., 24 June 2009. Accessed: 30 Mar. 2013. http://forward.com/articles/108456/carving-our-niches-at-summer-camp/.

Neusner, Noam. 5 April 2013. Telephone interview.

Newman, Andy. "Outsourcing Comes to Summer Camp." *The New York Times.* N.p., 9 July 2009. Accessed: 11 Feb. 2013.

Nicolai, Kevin. "Sailing." Message to the author. 13 Oct. 2012. E-mail.

"1970-1999: The End of the Century, Three Directors." www.campdudley.org. N.p., n.d. Accessed: 23 Sept. 2012. http://campdudley.org/wp-content/uploads/2011/08/1970-1999-History.pdf.

Noah, Timothy. "You Are How You Camped: What Your Enjoyment of Sleep-away Camp, or Lack of Same, Says about Your Character." *Slate Magazine.* N.p., 23 July 2010. Accessed: 24 Dec. 2012.

Norvell, Lucy J. "Play at Summer Camp." Seacoast Online. N.p., 15 Feb. 2013. Accessed: 23 Feb. 2013.

Ogilvie, Jessica P. "Welcome to Camp Wannabe a Kidagin." *Los Angeles Times,* 18 May 2013. Accessed: 18 May 2013. http://www.latimes.com/health/la-he-color-wars-20130518,0,2269399.story.

Orecklin, Michele. "The Purpose-Driven Summer Camp." *Time,* 25 May 2005. Accessed: 04 Nov. 2012. http://www.time.com/time/magazine/article/0,9171,1064447,00.html.

Oscar, Amy. "A Fine Romance: Couples Find Love of a Lifetime at Jewish Summer Camp." N.p., July-Aug. 2009. Accessed: 30 Mar. 2013. http://www.jewishrockland.org/page.aspx?id=202324.

Ozier, Lance. "Camp: At the Crossroads of America's Past and Future." American Camp Association, June-July 2012. Accessed: 09 Sept. 2012. http://www.acacamps.org/campmag/1207/camp-crossroads-americas-past-future.

Paris, Leslie. *Children's Nature: The Rise of the American Summer Camp.* New York: New York University Press, 2008.

Paris, Leslie. "Please Let Me Come Home." *The American Child: A Cultural Studies Reader.* Ed. Carloine Levander and Carol Singley. N.p.: n.p., n.d. 246-61. Print.

Parmley, Kali. Personal communication. 29 October 2012.

Parsons, Chris. Personal communication. 4 February 2013.

Pearse, Jack. "Camp Songs—History and Traditions." American Camp Association, July-Aug. 2010. Accessed: 09 Sept. 2012. http://www.acacamps.org/campmag/1007/camp-songs-history-and-traditions.

Peavy, David L. "A Bibliography of the Boy Scouts of America." www.paxtu.org. N.p., 22 Aug. 2010. Accessed: 30 Aug. 2012. http://www.paxtu.org/Paxtu_-_BSA_Bibliography_-_Part_E_-_100822.pdf.

Peterson, Allan. Personal communication. 24 March 2013.

Peterson, Christie. Personal communication. 30 August 2012.

Peterson, Christina. "Book interview." Message to the author. 7 Feb. 2013. E-mail.

"A Place With Real Stars." *The New York Times.* N.p., 02 Apr. 2006. Accessed: 03 Mar. 2013. http://www.nytimes.com/2006/04/02/opinion/nyregionopinions/LIfreshair.html?ref=freshairfund

Potok, Chiam. "Chaim Potok Writes about Going to Summer Camp." Untitled Document. N.p., n.d. Accessed: 26 Jan. 2013.

"A Quick Look at Trail Blazer Camps." www.trailblazers.org. N.p., Mar. 2011. Accessed: 3 Mar. 2013. http://www.trailblazers.org/docs/history.pdf

Rich, Frank. "Camp Visiting Day." *The New York Times,* 24 July 1994. Accessed: 27 Apr. 2013. http://www.nytimes.com/1994/07/24/opinion/journal-camp-visiting-day.html.

Rimer, Sara. "A Last Goodbye to Camp, and to Just Be a Girl." *The New York Times.* N.p., 1 Sept. 1993. Accessed: 19 Jan. 2013.

Rock, JK. "Celebrating Summer Camp." Message to the author. 20 Mar. 2013. E-mail.

Rogers, Mary. "Where the Internet Ends: What Camp Teaches 21st Century Kids." *American Camp Association.* N.p., 23 Apr. 2013. Accessed: 02 June 2013. http://www.acacamps.org/blog/word-peg/where-internet-ends-what-camp-teaches-21st-century-kids.

Rohrlich, Marianne. "When the 'Aisle' Is Slippery and Buggy." *The New York Times,* 21 Sept. 2012. Accessed: 28 Oct. 2012. http://www.nytimes.com/2012/09/23/fashion/weddings/summer-camps-as-destination-weddings.html?pagewanted=all&_r=0.

Rollin, Lucy. *Twentieth-Century Teen Culture by the Decades.* Westport: Greenwood, 1999. Print.

Rosenzweig, Michael. "Summer Camp Got in the Way of Blogging." *Boulder Jewish News.* N.p., 9 Sept. 2012. Accessed: 07 Apr. 2013. http://boulderjewishnews.org/2012/summer-camp-got-in-the-way-of-blogging/.

Russell, Lindsey Mead. "Camp." Web log post. A Design So Vast. Lindsey Mead Russell, 29 July 2011. Accessed: 1 Aug. 2012. http://www.adesignsovast.com/2011/07/camp/.

Russell, Lindsey Mead. "Celebrating Summer Camp." Message to the author. 30 April 2012. E-mail.

Russell, Lindsey Mead. "My Little Soul Mate." Web log post. A Design So Vast. Lindsey Mead Russell, 26 July 2011. Accessed: 2 Aug. 2012. http://www.adesignsovast.com/2011/07/my-little-soul-mate/.

Sales, Amy L., and Leonard Saxe. *How Godly Are Thy Tents: Summer Camps as Jewish Socializing Experiences.* Hanover: University of New England, 2004. Print.

Sangster, Andy. "Longer Camp Sessions: Disappearing Dinosaur or Timely Treasure?" *American Camp Association.* N.p., Nov.-Dec. 2011. Accessed: 16 Mar. 2013.

Scheff, Nancy B. "Romance at Ramah." *Ramah Marriages.* N.p., n.d. Accessed: 30 Mar. 2013. http://www.campramah.org/content/ramahmarriages.php.

Schweinhart, Tom. "The Camp Community and the World Community." *American Camp Association.* N.p., Mar.-Apr. 2002. Accessed: 25 Mar. 2013. http://www.acacamps.org/members/knowledge/participant/cm/023camp.

"Scouting." Boy Scouts of America. N.p., 2013. Accessed: 15 June 2013. http://www.scouting.org/.

Seabrook, John, Harry Seabrook, Sophie Pera, Harry Hurt, III, James Villas, and Alix Browne. "Camp Tales." *Town & Country,* June-July 2012: 92+. Accessed:

"Camp Care Packages by Sealed With A Kiss (SWAK)." N.p., n.d. Accessed: 31 Aug. 2012. https://www.eswak.com/pages/home.

"The Seaside Boarding House for Working Women". *The New York Times.* N.p., NYTimes.com,. 04 Aug. 1874. Accessed: 03 Mar. 2013.

"Series - Private Issue Boy Scout Postcards." N.p., n.d. Accessed: 26 Jan. 2013.

Shafrir, Doree. "Inside Visiting Day at Trail'™s End Camp." *New York Magazine.* N.p., 2 Aug. 2009. Accessed: 20 Jan. 2013.

Shalof, Tilda. "Celebrating Summer Camp." Message to the author. 28 Apr. 2013. E-mail.

Shalof, Tilda. *Camp Nurse: My Adventures at Summer Camp.* N.p.: Random House Digital, 2010. Google Books. 4 May 2010. Accessed: 15 June 2013. http://books.google.com/books?id=-8wn7-r3cTUC.

Shuter, Holly Zax. Personal communication. 14 July 2012.

Sifferlin, Alexandra, Alice Park, and Maia Szalavitz. "Summer Camp: Great for Kids, Maybe Even Better for Parents." *Time,* 3 Aug. 2012. Accessed: 22 Sept. 2012. http://healthland.time.com/2012/08/03/summer-camp-great-for-kids-maybe-even-better-for-parents/.

Simonoff, Eric, ed. *Sleepaway: Writings on Summer Camp.* New York: Riverhead Books, 2005.

Singer, Natasha. "Summer Camps Are Facing New Economics." *The New York Times. The New York Times,* 10 July 2011. Accessed: 23 Dec. 2012.

Singer, Sarah. "Some Enchanted Summer..." *Washington Jewish Week,* 28 Aug. 2008: B14-15. Print.

Smith, April. "Off to Summer Camp." *The New York Times,* 26 Apr. 1981. Accessed: 27 Mar. 2012.

Smith, Mark K. "Summer Camps, Camp Counselors and Informal Education." The Informal Education Homepage. N.p., 2000. Accessed: 23 Sept. 2012. http://www.infed.org/association/sum-camp.htm.

Smith, Peg L. "The Great Education Debate: Camp Has A Place In Childhood Development." *Parents & Families.* N.p., n.d. Accessed: 31 Mar. 2013. http://www.campparents.org/case-for-camp/great-education-debate.

Snow, Bonnie M., Betty Nale, Elinor Rust, Art Farnham, John Worgan, Mary Lou Brier, Robert Melcher, Ann Hammatt, Ruth Linden, Jeanne Stage, Heidi Hagenbuckle, Bob Miller, Bonnie Lincoln, and Richard Marvin. *The Camps of Orleans, 1900-1988.* Orleans: Best Read Guide, 1997. Print.

Sokolsky, Marla. "Article from The Forward." Http://boiberik.media.mit.edu. N.p., 29 May 1998. Accessed: 20 Feb. 2013.

"Sporting and Recreational Camps." *Highbeam Business.* N.p., 2012. Accessed: 04 Nov. 2012. http://business.highbeam.com/industry-reports/personal/sporting-recreational-camps.

Steinberg, Don. "Rites of Passage: A Summer at Camp Kweebec" *Philadelphia Magazine.* N.p., July 2012. Accessed: 29 Mar. 2013. http://www.phillymag.com/articles/rites-passage-summer-camp-kweebec/2/.

Stern, Andy. "Sailing." Message to the author. 26 Nov. 2012. E-mail.

Sudduth, Carol. "Camp traditions." Message to the author. 25 March 2013. E-mail.

"Summer Camp." *Rookie.* N.p., 10 June 2013. Accessed: 15 June 2013. http://rookiemag.com/2013/06/summer-camp/.

"Summer Camp: Board Game," 2003. *Board Game Geek.* N.p., n.d. Accessed: 04 May 2013. http://boardgamegeek.com/boardgame/7069/summer-camp.

"Summer Camps." *Discover Archery.* N.p., n.d. Accessed: 02 Nov. 2012. http://www.discoverarchery.org/from-the-basics-to-the-podium/summer-camps/.

"Summer Camps of Lake Winnipesaukee." Lake Winnipesaukee Historical Society. N.p., n.d. Accessed: 02 Mar. 2013.

"Summer Camp Outcomes Study." N.p., 2001. Accessed: 31 Mar. 2013. http://www.scouting.org/About/Research/SummerCampOutcomes.aspx.

Swindle, Dawn. "Camp Traditions: Memories in the Making." *American Camp Association.* American Camp Association, May-June 2010. Accessed: 09 Sept. 2012. http://www.acacamps.org/campmag/1005/camp-traditions.

Tergesen, Anne. "The Best Summer Camps for Grown-Ups." *The Wall Street Journal.* N.p., 18 Mar. 2013. Accessed: 23 Mar. 2013. http://online.wsj.com/article/SB10001424127887324610504578275744143657034.html.

"13 Things Your Kid's Camp Counselor Won't Tell You." *Readers Digest.* N.p., July 2008. Accessed: 02 Feb. 2013.

Thompson, Michael. "Back to Where You Once Belonged: Risk and Choice at a Creative Arts Camp." *American Camp Association.* N.p., Nov.-Dec. 2008. Accessed: 04 Nov. 2012. http://www.acacamps.org/campmag/issues/0811/thompson.

Thompson, Michael. "Should I Be Sending My Children to Camp?" *The Huffington Post.* TheHuffingtonPost.com, 25 June 2012. Accessed: 16 Mar. 2013.

Thurber, Chris. "Camp Forum: For Campers/Parents: Camp Scholar: Single-Sex or coed?" *My Summer Camps.* N.p., 8 Aug. 2005. Accessed: 17 Mar. 2013. http://www.mysummercamps.com/forum/For_Campers/Parents_C1/Camp_Scholar_F16/Single-Sex_or_Coed_P194/.

Thurber, Kathy. "Riding Programs at Camp: Enrichment of a Different Kind." *American Camp Association.* N.p., Mar.-Apr. 2004. Accessed: 04 Nov. 2012. http://www.acacamps.org/members/knowledge/program/cm/043riding.

"To An Old Camper." N.p., n.d. Accessed: 29 Dec. 2012.

Tobias, Scott. "The New Cult Canon: Wet Hot American Summer." AV Club Live. N.p., 11 June 2008. Accessed: 27 Jan. 2013.

Tucknott, Renee. "Celebrating Summer Camp." Message to the author. 1 May 2012. E-mail.

Umberger, Mary. "Greetings from Camp Not-gonna-open-again." *Chicago Tribune.* N.p., 09 July 2006. Accessed: 19 Jan. 2013.

"Urban Dictionary: Sleepaway Camp." *Urban Dictionary.* N.p., n.d. Accessed: 02 Oct. 2012. http://www.urbandictionary.com/define.php?term=sleepaway camp.

"Urban Dictionary: Summer Camp." *Urban Dictionary.* N.p., n.d. Accessed: 02 Oct. 2012. http://www.urbandictionary.com/define.php?term=summer camp.

Van Slyck, Abigail A. "Connecting with the Landscape." *Designing Modern Childhoods: History, Space and the Material Culture of Children.* Rutgers University Press, 2008. 23-44. Print.

Van Slyck, Abigail Ayres. *A Manufactured Wilderness: Summer Camps and the Shaping of American Youth, 1890-1960.* Minneapolis: University of Minnesota, 2006. Print.

Van Slyck, Abigail A. "Housing the Happy Camper." Http://www.mnhs.org/collections/index.htm. Minnesota Historical Society, Summer 2002. Accessed: 31 Aug. 2012. http://collections.mnhs.org/MNHistoryMagazine/articles/58/v58i02p068-083.pdf.

Villanueva, Jari A. "24 Notes That Tap Deep Emotions." N.p., n.d. Accessed: 29 Dec. 2012.

Vorkink, Christiaan P. "Ernest Thompson Seton and the Woodcraft Indians." YMCA Camp Belknap, n.d. Accessed: 29 Aug. 2012. http://www.campbelknap.org/pages/woodcraft_history.htm.

Wachs, Kathie. "Camp Questions." 15 May 2012. E-mail.

Wack, Henry Wellington. *The Camping Ideal: The New Human Race.* New York: The Red Book Magazine, 1925.

Walsh, Dianna Lamb. Personal communication. 5 September 2012.

Ward, Carlos E. "Organized Camping and Progressive Education." Archive.org. N.p., n.d. Accessed: 29 Dec. 2012.

Warner, Judith. "Camp Codependence." *The New York Times.* N.p., 31 July 2008. Accessed: 01 Feb. 2013.

Warner, Judith. "Loosen the Apron Strings." *The New York Times.* N.p., 20 July 2006. Accessed: 19 Jan. 2013. http://www.nytimes.com/2006/07/20/opinion/20warner.html?_r=1&

"The Way Childhood Should Be: Maine Summer Camps." *Maine Experience.* Maine Public Broadcasting Network. MPBN, Portland, Maine, n.d. Television.

"WayBack. Summer Vacation. Summer Camp | PBS KIDS GO!" n.d. Accessed: 09 Sept. 2012. http://pbskids.org/wayback/summer/features_summer.html.

Weisse, Allen B. "Speaking Personally: Summer Camp." *The New York Times.* N.p., 24 Aug. 1980. Accessed: 19 Jan. 2013.

Werlin, Jessica. Personal communication. 9 June 2012.

"Wet Hot American Summer." IMDb. IMDb.com, n.d. Accessed: 27 Jan. 2013.

"Wet Hot American Summer—Official Web Site." N.p., n.d. Accessed: 27 Jan. 2013.

Whitley, Peggy, Becky Bradley, Bettye Sutton, and Sue Goodwin. "1990–1999." *American Cultural History,* Lone Star College-Kingwood Library. Last modified February 2011. http://wwwappskc.lonestar.edu/ popculture/decade90.html.

Whitley, Peggy. "1900–1909." *American Cultural History.* Lone Star College-Kingwood Library, 1999. Accessed: 7 Feb. 2011.

Whitley, Peggy,. "1910–1919." *American Cultural History.* Lone Star College-Kingwood Library. Last modified November 2008. http://wwwappskc.lonestar.edu/popculture/decade10.html.

Whitley, Peggy. "1980–1989." *American Cultural History.* Lone Star College-Kingwood Library. Last modified September 2008. http://wwwappskc.lonestar.edu/popculture/decade80.html.

"Why Camping Is Important." N.p., n.d. Accessed: 12 May 2013. http://www.friendsofcrowellhilaka.org/camping_reasons.htm.

Wolk, Josh. Personal communication. 21 March 2013.

"Women Need Teamwork." *The New York Times.* N.p., 12 July 1912. Accessed: 1 Feb. 2013.

"The Woodcraft Way." The Ernest Thompson Seton Pages. N.p., 2012. Accessed: 22 Feb. 2013.

Yerkes, Rita. "His Story, Her Story, Our Story: 100 Years of the American Camp Association." *American Camp Association.* N.p., Jan.-Feb. 2010. Accessed: 09 Sept. 2012. http://www.acacamps.org/campmag/issues/1001/his-story-her-story-our-story-100-years-american-camp-association.

"Yesterday, Today, Tomorrow...For Good." *The Y: History.* N.p., n.d. Accessed: 09 Mar. 2013. http://www.ymca.net/history/1870-1890s.html.

"YMCA of Pierce and Kitsap Counties." *History of Camp.* N.p., n.d. Accessed: 06 Apr. 2013. http://www.campseymour.org/history-camp.

"Youth Development Organization - Youth Programs ." 4-H. N.p., n.d. Accessed: 17 Mar. 2013. http://www.4-h.org/about/youth-development-organization/.

Zeder, Jeri. "Summer Camps." *My Jewish Learning.* N.p., n.d. Accessed: 03 Feb. 2013.

Index